RURAL SOCIETY IN THE
AGE OF REASON

CONTRIBUTIONS TO GLOBAL HISTORICAL ARCHAEOLOGY

Series Editor:
Charles E. Orser, Jr., *Illinois State University*, Normal Illinois

---

AN ARCHAEOLOGICAL STUDY OF RURAL CAPITALISM AND MATERIAL
   LIFE: The Gibbs Farmstead in Southern Appalachia, 1790–1920
Mark D. Groover

ARCHAEOLOGY AND CREATED MEMORY: Public History in a National Park
Paul A. Schackel

AN ARCHAEOLOGY OF HISTORY AND TRADITION: Moments of Danger in the
   Annapolis Landscape
Christopher N. Matthews

AN ARCHAEOLOGY OF MANNERS: The Polite World of the Merchant Elite of
   Colonial Massachusetts
Lorinda B.R. Goodwin

AN ARCHAEOLOGY OF SOCIAL SPACE: Analyzing Coffee Plantations in
   Jamaica's Blue Mountains
James A. Delle

DOMESTIC ARCHITECTURE AND POWER: The Historical Archaeology of
   Colonial Ecuador
Ross W. Jamieson

HISTORICAL ARCHAEOLOGIES OF CAPITALISM
Edited by Mark P. Leone and Parker B. Potter, Jr.

THE HISTORICAL ARCHAEOLOGIES OF BUENOS AIRES: A City at the End
   of the World
Daniel Schavelzon

A HISTORICAL ARCHAEOLOGY OF THE OTTOMAN EMPIRE: Breaking New
   Ground
Edited by Uzi Baram and Lynda Carroll

MEANING AND IDEOLOGY IN HISTORICAL ARCHAEOLOGY: Style, Social
   Identity, and Capitalism in an Australian
Heather Burke

RACE AND AFFLUENCE: An Archaeology of African America and Consumer
   Culture
Paul R. Mullins

RURAL SOCIETY IN THE AGE OF REASON
An Archaeology of the Emergence of Modern Life in the Southern Scottish
   Highlands
Chris Dalglish

RURAL SOCIETY IN THE AGE OF REASON

An Archaeology of the Emergence of Modern Life in the Southern Scottish Highlands

by

Chris Dalglish

University of Glasgow, Glasgow, United Kingdom

Kluwer Academic/Plenum Publishers
New York, Boston, Dordrecht, London, Moscow

Library of Congress Cataloging-in-Publication Data

Dalglish, Chris.
   Rural society in the age of reason : an archaeology of the emergence of modern life in
the southern Scottish Highlands/by Chris Dalglish.
      p.   cm. — (Contributions to global historical archaeology)
   Includes bibliographical references and index.
   ISBN 0-306-47725-4 (hardbound); ISBN 0-306-47772-6 (paperback)
   1. Highlands (Scotland)—Social life and customs.   2. Material
culture—Scotland—Highlands.   3. Highlands (Scotland)—Social conditions.
   4. Highlands (Scotland)—Rural conditions.   5. Land settlement—
Scotland—Highlands.   6. Country life—Scotland—Highlands.
   7. Highlands (Scotland)—Antiquities.   I. Title.   II. Series.
DA880.H6D35 2003
941.1′5—dc21

                                                                              2002043451

HB: 0-306-47725-4
PB: 0-306-47772-6

© 2003 Kluwer Academic/Plenum Publishers, New York
233 Spring Street, New York, New York 10013

http://www.wkap.nl

10 9 8 7 6 5 4 3 2 1

Printed in the United States of America.

Preface

My interest in the archaeology of the Scottish Highlands began long before I had any formal training in the subject. Growing up on the eastern fringes of the southern Highlands, close to Loch Lomond, it was not hard stumble across ruined buildings, old field boundaries, and other traces of everyday life in the past. This is especially true if you spend much time, as I have done, climbing the nearby mountains and walking and driving through the various glens that give access into the Highlands. At the time, I had no real understanding of these remains, simply accepting them as being built and old.

After studying archaeology for a few years at the University of Glasgow, itself only a short commute from the area where I grew up, I became acutely aware that I still had no real understanding of these familiar, yet enigmatic, buildings and fields. This and a growing interest in Scotland's historical archaeology drove me to take several courses on the subject of *rural settlement studies*. These courses allowed me to place what I now knew to be houses, barns, mills, shieling (transhumance) settlements, rig-and-furrow cultivation, and other related remains in history. Overwhelmingly, they seemed to date from the period of the last 300 years. I also began to understand how they all worked together as component parts of daily rural life in the past.

While an undergraduate, I undertook to write a dissertation on this period of archaeology on Loch Lomondside and later began research towards a Ph.D. in the subject. By the time I came to start that Ph.D. research I had come to find the empirical nature of much work in Scottish rural settlement studies unsatisfying. Such past work is of course invaluable for the data and empirical interpretation it provides. However, when compared with the issues discussed by documentary historians of this period—issues like the Highland Clearances, agricultural Improvement and commercialization, and the demise of clanship—a wide gap in interpretation becomes obvious. Having studied prehistory and having developed an interest in historical archaeology outside of Scotland, my interest became the exploration of the social archaeology of the Highlands; to move beyond an empirical understanding to an understanding of how people's houses and fields formed an integral part of their social life.

My approach to this social archaeology of Scotland's recent past has therefore grown from a background in Scottish historical archaeology, and in particular the field of rural settlement studies. It has been influenced by recent work in British prehistory and, leading from there, by readings in anthropology and social theory. Equally important for me have been the ways in which other historical archaeologists, in Britain and around the world, have tackled the major social issues of the modern era, particularly that of capitalism. I can remember at one point being surprised, but excited, to find that work on contemporaneous archaeology as far afield as the United States or Australia had something to offer in understanding the Scottish Highlands.

I hope that this brief biography will go some small way to explain how this book came to be as it is. The book has grown from my Ph.D. thesis, though with substantial revisions. It has been written with two main audiences in mind. Firstly, there are the growing number of those in Scotland and in the British Isles as a whole interested in the archaeology of the recent past. My hope here is to offer something to fuel discussion of how we continue to progress this archaeology with a social agenda foremost in our minds. Secondly, the book is aimed at historical archaeologists and others in other parts of the world. I am glad that this book is published in the *Contributions to Global Historical Archaeology* series for a number of reasons. I have already mentioned my own debt to the work of archaeologists in other countries and continents. I hope that this book offers a return contribution in making more widely known Scottish material from a period when Scots, for good or bad, were playing a significant role in shaping the modern world. I also hope that it offers a contribution to the more general, theoretical debate on the construction and constitution of capitalist societies.

Acknowledgments

As this book has grown out of my Ph.D. thesis, I wish to acknowledge those who gave support and advice both during my time as a research student and subsequently in the drafting of this book. First, my parents, Janet and Ian, have proved a constant source of support and encouragement and continue to show an interest. In the same breath, and for the same reasons, I wish to thank Katinka, who also persevered with draft versions of the text, and provided invaluable critical comment, help with the illustrations, and general moral support. It has taken some time to progress from the initial unpublished thesis to a stage where I am happy with this text as it is and, with major re-writes and changes in direction, this has been a labor-intensive process. It would have been much harder to achieve the end result without everyone's continued understanding and encouragement.

Matthew Johnson, of the University of Durham, read a draft of the text and I am grateful to him for his positive, incisive, and constructive comments.

Both during the period of my original research and since, I have benefited immeasurably from discussions with members of the academic staff of the University of Glasgow Department of Archaeology, most notably Stephen T Driscoll and Alex Morrison. It was Alex Morrison who first sparked my academic interest in the recent past of the Scottish Highlands and Stephen Driscoll who supervised my subsequent research in such a way that I was free to take it in the direction I wanted, though encouraged to think critically. He also kindly provided material for Figures 8, 9, 15, and 16 and permission to reproduce it. I have also learnt much from working and conversing with the staff of Glasgow University Archaeological Research Division, and in particular I would like to single out John A Atkinson, Olivia Lelong, and Gavin MacGregor. Whilst studying at the University of Glasgow, I benefited from the interest of my peers in my own work, their willingness to discuss their research, and their practical assistance and advice. For numerous discussions and all their help I wish to thank Martin Carruthers, Meggen Gondek, Caroline Hale, Stuart Jeffrey, and Kylie Seretis in particular.

Terry Nelson provided much practical assistance and advice that allowed me to complete my Ph.D. In particular, he steered me through the minefield of computer technology—no small feat in my case.

Murdo MacDonald of the Argyll and Bute District Archive, Lochgilphead, and Mike Davis, of Argyll and Bute Libraries, were both extremely helpful in leading me to significant manuscript sources. Figures 5 and 13 are based on copies of material kindly supplied by Murdo MacDonald.

The staff of various other institutions also deserve thanks. The National Monuments Record of Scotland has proved a vital source of information and the staff of the Royal Commission on the Ancient and Historical Monuments of Scotland have always proved helpful. Figures 4, 6, 7, 10, and 14 are based on material supplied from the National Monuments Record and reproduced with the permission of the Royal Commission. Of the many libraries and archives where I have conducted research, the Mitchell Library in Glasgow and Glasgow University Library deserve special mention.

I hope you all think the end result is worthwhile.

Contents

CHAPTER 1 Introduction 1

Subject 1
Approach 6
Structure 9

CHAPTER 2 Rural Settlement Studies: A Critical History 13

Rural Settlement Studies as Ethnology 15
Rural Settlement Studies as Folk Life 23
Rural Settlement Studies as Historical Archaeology 27
Archaeology, Documents, and the Writing of Social History ... 32
An Active Archaeology of Improvement 36

CHAPTER 3 Capitalism and Society 39

Archaeology and Capitalism: The Georgian Order 40
Beyond the Georgian Order: Society and the Individual 51
The Constitution of Society and Social Change 59
Ideology, Material Culture, and Routine Practice 68
Capitalism, Capitalist Society, and Archaeology 75

CHAPTER 4 The Changing Material and Routine Environment . 79

The Pre-Improvement Material Environment 80
Settlement 81
Landscape 90
Domestic Space 97
The Material Environment of Improvement 103
Settlement 103
Landscape 114

Domestic Space 120
Changing Routine Practice with Improvement 123

CHAPTER 5   Improvement and Enlightenment 129

Improvement and the Scottish Enlightenment 130
Enlightenment Historiography: The Stages of Society 134
Human Nature, the Commercial Age, and Human
    Independence 138
Exemplars for Improvement: Lowland Scotland and England . 141
    Settlement 141
    Landscape 143
    Domestic Space 145
    Routine Practice 147
A Partial Understanding of Improvement 149

CHAPTER 6   Improvement and the Landowner 153

Clanship as a Socio-Political System 155
Duthchas and Oighreachd in Kintyre 158
    Kintyre and the Lordship of the Isles 158
    Forfeiture and Unrest: Kintyre and the Decline of the
        Lordship of the Isles 160
    Clan Campbell and Clan Donald from the Late Sixteenth
        Century 162
    Kintyre in the Seventeenth Century: Campbell Territorial
        Expansion and Resulting Civil Unrest 164
    The Legacy of Unrest: Improvement and the Civilizing of
        Kintyre 167
    Summary 170
Improvement in Kilfinan and the Emergent Middle Class 171
    The Landholding History of Kilfinan 174
    Urban Society and the Emergent Middle Class 181
    Improvement and the Establishment and Maintenance of
        Middle Class Status 185
Improvement as a Strategy in Resolving Social Contradiction 191

CHAPTER 7   Improvement and the Farming Population 193

Narratives of Response to Improvement 195
Archaeology and the Dynamics of Improvement 199

Dual Material Response to Improvement 200
Improvement and the Horizontal Division of the Farming
    Community 205
Regional Variation in the Construction of Modern Highland
    Society 210
The Dynamics of Improvement 214

CHAPTER 8   Conclusion 217

Improvement, the Material Environment, and Routine Practice 217
Improvement and the Negotiation of Society 222
Resistance and the Asymmetry of Society 228

References 233

Index 247

Introduction | 1

SUBJECT

Rural Society in the Age of Reason. This book is an exploration of the emergence of modern society in the southern Highlands of Scotland, traceable directly to the eighteenth century, though not to be understood without reference to the centuries before.

Understanding the emergence of modern society is to understand how today's social relationships came to be structured as they are. I will be particularly concerned with the growth to predominance of capitalism, which will be understood in a specific and sociological sense as a form of relationship conducted between autonomous individuals. With capitalism, the central place of the individual, defined in isolation from wider society, relates to individualized notions of private property and land ownership, land rights and tenancy. Questions of land rights and ownership have long been central to the history of the recent past in the Highlands and, in many areas, are issues that continue to be disputed.

My main focus will be the process of Improvement in the eighteenth and nineteenth centuries, though this period must be placed in a longer-term context. Improvement involved fundamental change in the ways people engaged with each other. It privileged the individualized relationships of capitalism over those of community or kin. In restructuring the ways people interacted, Improvement involved significant change to the physical environment, to the structure of settlement, to the agricultural and wider landscape, to domestic space. Such physical changes related to changing routine, everyday practices, including changes to the ways in which fields were worked, livestock shepherded, meals consumed, guests entertained, and much else. Improvement involved the commercialization of agriculture, the rise to prominence of the lease system and of private property.

The process of Improvement will be explored through two case studies, focusing on the peninsula of Kintyre and on the parish of Kilfinan in Cowal (see Figure 1). Kintyre projects from the southwest mainland of Argyll into the Atlantic and toward Ireland, which is only 22km distant at closest (see RCAHMS 1971:1–3 for an introduction to the area;

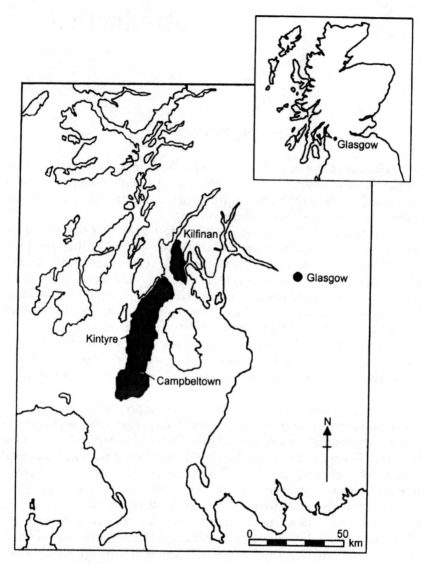

Figure 1. The locations of Kintyre and Kilfinan.

see Figure 2). The peninsula is some 65km long and varies in breadth from 9 to 15km along most of its length. It is connected to the mainland by a 1.5km wide isthmus between East Loch Tarbert and West Loch Tarbert. A spine of peat-covered high ground (up to 455m in height) runs down the middle of Kintyre and is severed to the south by a Lowland

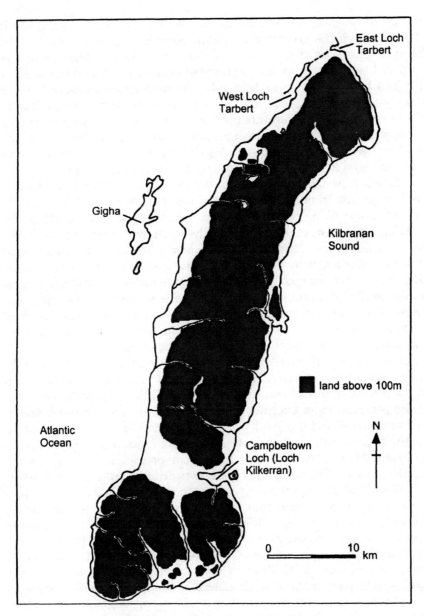

Figure 2. The peninsula of Kintyre.

plain, the Laggan, connecting the east and west coasts. To the south of the Laggan the ground rises again, formed in part by the Mull of Kintyre. For most of the length of the peninsula, the high ground is bordered to the west by an interrupted coastal plain and the shelf of a raised beach. On the eastern side, the high ground descends more steeply to the shore, with only occasional patches of more gradually sloping ground. The interior of the high ground is penetrated by a number of glens. I will concentrate in particular on southern Kintyre, as this is where the Campbell House of Argyll's estate was concentrated, and it is the social history of this estate that is my primary concern.

Kilfinan parish lies in the southwest corner of Cowal, a block of land projecting from the southern mainland of Argyll and lying to the east of Kintyre. The parish has a maximum length of some 23km and is 9.5km at widest. It is bounded to the south and west by Loch Fyne, across which it faces Kintyre and Knapdale. To the east it is bounded in its southern half by the Kyles of Bute and in its northern half by Glendaruel. For the most part, the ground is rough and hilly, to a maximum height of 454m. However, there are pockets of low-lying and more gently undulating ground in coastal areas and, thus, confined to the western and southeastern parts of the parish. The low ground of Glendaruel falls just outside of the parish boundary.

Kintyre is of interest for specific historical reasons. Firstly, Improvement began early there. Secondly, its largest estate belonged at the time of Improvement to the Campbell Dukes of Argyll, but much of the peninsula had traditionally been Clan Donald territory. Access to its resources and the loyalty of its population had been disputed for centuries prior to Improvement and a consideration of Kintyre allows an exploration of the idea that Improvement was a strategy of some landlords in settling such social and territorial disputes in their favor.

Historically, Improvement came to Kilfinan much later than Kintyre, perhaps a half-century or more later. This chronological difference relates to the different social and historical contexts of Improvement in the two areas. The comparison between Improvement in Kintyre and Improvement in Kilfinan will show that it was not a monolithic process. In Kilfinan, a key context for Improvement on the landowner's part is their involvement in emergent middle class society. Through Improvement, various landowners sought to restructure the rural community in such a way as to establish and maintain their position within the middle class.

As will be made clear, the progress of Improvement varied significantly between and within these two areas. This is a result of the fact that Improvement, far from being a process conceived of by a

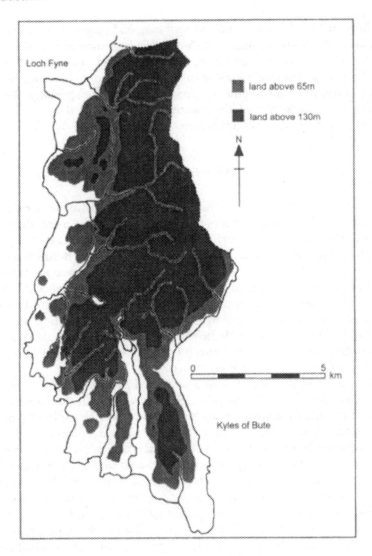

Figure 3. The parish of Kilfinan.

select group of landowners and implemented in a vacuum, was a process involving the unequal interaction of a multitude of individuals and social groups. Just as important to our understanding of Improvement are the actions of the tenant farmer, smallholder, and landless farm laborer. Perhaps *Rural Society in the Age of Reason*, with its connotations of commercialization, rationalization, and Enlightenment should read *Rural Society in the Age of Reason?* Improvement involved a fundamental transformation of the physical environment and of social practice, but it was not a uniform, monolithic, and uncontested experience. This said, it should be borne in mind throughout that not everyone had an equal part in the determination of society. So, perhaps the lack of a question mark in my title is apposite after all as it recognizes the greater power to act of the Improving landlord.

APPROACH

I could define this book within the Scottish tradition of *rural settlement studies*. This term is widely accepted as defining a sub-discipline within archaeology and historical geography that focuses on the period from the Middle Ages to the near present (the use and definition of the term are evident in volumes like the recent *Townships to Farmsteads. Rural Settlement Studies in Scotland, England, and Wales* (Atkinson et al. [eds.] 2000)). In Scotland, the process of Improvement has long been a primary thematic concern of rural settlement studies, although the dearth of knowledge on Medieval settlement increasingly competes for attention. In studying Improvement, this book has traditional disciplinary subject matter at its core.

The approach I have taken also has its roots in past rural settlement studies, partially at least. Such studies will be thematically explored in full in chapter two, but here I wish to highlight one of their established strengths, their holistic and interdisciplinary character. Despite the name, rural settlement studies have traditionally had a holistic outlook. They have not been confined to the material aspects of settlement, but, as a matter of course, have considered various forms of material culture, landscape, custom, tradition, superstition and folk-lore, farming practice, social institutions, and much else. An interdisciplinary approach is usual, drawing on archaeology, historical geography, ethnology, folk life studies, and many branches of history. In keeping with this tradition, although I am primarily concerned with the material aspects of society, this archaeology will be approached from a broad inter-disciplinary perspective.

This said, in certain important ways I hope to break from the flow of past work. The politics of Improvement are a major concern in what is to follow. On the whole, archaeologists have previously ignored them. The low level of interest in this regard is somewhat surprising considering the strength of feeling attached to different historical narratives of Improvement, especially where these tell of the clearance of the population from the land. Many deserted settlements and landscapes exist and survive as such because of the dispossession and eviction of their inhabitants. When I say I am interested in the politics of Improvement, I am not just concerned with the usual material of political history, such as relations between the clans, kindreds, and landowners of the Highlands, or the place of the Crown in the region's history, for example. All social relations are political and I am just as concerned with the negotiation of interests between tenant and landlord, between subtenant and tenant, and between whomever else. Past rural settlement studies have largely seen Highland society as socially coherent and culturally homogenous, with social structure and social change managed and controlled by a landowning elite and largely uncontested. I will argue that this was not necessarily the case and that through rural settlement studies we can explore social conflict and the relationships between different groups within Highland society.

Despite its inter-disciplinary approach, this book is above all an archaeology of Highland society. This is because I explore the constitution and reconstitution of social relations in the Highlands through the construction and reconstruction of the material environment and the re-ordering of related routine practices. Improvement will also be understood with reference to contemporary abstract ideological statements aiming to justify the social changes it entailed. However, the basic materiality of Improvement cannot be denied. Improvement was a process involving drastic change to the physical environment. This is not to say that such physical change should be privileged above its social, historical, and ideological context, but to argue that Improvement is an archaeological concern if we realize that it was a transformation of the daily lives of the farming population in no small part achieved through change to the physical environment.

If, as an archaeological project, this book is to fulfill the need for a dynamic social history of Improvement, the physical environment must, of course, be argued to play a significant role in the structuring of society. All but the most recent of rural settlement studies have preferred to leave the writing of social history to documentary historians, subscribing, often uncritically, to their narratives. Many rural settlement studies have, thus, constrained themselves with empiricism. I will not argue that documentary history is to be ignored by the archaeologist of Improvement, quite the contrary. I do hope to show that the archaeological resource can be used to *write* a social history of Improvement. The way I have attempted to do this draws inspiration from the holistic/interdisciplinary approach to the past, and from recent work in *the archaeology of practice* and *the archaeology of capitalism*.

The archaeology of practice has become prominent in British pre-history (see Hodder 1999:132–137 for a brief introduction), though it is less so in the archaeology of later, historical periods. Some studies in historical geography have taken a similar approach (Pred 1986 is particularly relevant to studies of Improvement). In one form, archae-ologies of practice argue as a basic premise that material culture struc-tures and is structured by routine practice, or the way in which people interact with each other and their environment on a day-to-day basis. Routine practice is fundamental to our understanding of society as peo-ple assess explicit ideological statements, used by some social groups to explain and justify asymmetrical social relationships, in relation to their routine experience of the social and material environment. Some statements appear as common sense, where others do not, because they accord with routine experience of the world. For example, I will argue later that explicit concepts of the clan in the Highlands, as a community, made sense to the mass of the population in relation to their daily rou-tine structured around communal activity. We can go further than this and consider that routine relationships, in the ploughing of the fields for example, impacted on other relationships, between clan-gentry and clan. With the connection between routine practice and the material environment, and with the links between everyday social relations and ideology and between different types of social relationship themselves, it is clear that archaeology has an important role in our understanding of the politics and constitution of past societies.

Archaeologies of capitalism have perhaps been most associated with American Historical Archaeology, although some important work has emerged from Britain in recent years. There is no absolute consen-sus as to what should constitute an archaeology of capitalism, but one central theme is the rise of the individual over the community. There are various understandings of this process, and I favor one that focuses on the ways in which social relations are constituted. For example, from this understanding we might look at how individuals were demarcated within and as part of the community or kin-group prior to capital-ism, and how, with capitalism, they came to relate to others as an au-tonomous self, an individual divorced from the community or kin-group.

This book is aimed at several groups of people, including Scottish rural settlement scholars, other Scottish and British archaeologists, geographers and historians, and historical archaeologists in other parts of the world. As such, some parts of the text may go into detail already familiar to some. I hope, though, that most will also find something new and of interest.

STRUCTURE

I have already begun to discuss the relationship of this book to Scottish rural settlement studies. Understanding the history of the subject and the present nature of research is basic in setting the scene and in progressing any discussion of where we might go from here. As such, Chapter 2 is a review of past work in the subject with particular emphasis on the implicit and explicit theoretical constructs that have shaped accounts of rural settlement, landscape, and society. My concern, therefore, is not simply to describe past work, but to understand why it took the form it did. Two main themes of the chapter are the rise of historicity and of the modern archaeological approach. In the mid-nineteenth century, rural settlement studies were concerned with ahistorical material and social forms as examples of the survival of the prehistoric past into the present. This view has gradually been amended to one where rural settlement studies are concerned with historically situated accounts of their material. Partly as a result of the rise of historicity, rural settlement studies have become a mainstream archaeological concern. Previously such studies had been the province of folk life scholars or carried out by prehistorians to provide analogy for use in their own work. These two themes of the rise of historicity and of the modern archaeological approach describe the context of any current study. Most such studies, however, are inadequate in that they are strictly empirical in nature. The chapter concludes with a discussion of the few theoretically informed works within the subject and begins to suggest how we might move beyond mere description to the active creation of history.

This theme is picked up in Chapter 3, which discusses the general theoretical constructs that inform the rest of the book and form an explicit expression of the way in which I have tried to break from empiricism and the uncritical acceptance of traditional narratives of Improvement. Capitalism will be understood as a form of social relations, central to which is the way in which people position themselves to others as autonomous individuals.

In understanding the emergence of capitalism, I will consider that people brought about change and that they did so actively. This is not to say they did so freely. The possibilities for change were both constricted and enabled by existing social practice. The exercise of control over the conditions of existence was also conditioned by relations of power. People are influenced, enabled, and restricted, positively or negatively, by those with whom they interact.

The manner in which society is constituted and in which social structure is maintained or altered can be defined analytically in terms of a network of social relations, in terms of practical knowledge of how to engage with others, and in terms of explicit understandings of society, or ideology. These three elements impact on each other, each reflexively justifying or undermining the other. People act in complex ways to address their own interests, which are rooted in the past and constructed and pursued, successfully or not, with reference to others. The distinction of ideology and social relations and the separation of different forms of social relation are abstractions of this process.

Capitalism should not be seen as a universal, homogenous process. Rather, the social relations of capitalism were actively created in specific historical contexts. Because of this, capitalism can describe certain social relationships or aspects of those relationships that existed alongside other relationships and other understandings of the world. Capitalist society in a broad sense can, at one and the same time, accommodate capitalism and other social relations structured in quite different ways. That such a society can still be called capitalist, though, underlines the significance of asymmetrical relations of power in all social interaction. It should also be remembered that the distinction of the social relations of capitalism from other forms of social relationship is in no small part an analytical one, and different forms of social relationship are not strictly separate.

Chapter 4 outlines change in the material environment and routine practice with Improvement in the study areas. Pre-Improvement routine practice was communal and familial, in that much daily experience was as part of a farming community or a family. This produced a sense of the community and a sense of the family, where sense is understood as a form of practical, non-discursive knowledge. Routine practice with Improvement was individual, in that much experience was apart from the community or the family. This relates to a sense of the individual.

Understanding the process of Improvement requires the restoration of its links with Scottish Enlightenment thought, which provided an explicit ideology for Improvement, as discussed in Chapter 5. The Scottish Enlightenment, flourishing in the eighteenth century, was the Scottish contribution to a much wider process involving the transformation of thought in a wide range of disciplines, including philosophy, history, the physical sciences, and much else. While it is fair to describe the Enlightenment in part as an intellectual movement, it should not be separated from its political, social, and material context.

Scottish Enlightenment social theory argued that society naturally and inevitably progressed through stages, eventually reaching the end point of the Commercial Age. The Commercial Age was above all associated with England, and Lowland Scotland was considered to be in transition to that point. Improvement, as the process that brought the Commercial Age to the Highlands and restructured Highland society along more English or Lowland lines, was therefore professed as desirable and even inevitable by Enlightened landowners. Large-scale material and social change were justified through a disposition of independence, which stressed that people were free to alter the conditions of their existence.

Improvement cannot be explained by its ideological context alone, however. In manipulating the routine environment to undermine the community and family and to privilege the autonomous individual, landowners in the study areas had concrete political and social motives and these are explored in Chapter 6. The sense of community engendered in pre-Improvement routine practice made knowable the clan as an ideological construct. The communal structuring of people's everyday lives concurred with the social relations of the wider community of the clan. The sense of family made hereditary tenure appear as common sense. Daily experience of life as part of the family was in contradiction to individualized landlord-tenant-subtenant relations. The House of Argyll in Kintyre sought to undermine pre-Improvement routines because their ownership of estates there as private property was threatened by the farming population's continued adherence to their clan and their claims to land as their hereditary right. Improvement, in this case, was aimed at resolving a centuries old contradiction in west Highland society, that between the communal and hereditary on the one hand and the individual on the other.

In Kilfinan, I will focus on a different constellation of social contradictions at the root of Improvement. There was a contradiction between the landowners' membership of the emergent middle class and their ownership of Highland estates, organized along only partially commercialized lines. The continued inclusion of these landowners within the middle class required the Improvement of their estates, which were seen as backward in terms of Enlightened progress. The social organization of the estates contradicted the individualized nature of middle class relationships. Improvement in Kilfinan was not simply about the maintenance of a given landlord's middle class status, though. In the nineteenth century, new and established landowners alike faced potential conflict with their tenantry, who might expect some right to occupancy of the land in contradiction to the increasingly commercial nature of the estate as an asset for rationalization and exploitation. As for Kintyre, though in a slightly different historical context, Improvement in Kilfinan acted to secure the landowner's ownership of an estate as private property and to underpin their continued commercial exploitation of that estate.

Improvement was not a straightforward imposition of the landowner's will, though. As discussed in Chapter 7, the farming population engaged with Improvement in diverse ways. Their response was structured by a concern for continued occupancy of the land, meaning their continued residency upon a holding and use of its resources. Their response was contingent on how it affected their land rights. Where these were secure under the lease system, in relation to individual concepts of ownership and tenancy, and within individualized relationships, Improvement was perhaps more readily accepted. Where they were not secure, Improvement might be resisted and it might be resisted in the maintenance of non-individualized routine relationships. However, people, whether landlords, tenants, sub-tenants or whatever, were not simply free to act with regard to Improvement. They acted with reference to others and their scope for action was constrained or expanded by their relative position within a network of asymmetrical social relations.

Rural Settlement Studies
A Critical History

Rural settlement studies in Scotland have a long and varied history with substantive beginnings in the mid-nineteenth century. At times, and especially in the late nineteenth century, such studies were prominent in mainstream archaeology and played a key role in theoretical discussion within the subject. Despite this, reviews of the subject have been few and limited (e.g., Morrison 2000). None have discussed the theoretical constructs governing past analysis. More often we are given a descriptive list of previously published works or field projects and the emphasis is firmly upon work of the last forty to fifty years. It is my aim in this chapter to consider the various and changing theoretical underpinnings of past work in the subject. It is also my aim to bring to explore the extensive pre-1960 literature, which has previously been discussed in a cursory manner.

Highland rural settlement studies are discussed here in terms of three schools or theoretical orientations. The first is referred to as *Rural Settlement Studies as Ethnology* and refers to work undertaken largely in the second half of the nineteenth century and characterized by the analysis of Highland rural settlement for the provision of ethnological analogy. Such studies were intended to be used as analogy in writing prehistory and to put the latter discipline on a more scientific footing. The nineteenth century Highlands and Islands were seen to be characterized by the direct survival of the past into the present in material and social terms. This, naturally, characterized Highland and Island society and its material environment as static over millennia, a truth especially held for the Western Isles.

The second main theoretical orientation is referred to below as *Rural Settlement Studies as Folk Life*, beginning in the early decades of the twentieth century and continuing to the present. Folk Life studies are informed by the theoretical structure of the ethnological approach, though with more of a concern for a historical, changing past. Since the 1920s, documentary sources have increasingly been employed in a consideration of rural settlement that allows some degree of change and plays down the direct links to prehistory. However, this transformation has not been complete and such studies still often maintain a view of rural settlement and society as largely static.

The third main orientation discussed is referred to as *Rural Settlement Studies as Historical Archaeology*. This encompasses a tradition prominent from the 1950s to the present. "Historical" here not only refers to the fact that the material in question is from a period also covered by documentary sources, but also carries the added connotation that the previous view of settlement and society as static, or ahistorical, is rejected. Archaeology as a term is used not just to suggest the analysis of material culture, common to all approaches, but the nature of that analysis. With *Rural Settlement Studies as Historical Archaeology* the empirical aspect of rural settlement studies is brought in line with mainstream modern archaeological practice in that this approach is characterized by methodologically coherent survey and excavation, previously largely lacking.

The boundaries drawn here, between these three different approaches, are not absolute. The first approach does to some extent sit apart from the other two in chronological terms. However, there are clear theoretical links between the ethnological and folk life approaches. The folk life and historical archaeology approaches have run alongside each other for the last fifty or so years. Their mutual interest and partial compatibility is underlined by the fact that papers relating to both schools occur in the same journals, *Folk Life* for example, and the works of one are referenced in those of the other.

However, from an analytical perspective these divisions *are* necessary to achieve clarity in tracing the history of the subject and, in particular, the themes of the rise of historicity and the modern archaeological approach in particular. These themes largely set the agenda for any current archaeological consideration of Highland rural settlement and landscape.

This chapter concludes with a discussion of the relationship between history and archaeology within rural settlement studies and an account of the few recent theoretically informed works. These are discussed in order to set the agenda for the rest of the book. Recent archaeological studies of rural settlement have largely been empirical in nature, primarily excavation and survey reports or syntheses of these. Use of documentary sources by archaeologists has been limited to the consideration of empirical questions. Where the social history of the period is considered at all, narratives derived from documentary history are pasted into the archaeological report. As such, archaeologists have not played an active role in constructing the recent history of the Highlands.

As we shall see, this has begun to change and there is a minority of archaeologists attempting to write new histories of the Highlands. However, I will suggest that they portray Highland society as normative, which is to say that belief and understanding of the world is portrayed as universal and uniform. I will argue that it is necessary for us to overcome this problem and to explore the dynamic nature of Highland society in the recent past and the material environments from and through which social relationships were contested. The concern of archaeology with the material world and the possibilities this allows for a consideration of routine social practice gives archaeology a potentially prominent role in considering the diverse and often conflicting understandings of the world that may have existed in the past and the ways in which people created, maintained, or transformed their relationships with others.

It should be noted that the term *rural settlement studies* is a widely used shorthand for the study of the material aspects of past rural society in Scotland and such studies are not confined to settlement alone.

RURAL SETTLEMENT STUDIES AS ETHNOLOGY

The first studies of Highland rural settlement and landscape of recent centuries are contemporary travelers' accounts and other eyewitness descriptions. The earliest substantial account of this type was Martin Martin's *A description of the Western Islands of Scotland* (Martin 1994 [1695]). This was followed in the eighteenth century by a series of similar accounts including, most famously, those of Captain Burt, Thomas Pennant, Dr. Johnson, and James Boswell (Levi [ed.] 1990; Simmons [ed.] 1998a; 1998b). This tradition continued into the nineteenth century, with the publication of the journals of Dorothy Wordsworth and Lord Teignmouth, for example (Teignmouth 1836; Thin [ed.] 1981).

Many of these works are the travel journals of individuals with varied backgrounds. Some were English (Johnson, Pennant, Wordsworth, and Teignmouth), but others were Scots (Boswell and Martin). Many such accounts described flying tours of the region, but some were written from the perspective of people native to the area (Martin). Not all were travel journals, however. Burt's contribution came as a series of *Letters from A Gentleman in the North of Scotland to his Friend in London*, as the original title ran. He was stationed in Inverness in the period between the Jacobite rebellions of 1715 and 1745.

These accounts contain, amongst much else, descriptions of settlement and landscape in the Highlands and Islands, but the journals are not simply descriptive. They are frequently pejorative. Thus Pennant's description of the houses of Islay:

> A set of people worn down by poverty: their habitations scenes of misery, made of loose stones; without chimneys, without doors, excepting the faggot opposed to the wind at one or other of the apertures, permitting the smoke to escape through the other, in order to prevent the pains of suffocation. The furniture perfectly corresponds: a pothook hangs from the middle of the roof, with a pot pendant over a grateless fire, filled with fare that may rather be called a permission to exist, than a support of vigorous life... (Pennant, in Simmons [ed] 1998b:217)

Such morally loaded descriptions are also found in the works of the later, nineteenth century ethnological approach to rural settlement. However, earlier accounts like Pennant's are not analytical in the sense that the later work is. Further, the context of rural settlement as evidence of the survival of prehistoric social and material traits into the present, the major theoretical underpinning of that later work, is not manifest in the travelers' accounts. These accounts evidence the beginnings of some important assumptions informing later thinking on Highland settlement and society, though their conceptual and methodological background were also distinct.

The flurry of work on Highland rural settlement from the mid- to late-nineteenth century can be understood not so much as reflecting an interest in the recent past of the Highlands for its own sake, but as being related to the study of prehistory. Contemporary theory stressed that an understanding of the distant past could better be achieved through ethnological analogy. For instance, J Y Simpson in his "Address on Archaeology" to the Society of Antiquaries of Scotland in 1860 stated:

> In our archaeological inquiries into the probable uses and import of all doubtful articles in our museums or elsewhere...[l]et us, like the geologists, try always, when working with such problems, to understand the past by reasoning from the present. Let us study backwards from the known to the unknown. In this way we can easily come to understand, for example, how our ancestors made those single-tree canoes, which have been found so often in Scotland, by observing how the Red Indian, partly by fire and partly by hatchet, makes his analogous canoe at the present day; (Simpson 1862a:31)

It was not just that the material culture of such societies as the Red Indian (*sic.*) showed superficial resemblances to that of past societies in Scotland. The connection was seen to run deeper than this:

... there are in reality two kinds of antiquity, both of which claim and challenge our attention. One of these kinds of antiquity consists in the study
of the habits and works of our distant predecessors and forefathers, who
lived on this earth, and perhaps in this segment of it, many ages ago. The
other kind of antiquity consists of the study of those archaic human habits
and works which may, in some corners of the world, be found still prevailing
among our fellow-men—or even among our fellow-countrymen—down to the
present hour, in despite of all the blessings of human advancement, and the
progress of human knowledge. (Simpson 1862a:32–33)

The material culture of some contemporary societies is not just su-
perficially similar to that of some past societies. The two are intimately
linked, as the former is the survival of the latter into the present. It *is*
the past, in the present.

This close alignment between prehistoric archaeology and ethnography was generally prevalent in western Europe and the United States
in the 1860s and 1870s, and was promoted by the shared commitment
of the two disciplines to an evolutionary approach (Trigger 1989:110).
The ultimate basis of this alignment was the belief in unilinear cultural
evolution evolved by Enlightenment philosophers, a belief that allowed
the equation of past and contemporary societies seen to be in the same
stage of cultural development in terms of a stadial evolutionary scheme
(Trigger 1989:59, 110).

Significant here is the fact that aspects of nineteenth century
Scottish society and material culture, those archaic works of our fellow-
countrymen, were seen to be examples of the past in the present and,
therefore, worthy of study towards a greater understanding of prehistory. Archaic habits and works were seen to persist to their greatest
extent in the Western Isles. So it was that, from the late-eighteen fifties
until the turn of the century, a series of archaeological and ethnographic
studies were carried out there with a view to understanding and recording aspects of the archaic society then inhabiting the area. The ethnological approach continued in cases into the early twentieth century
(e.g., MacKenzie 1904; Curwen 1938), and such later studies sometimes explicitly ascribed to a theoretical approach like that outlined by
Simpson and described above (e.g., Curwen 1938:261).

The ethnological approach often focused on shieling (summer
pasture) sites, especially the beehive structures of the Western Isles, as
most reminiscent of prehistoric forms. Analysis of shielings and other
related sites was often pursued through excavation, as on St Kilda (Muir
1860). Particularly notable is the work of Captain (or Commander) F W L
Thomas (1860; 1868). As an example, I will discuss his paper "On the
Primitive Dwellings and Hypogea of the Outer Hebrides" (1868).

Thomas' study of Hebridean dwellings explicitly follows Simpson's suggestion that prehistorians should work backwards from the known to the unknown. He makes this context clear:

> Proceeding from the centers of civilization on the east coast of Scotland towards the north and west, the cottages of the peasantry become still more simple in form and poor in comfort, until on the shores of the Atlantic there are dwellings so primitive, that we appear to reach backward to the Stone period almost at once. (Thomas 1868:154)

To illustrate his point, Thomas goes on to describe a number of blackhouses (dwellings) in the Hebrides, providing annotated plans and drawings from photographs. These houses are seen as recent examples of "a very old style" (Thomas 1868:156) and specific features, such as the thickness of the walls, are drawn on as being of great archaic importance, being evident in recent and ancient forms of dwelling alike (Thomas 1868:157–158).

Perhaps most interesting in this context, however, is his discussion of shieling structures. Describing his experience of entering one such structure inhabited at the time of his visit, he says:

> The situation was delightful to an archaeologist, for he found himself almost introduced to the Stone period: the dwelling of moor-stones and turf, without one morsel of wood or iron, no other tool required than a wooden spade; baskets of bent, docks, or straw; straw or hair ropes for an unwilling cow; and a very few years before the present time, both cooking and milk vessels made on the spot from the first clay that could be found. (Thomas 1868:162)

The interesting aspect of his discussion is the context in which he places shieling structures. Certain architectural traits, most notably the corbelled stone roof that gave rise to the term beehive, are seen to be common to these structures and other, older ones. Such perceived formal similarities between the beehive shieling and certain prehistoric forms, such as *Pict's houses* (i.e., wheelhouses) and *hypogea* (i.e., souterrains), are taken to demonstrate the survival of the past into the present. This assumption allows Thomas to use information gathered on the use of space in the shieling to aid interpretation on the use of space in the wheelhouse. For instance, it allows him to calculate the number of people who could have slept in the latter with reference to the number in the former, related to floor space. Also significant is the fact that Thomas notes that while souterrains existed in the Lowlands, beehive dwellings did not (Thomas 1868:187–189). It is no surprise, then, that his interpretation of these souterrains is based on examples from the Western Isles. It is there that the principles governing their construction and use were seen to survive and, thus, to be accessible to the archaeologist.

An evolutionary interpretation of the archaeological record was not the only accepted theoretical framework at the time (Trigger 1989: 102–103). From the 1830s, the doctrine of degenerationism became increasingly popular. In an extreme form, this held that humanity originally existed in a state far superior to that of modern savages. Generally, it questioned the unilinear evolutionary scheme discussed above. The study of Scottish Highland and Island rural settlement still played a role within this different context.

Particularly significant is Arthur Mitchell's *The Past in the Present: What is Civilization?* (1880). Mitchell was prominent in the Scottish archaeological community being, in 1880, Professor of Ancient History to the Royal Scottish Academy and Secretary of the Society of Antiquaries of Scotland. In the preface he sums up his aims in writing:

> ...in showing how often the Past is seen in the Present—how many neo-archaic objects and customs exist among us—I have sought and found opportunities of showing that the methods followed in archaeological inquiries should be as strict as those which are deemed necessary in other departments of science....I have endeavored, in a special manner, to show that strict methods should be followed in those archaeological inquiries which are at the same time anthropological, because in them there seems to be a special liability to fail in seeing the whole significance of the observations from which conclusions are drawn as to the antiquity and condition of the so-called Primeval Man. (Mitchell 1880:v–vi)

Mitchell is referring to the tendency, seen above, for contemporary primitive societies to be viewed as equivalent in most respects to past societies, within a linear evolutionary scheme. He argues at length that study of those contemporary societies in fact suggests that a form of evolutionary degenerationism can be seen. In this context, he uses the term "neo-archaic objects" to separate primitive material culture of the present from that of the past. However, as the quotations below make clear, there was still seen to be a concrete link between past and present. Mitchell was not interested in severing that link, but in discussing how it might best be understood.

A second main thread in Mitchell's argument is that while contemporary primitive societies produce material culture that is at first glance simple and uncivilized, it is in fact not a product of people of low intelligence. Furthermore, it need not be less effective than modern equivalents in accomplishing those tasks necessary to procure a living.

Mitchell breaks the investigative link existing between ethnography and archaeology, as contemporary primitive societies are no longer seen as directly equivalent to those of the past. Direct comparisons between the two are problematic. He then proceeds to re-constitute the link between the two disciplines along different lines. Ethnological studies can warn against certain assumptions about past societies. Primitive material culture does not necessarily imply inferior intellect; neither need it be less effective in its role than modern, civilized equivalents. The final point he argues is that rude and high forms of material culture can occur in the same period and in the same nation. The nation can be civilized while not all of its parts seem to be so. This again provides a warning to the prehistorian, in that uncivilized material culture may come from a civilized society. So, while direct comparison between prehistoric and neo-archaic societies is problematic, ethnological studies have value in indirect comparison, most notably in refining the archaeologist's general assumptions about "primitive" societies.

Mitchell draws on several case studies to illustrate his points. Most of these concern the customs and material culture of the Scottish Highlands and Islands in the nineteenth century. He draws on personal experience and on many of the studies noted above. A whole chapter is devoted to the description of "The Black Houses and the Beehive Houses of the Hebrides" (Mitchell 1880:48–72). The Hebridean blackhouse is discussed with reference to the fact that, although it is of rude construction, the intelligence and relative capacity of culture of its builders are not displayed in the primitive nature of the architecture:

> I shall not dwell on the general wretchedness of these dwellings—the absence of privacy and separation of the sexes, the presence in the house of the cattle and their accumulated dung, the want of comforts, etc. For my present purpose it is sufficient if I draw attention to certain features of the building, which seem to me to be of special interest and importance. These are: (1) The thickness of the wall—often six or seven feet; (2) The way in which the wall is built—two facings of dry stone with turf between; (3) The very low door—often barely five feet high; (4) The absence of any light hole or window; and (5) The want of overlapping of the wall by the roof, so that such rain as does not simply wet the roof or fall through it, runs down into the body of the wall. To this last feature, more perhaps than to any of the others, I attach importance. If it were to be accepted as indicative of the intellectual state of the people, that state would certainly be of the very lowest.... To suppose, indeed, that the Lewis arrangement is really the outcome of ignorance and stupidity, is to suppose a degree of ignorance and stupidity which have scarcely been found among any people on the face of the earth.... In point of fact, however, this plan of roofing the Lewis houses is not an expression of want of mind or want of knowledge. The people who adopt it know perfectly well the effects and advantages of making the

roof throw the rain over the wall. Why they do not act up to the measure of their knowledge may be a puzzle, but it is beyond all question that it does not arise either from want of capacity or want of culture. (Mitchell 1880:54–55)

Beehive houses of the Western Isles are also of interest to Mitchell in demonstrating degenerationism. His discussion draws on the perceived architectural link between them and the wheelhouse and the former is seen to be a degenerate form of the latter (Mitchell 1880:58–72). That the two forms of structure are connected, however, is underlined by the fact that Mitchell applies the term beehive house to both. He describes the wheelhouse at Meall na Uamh, Huishinish, South Uist in these terms:

> ... [it] exhibits the same architectural style and knowledge as the simpler beehive houses which have been noticed. But it is vastly more pretentious—altogether a larger conception, and designed for a larger purpose. It is a handsome building and involves much clever planning. It may have been the palace or reception-hall of an ancient chief. (Mitchell 1880:69)

This example is explicitly linked to then contemporary beehive houses in the following terms:

> The handsome beehive building, which I have just described, is ... believed to be older than any of which I have spoken. In other words, as this kind of dwelling passed out of use, it appears to have undergone a degradation or debasement. ... If it is unlikely that we shall ever again have one of these simple beehive houses built in Scotland, it is infinitely more unlikely that we shall ever have one of the size and complicated design of that at Meall na Uamh. (Mitchell 1880:70)

Whether rural settlement of the nineteenth century Scottish Highlands was studied in terms of a linear evolutionary scheme or with reference to degenerationism and other agendas, this period of study is characterized by the fact that the material was not studied for itself. Throughout, the agenda was to place the study of prehistory on a more secure footing. In this light, such settlements were not historically situated and, as a result, their study in relation to cartographic or documentary material and to their proper historical context was hampered. That this was the dominant approach can be seen by its prevalence in the *Proceedings of the Society of Antiquaries of Scotland*, where many of the papers mentioned above were published. Aspects of this line of thought are also evident in at least one major historical work of the period (Skene 1880:Chapter 10, especially 393–394).

However, empirical study of Highland and Island rural settlement was begun. The published accounts of this period of study provide us with a record of these settlements in use and in this sense they are invaluable. They are also useful as expressions of one set of contemporary perceptions of Highland rural society.

As we shall see below, the ahistorical nature of these studies formed a major part of their legacy to the twentieth century. There is, however, another defining characteristic of the nineteenth century work that is worth considering as a basic structuring theme of subsequent studies. This is its holism. Studies of material culture other than settlement and studies of other, non-material, aspects of society accompanied the work discussed above. The majority of these other studies took place within the theoretical frameworks already described.

J Y Simpson, who defined the agenda for studying the past in the present, penned "Notes on some Scottish Magical Charm-Stones, or Curing-Stones" (1862b). In this, magical charms are related to their various functions in a timeless and cross-cultural manner. These charms exist in the present as they did in the past and their function in the present can be taken as a guide to their function in the past. Arthur Mitchell and others also wrote of Scottish superstitions (e.g., Mitchell 1862; Stewart 1888). These were of interest primarily as relics of antiquity (Mitchell 1862:288).

There were other studies relating to moveable material culture. In these, many forms of material were considered, including querns, *craggans* (pots), *crusies* (lamps), and *impstones* (fishing weights) (e.g., Goudie 1888; MacAdam 1881; McGregor 1880).

Perhaps the two key works here are Mitchell's *The Past in the Present*, introduced above, and G L Gomme's introductory address to the Glasgow Archaeological Society, "Archaic Types of Society in Scotland" (1890). Mitchell's book discusses a wide range of material and other characteristics of Highland/Island society in relation to the survival of archaic social and material forms into the late nineteenth century. This is also the agenda of Gomme's paper. It is clear from these two works that it is not just settlement studies, but also related material culture and social analyses, that were carried out at the time within the past in the present framework. Gomme's paper deals with the survival of archaic social organization in both Highland and Lowland Scotland. In his analysis of the Highlands (Gomme 1890:157–164), he considers that the archaic nature of society there is to be seen in kin-based, communal forms of social organization as well as in material culture. He makes explicit the links between settlement, other forms of material culture, tradition and superstition, and social organization.

RURAL SETTLEMENT STUDIES AS FOLK LIFE

As I have suggested, aspects of the ethnological approach to rural settlement studies formed the basis of the subsequent folk life approach. The essential feature of the late nineteenth century approach that informed that of folk life scholars was its holistic outlook. There was also the partial legacy of a lack of historical contextualization. Both themes can be seen in Iorwerth Peate's introduction to the first volume of the journal *Folk Life* (Peate 1963). This journal was established by the Society for Folk Life Studies in the early 1960s and is concerned with the British Isles as a whole. However, papers on the Highlands were published regularly in its early years (e.g., Cregeen 1965; Dunbar 1965; Fenton 1968; 1974; Storrie 1967) and the agenda of the Society and its journal are therefore relevant. Peate explained that:

> The Society aims to further the study of *traditional* ways of life in Great Britain and Ireland and to provide a common meeting point for the many people and institutions engaged with the *varied aspects* of folk life. (Peate 1963:4; my emphasis)

The subject of study is traditional ways of life. The use of the word traditional implies a lack of historicity: "Tradition is the factor which maintains the link between those habits [of living] in present and past times" (Peate 1938:321). The holistic nature of study is captured in the reference to its varied aspects. Peate had outlined the pre-War fragmentation of published folk life studies throughout archaeological, anthropological, and other journals as a result of their wide ranging focus and lack of an appropriate, consolidated outlet (Peate 1963:3).

Although the basis of Highland folk life studies lay in part in the preceding period, there were also changes in theory and in practice. Despite the focus on traditional ways of life, a limited degree of historicity was in fact restored, but only with regard to the transition from traditional to modern society. This came from, and resulted in, the study of this traditional material and cultural life with reference to relevant historical documents. The folk life approach grew from early works like Isabel Grant's *Every-Day Life on an old Highland Farm, 1769–1782* (1924), based on the account book of a Strathspey farm.

However, historic specificity and the consideration of change are largely confined to the period of agricultural Improvement, when the traditional way of life began to disappear. Pre-Improvement society is seen as static, where Improvement brings movement and change.

In terms of changing practice, folk life studies are not usually accompanied by a program of fieldwork, in contrast to the previous tradition. The reasons for this are unclear. However, the emphasis on a wide range of cultural topics, reliance on documentary and oral history, and a disciplinary distinction from archaeology were no doubt contributory.

Looking at the holistic nature of study first, this is clearly evident from the content pages of perhaps the two best-known folk life works, Isabel Grant's *Highland Folk Ways* (1995 [1961]) and Alexander Fenton's *Scottish Country Life* (1999 [1976]). *Highland Folk Ways* contains much information on house architecture and settlement morphology (Chapters 3 and 7). This analysis of the fabric of settlement is complemented by discussion on farmland and the wider landscape (Chapters 3 and 5). Consideration of material culture does not end there. There is a chapter on the moveable objects within the house (Chapter 8), as well as information on the material aspects of craft, economy, transport and much else throughout the book. This concern with the material is placed within the context of a consideration of other aspects of culture. For instance there are chapters on "The People Who Lived on the Land" (6), "The People's Daily Round and Common Tasks" (9), "Food, Physic and Clothing" (14), "Sports and Festivals" (15), and "Seasons and Great Occasions" (16).

Scottish Country Life likewise contains sections on house architecture and landscape organization (Chapters 1 and 11). The rest of this book is more concerned with the practicalities and economy of farming than is Grant's, which has a wider cultural scope. So, *Scottish Country Life* contains chapters on "Tilling the Soil" (2); on the harvesting and processing of grain (3,4,5); on the various crops cultivated (6,8); on the pastoral economy (7,9); on food, fuel and transport (10,12 and 13 respectively); and, on the organization of the farming community (14).

One result of taking a holistic approach was that any consideration of Highland rural settlement and landscape placed that material within a rich social and cultural context. With the folk life approach, however, the timeless nature of Highland rural society, where the past and present merged seamlessly, was partially replaced by an historic past. Change became an issue where continuity had often previously been argued or assumed. As suggested above, though, this theoretical reorientation was largely confined to considerations of the period of agricultural Improvement.

Isabel Grant's earliest substantive study is an analysis of the account book of a Strathspey farm in the later eighteenth century (Grant 1924). This source provides the basis for a discussion of the changing material, social and economic structure of that area at the time.

This stands in contrast to the assumed unchanging nature of Highland society that had informed earlier studies:

> The historical value of the Account Book is greatly enhanced by the date at which it was written. William Mackintosh of Balnespick [its author] happened to live through the most crucial time in the whole history of the Highlands, for by 1769 not only had the new system of agriculture... which we speak of as the 'Agricultural Revolution', begun to permeate the wilder and more backward uplands of Badenoch, but the whole social, political and mental life of the people was being rapidly changed... (Grant 1924:3)

The approach was historical and admitted the changes that had occurred in Highland society in recent centuries. This philosophy is evident elsewhere. For instance, Grant later gave an account of the stages of development of the interior of Highland houses, especially concerned with the placing of the hearth (Grant 1995:160–163). The use of space within Highland houses was considered to have gone through changes. It was not simply a story of the continuity of the prehistoric past into the present. Fenton (1999:Chapter 11) draws more explicit links between agricultural Improvement and the changing layout of the house, although his analysis is not limited to the Highlands alone. In fact, it is probably the restoration of a degree of historicity to the subject that allowed the widening of the geographic sphere of study. Nineteenth century writers largely concerned themselves with the far north and west of Scotland, as the area in which past material and social organization had survived most notably. The introduction of a more historical basis was accompanied by a consideration of other Highland areas (e.g., Grant 1995; Martin 1987) and of Scotland as a whole (Fenton 1999). However, some late nineteenth century studies had begun to consider archaic survivals outside of the north and west (e.g., Gomme 1890).

The above implies that the distinction between nineteenth century studies and folk life studies in theoretical terms is not necessarily that great. The fact that nineteenth century archaeologists confined the geographical extent of their studies to the far northwest, where archaic survivals were at their greatest, suggests they recognized change as having taken place throughout the rest of the country. They did not look at other areas, on the whole, because they were of little use in providing information for analogy with prehistory. They perceived both traditional and modern society within Scotland, but both were largely mutually exclusive.

With folk life studies the split between traditional and modern is maintained. However, the relationship between the two is now more chronological than spatial. Modern, Improved society and material

culture replaced its traditional counterpart in time. Folk life conceptions of the traditional and the modern do have much in common with
those of the nineteenth century, despite the differences already outlined. In folk life studies the explicit statement that the present and
prehistory are directly connected is not made. However, the lack of consideration of change in material culture and society before the period
of Improvement by implication suggests that traditional culture and
society was unchanging. Grant's *Highland Folk Ways* is "a picture of
this [Highland folk] life, within the period for which we have records
and traditions" (Grant 1995:xiii). The records in question, however, are
largely used in considerations of political and social phenomena (e.g.
Chapter 2, The Clans) that are kept apart from the material and social
aspects of everyday life. Her account of the clans traces their history
back to the twelfth century (Grant 1995:15). Alongside this, a chronological framework for each of the various chapters on aspects of everyday life is absent. We are simply presented with statements such
as: "The actual cultivation of the land was done by groups..." (Grant
1995:44). This encourages the reader to graft the temporal framework
of a (much-simplified) political and social history onto a consideration
of everyday practice and its associated material culture. Material and
everyday life in the Highlands becomes static over the period from at
least the twelfth to the eighteenth centuries. It is worth noting here
the assertion by Peate that rural populations are characterized by im-
mobility and primitiveness, and that modern conditions have affected
rapid transformations of the countryside (Peate 1938:321).

The description of pre-Improvement Highland society and material
culture as traditional can be seen as part of the process of characterizing it as unchanging in opposition to the fluid modern world. This
idea of the traditional in Highland and especially Gaelic-speaking society carries with it notions of an authentic, whole, and socially cohesive
society (MacDonald 1997:3–6) that perhaps explains in part the attrac-
tiveness and popularity of folk life accounts. This popularity is despite
academic condemnations of key folk life works (e.g., Evans 1961). The
success of these studies should perhaps be understood within a wider
context of the appropriation of stereotyped aspects of the Scottish (and
especially Highland) rural past in the creation of modern identities, not
least the national (see Creed and Ching 1997:24–26 on this process in
general):

> ...there is clearly a national consciousness about rural lifestyle in
> Scotland...derived more from a contaminated and romantic viewpoint of
> 'ye olde Scotland' than from any academic debate. (MacKay 1993:50)

This may generally be true. However, the use of the word contaminated is unwarranted and is presumably intended to underline the apparent reality and objectivity of recent academic discourse on the subject.

RURAL SETTLEMENT STUDIES AS HISTORICAL ARCHAEOLOGY

In 1960, Horace Fairhurst made some important observations regarding the antiquity of the main characteristics of eighteenth century rural settlement and landscape (Fairhurst 1960). He gave a general descriptive account of the *clachan* (his term for deserted nucleated settlements of the eighteenth and nineteenth centuries) and its Lowland equivalent, the fermtoun. He noted some basic aspects of settlement morphology and house construction that are of regional or chronological importance. Of more significance, however, was his observation of a lacuna in Scottish settlement history between the Iron Age and the eighteenth century. Fairhurst recognized that this lacuna had previously been disguised: "In the absence of documentary proof...it must be admitted that we are largely projecting into a more distant past the conditions prevailing in the early eighteenth century" (Fairhurst 1960:73).

Pre-Improvement settlement form had been viewed as static in time and the projection of eighteenth century material culture characteristics into earlier periods had been seen as unproblematic. Fairhurst problematized the history of rural settlement prior to the eighteenth century.

The four decades subsequent to Fairhurst's paper have seen a number of general studies on the problem, that is our lack of knowledge, of rural settlement prior to the eighteenth century (e.g., Dunbar 1971; Fairhurst 1967; 1971; Laing 1969; Morrison 1977; Yeoman 1991; 1995:Chapter 8). The period in question has become known, in terms of settlement studies, as "the Invisible Centuries" or "a prolonged dark age" (Yeoman 1991; Fairhurst 1967:158, respectively) and Medieval settlement archaeology has become an established concern in Scotland, following from the growth of the subject elsewhere in Britain (Laing 1969:69). Further, the acronym MoLRS (Medieval or Later Rural Settlement) has become enshrined in the literature as a general term for post-Iron Age rural settlement, underlining the acceptance of the problem (e.g., Hingley [ed.] 1993; it could also be argued that the term MoLRS has become something of a euphemism and that, while it recognizes our lack of knowledge of Medieval settlement, it conveniently merges the Medieval with the later and allows us to side-step the issue. I owe this point to Olivia Lelong).

Archaeological excavation and survey have long been argued to be potentially important techniques in dealing with this problem (e.g., Dixon 1993; Fairhurst 1960; 1968; 1969; Fairhurst and Petrie 1964). However, for the Highlands and Islands, survey and excavation have only recently begun to extend our knowledge of Medieval rural settlement (e.g., Barrett and Downes 1993; 1994; 1996; Branigan 1997; Caldwell and Ewart 1993; Caldwell et al. 2000; Crawford 1983; James 1998; RCAHMS 1990:12–13 and *passim*; Sharples and Parker Pearson 1999). The results of these various fieldwork projects are certainly welcome, but it is difficult at this stage to assess their relevance outside of the particular site, region, or chronological range of focus. Having said this, settlement characteristics that may be diagnostic of the period between the Iron Age and the eighteenth century are beginning to be better understood (see especially Barrett and Downes 1993; 1994; 1996; Caldwell et al. 2000; Sharples and Parker Pearson 1999). Some historical geographers and historians have also begun to explore aspects of pre-eighteenth century rural settlement through documentary and cartographic sources, with some success (e.g., Dodgshon 1977; 1993a; 1998a; Smout 1996a; see Bangor-Jones 1993:36–37 for a brief overview).

Perhaps one reason for the general lack of field projects that are successful in locating Medieval settlement is the fact that most of these projects have been characterized by a vague methodology. They concentrate on locating the missing data through excavation of a visible deserted site of perhaps relatively recent date, usually fairly randomly selected, in the hope that earlier material *may* be recovered below. Promisingly, discussion has recently begun to focus on the development of more rigorous methodologies (e.g., Banks 1996; Banks and Atkinson 2000).

The specific results of all of these wide-ranging projects and studies are not of real concern here. Rather, they are of interest in showing an increasing concern with the changing nature of Highland, and Lowland, rural settlement. The idea that settlement and landscapes of the eighteenth and nineteenth centuries can be taken as representative of the end point in a continuum is now seriously challenged.

Recognition of this new past has ramifications for the ways in which we approach the subject of rural settlement. Some of these—the need to establish the nature of Medieval settlement and to construct methodologies in order to do so—we have just seen. There are also ramifications for how we view the relevant archaeological resource. Management and preservation issues in relation to MoLRS sites and landscapes are increasingly under discussion as their significance in writing the history of the period is realized (e.g., see Bangor-Jones 1993; Hingley 1993; 2000; Hingley [ed.] 1993:62–65; Mackay 1993; Swanson 1993; Turner 2000).

The other main characteristic of recent archaeological rural settlement studies is the renewed emphasis on fieldwork. As seen above, there was an amount of survey and excavation associated with rural settlement studies in the nineteenth century. That fieldwork was of its time and was, thus, sporadic, unmethodological, and frequently poorly documented and published. There has been little original fieldwork associated with the major folk life studies of the twentieth century.

In 1993, Donnie MacKay noted that there had been an amount of survey work on rural settlement in Scotland, but only a few excavations (MacKay 1993:43). At the time, this was generally true, and survey-specific projects continue to be important. Highland rural settlement made its first appearance in the Inventories of the Royal Commission on the Ancient and Historical Monuments of Scotland with the volumes on Argyll (RCAHMS 1971; 1975; 1980; 1982; 1984; 1992). In these, descriptive text, sometimes with accompanying plan surveys or photographs, is provided for one or two well preserved examples. The Commission volume for northeast Perth focused on understanding archaeological landscapes in that area (RCAHMS 1990). Surveys of multi-period landscapes included potential historic period settlement and field systems. Amongst these were the new Pitcarmick-type buildings, examples of which have since been excavated, producing radiocarbon dates in the mid first millennium AD (Barrett and Downes 1993; 1994; 1996; RCAHMS 1990:12–13 and *passim*). The landscape-oriented approach adopted in the northeast Perth volume is part of a wider interest in landscape studies in archaeology in general. Its potential for addressing the problems of pre-eighteenth century settlement is significant if the case of the Pitcarmick-type building is anything to go by. The Afforestable Land Survey of RCAHMS has also provided several useful recent surveys including areas of rural settlement (see Dixon 1993).

Surveys of MoLRS sites have also been conducted by a wide variety of other archaeological groups, both professional and non-professional (e.g., Gailey 1962a; Johnstone and Scott Wood [eds.] 1996; MacDonald [ed.] 1999; MacDonald and Scott Wood [eds.] 1995; 1996; 1998; 1999; Shepherd and Ralston 1981). Most of these surveys have concentrated on single settlement sites.

In 1993, when MacKay highlighted the prevalence of survey over excavation, it is true that there had only been a few prominent excavations (e.g., Fairhurst 1968; 1969; Stewart and Stewart 1988). This situation is beginning to change, though, and the excavation of rural settlement sites of the eighteenth and nineteenth centuries and exploration for and excavation of pre-eighteenth century settlement have become accepted archaeological pursuits in a number of contexts.

These aims are now often included in the agendas of wider ranging landscape projects. Indeed, it has been argued that the landscape context is essential to the understanding of MoLRS sites (Atkinson 1995). Landscape specific studies include the Dunbeath project, looking at the archaeology and history of a single estate in Caithness through time (Morrison 1996). SEARCH (Sheffield Environmental and Archaeological Research Campaign in the Hebrides) has conducted excavations on sites in the Western Isles dating from the Neolithic through to the nineteenth century and undertaken related survey work (Branigan 1997; Branigan and Foster 1995; Gilbertson et al. [eds.] 1996; Sharples and Parker Pearson 1999; Symonds 2000). The Ben Lawers Historic Landscape Project likewise has a wide chronological remit within a specific landscape, the north side of Loch Tay (Atkinson 2000). Geographically adjacent to Loch Tay, the Rannoch Archaeological Project also has a similar remit again (MacGregor 2000). The Loch Borralie area in northern Sutherland is a landscape rich in archaeological remains of varying character from a wide variety of periods from the Neolithic. It too forms the focus of a recently conceived landscape project that aims to record and contextualize the archaeology of past human interaction in a specific landscape context that naturally includes Medieval and more recent settlement (Lelong and MacGregor forthcoming).

There are also site-specific research projects in progress. For example, there is the excavation of an immediately pre-Improvement settlement at Easter Raitts, near Kingussie, Strathspey (Lelong and Wood 2000). Work there in recent years has targeted a number of dwellings, outhouses, and other features.

Excavation of rural settlement sites is now a concern in the context of developer-funded rescue archaeology, where fieldwork is executed by commercial archaeological field units (e.g., MacGregor et al. 1999; McCullagh and Tipping [eds.] 1998).

Considering excavation and survey together, there seems to have been something of an explosion in fieldwork in recent years. This may be due to a number of factors. The intellectual shift involving the problematization of pre-Improvement settlement history has provided a specific aim for much of this recent excavation and survey (e.g., see Fairhurst 1960; Fairhurst and Petrie 1964). Archaeological fieldwork has been seen as central to the problem of identifying and characterizing pre-eighteenth century settlement in the light of a lack of appropriate documentary material (Laing 1969:69). Until recently, historical sources have provided the most important advances in general terms (e.g., Dodgshon 1977; 1993a), but generally valid conclusions about Medieval settlement form and process are beginning to emerge from some of the most recent archaeological work (Barrett and Downes 1993; 1994; Caldwell et al. 2000; RCAHMS 1990; Sharples and Parker Pearson 1999).

As noted above, more prosaic influences have also brought about the recent increase in fieldwork as development threats have led to archaeological survey and excavation. This impetus to fieldwork may seem a straightforward consequence of increasing modern development. However, it is important to realize that the inclusion of rural settlement sites, especially those of the last few hundred years, within the remit of commercial archaeology itself requires the recognition of such sites *as* archaeology. The fact that RCAHMS only began to include such sites and landscapes in its inventories fairly recently underlines the fact that their acceptance as archaeology is a recent phenomenon. In the nineteenth century such material found its archaeological role in providing analogy for prehistoric studies. The study of rural settlement within folk life studies likewise separated the topic from traditional archaeological concerns. Rural settlement was for folk life scholars and too recent and familiar for archaeologists. Rural settlement was not archaeology. The legacy of nineteenth century to folk life studies included a tendency to extrapolate eighteenth century material conditions back into the past. The lack of field survey within folk life studies can be understood partially as a result of this.

The problematization of pre-eighteenth century settlement by scholars such as Horace Fairhurst from the 1950s played a key role in bringing rural settlement into the archaeological mainstream. The separation of the history of past settlement from tradition (folk life) and the appreciation that documents relevant to the study of that history were few made this an archaeological problem. The subject has no doubt also benefited from the general extension of archaeological concern to include recent material culture, like yesterday's refuse and beer cans (Rathje and Murphy 1992; Shanks and Tilley 1987).

Other reasons might be suggested for the increase in fieldwork concerning rural settlement. Upstanding structures are common on such sites and are perhaps assumed to be easy to understand, as houses, barns, tool sheds, and many other seemingly unproblematic spaces. This perhaps partly explains the popularity of deserted townships in the training of students in survey technique, but most of all, the upsurge in fieldwork concerning rural settlement and landscape in recent decades represents increasing interest in a historically situated archaeological account of the rural past of the Highlands. As we have seen, *this* past has become an important concern in several spheres other than archaeological fieldwork, whether driven by development or research. It has produced debate over the management of the relevant archaeological resource (e.g., papers in Hingley [ed.] 1993) and stimulated increasing academic interest (perhaps seen most notably in recent conferences and collections of papers on the subject, e.g., Atkinson et al. [eds.] 2000; Morrison [ed.] 1980).

However, despite the flurry of recent work, I would suggest that the archaeological remains of rural settlement are yet to be used to anything near their full potential in writing the Medieval and later history of the Highlands. Certain essential factors within recent approaches to the subject have limited the potential contribution of archaeologists to the debate on recent Highland society (see below). This potential contribution is at least as significant as that of the documentary historian, who has traditionally defined the research agenda for the period in question.

ARCHAEOLOGY, DOCUMENTS, AND THE WRITING OF SOCIAL HISTORY

Despite the restoration of historicity to the subject and the recent upsurge of interest in rural settlement, there has been almost no attempt to construct the recent social history of the Highlands from an archaeological perspective. This can be understood through a consideration of the relationship of history and archaeology in rural settlement studies and I will concentrate here on those studies relating to the eighteenth and nineteenth centuries.

The majority of rural settlement study is empirical in nature. Even the most recent of RCAHMS inventories simply give a physical description as the entry for an individual site, although there is some synthesis of this material in the introductions to the volumes (e.g., RCAHMS 1990:11–13, 95–171). A typical entry will categorize the structure or site, as a township or shieling for example. It will note the relationship of the archaeology to the local topography and the spatial inter-relationships of the archaeological elements of the site. It will give the dimensions of the various structures, give a description of construction techniques and fabric, and much more. Surveys carried out by organizations other than RCAHMS are usually equally empirically orientated (e.g., MacDonald and Scott Wood [eds.] 1999), as are many excavation reports (e.g., Fairhurst 1968; 1969; MacGregor et al. 1999: 17–44).

Admittedly, many such works are subject to a strict remit that is not of the excavator or surveyor's design. For instance, the excavations and survey at Tigh Vectican, Arrochar, were undertaken by a commercial archaeological field unit (Glasgow University Archaeological Research Division) on behalf of Argyll and Bute Council (the developer) under terms of reference supplied by the West of Scotland Archaeology Service, the archaeological monitoring body (MacGregor et al. 1999:5). The main aim was to establish and define the nature of the archaeological resource on the site in order to produce recommendations for mitigation during any subsequent development (MacGregor et al. 1999:6). In such circumstances, it is easy to understand why the report is largely confined to empirical statements. It is equally easy to understand why such an approach has been followed in a context where the prime objective is to teach students survey technique (e.g., Johnstone and Scott Wood 1996 [eds.]; MacDonald [ed.] 1999; MacDonald and Scott Wood [eds.] 1995; 1996; 1998; 1999).

Most empirical accounts do contain some historical component. This often takes the form of a brief chronological narrative detailing the main documentary and cartographic sources available that relate to the site (e.g., Johnstone and Scott Wood [eds.] 1996:27; MacGregor et al. 1999:8–17; RCAHMS 1990:95 and *passim*). This account is nearly always physically separated within the written report from that of the archaeology itself. The role of historical narrative within such reports is largely to refine our empirical understanding of the material culture. Documents can be used to date changes in the character of settlement or landscape, flesh out the archaeological bones by suggesting the potential functions of the various structures on a site or by giving information on past material culture now largely invisible archaeologically (organic materials, for example), or suggest the existence of other missing aspects of a site, such as its Medieval antecedents (e.g., Gailey 1962a; Fairhurst 1968; 1969).

Here, archaeological and documentary research are pursued together, but still largely apart, to further our empirical understanding. Most reference to the social aspects of a site or landscape is with this agenda in mind. The evidence given in the trial of Patrick Sellar, the notorious Sutherland factor associated with the clearance of a sizeable part of the population of that estate, is used in the Rosal excavation report to suggest where the structural wood in the houses came from (Fairhurst 1968:146).

It would be unfair to maintain that there has been absolutely no use of the archaeology of this period in discussing key social issues, such as clearance (e.g., Fairhurst 1968:142–143). However, such discussion is literally confined to half a dozen or so pages out of the hundreds of the combined reports. Further, where any account is given of the social history of a site or area it has largely been a case of uncritically lifting the traditional documentary historical narrative (of Improvement or clearance, for example) and pasting it onto the empirical archaeological account.

The result is that the role of archaeology in constructing the recent history of the Highlands has been an extremely limited one. Archaeological research has become an exercise in the illustration of narratives defined by documentary historians. Its main active role is to fill in the gaps where documentary evidence is lacking, as with Medieval settlement, or to confirm document-based hypotheses. Such a role is clear from the manner in which material culture is used within largely documentary-based research (e.g., Bil 1990; Stewart 1990). Archaeology here primarily maps and illustrates. As such, archaeological rural settlement studies tend to maintain a traditional historical account that often uncritically accepts the views of the Improvers themselves (MacKay 1993:46). This account has recently come under scrutiny from documentary historians who have increasingly focused on the question of overt resistance to Improvement and clearance (see Harvey 1990 for an overview).

Empirical archaeological research and the combination of documentary and material culture resources in the manner described have been useful. Such studies have formulated a basic understanding of settlement and landscape in physical and chronological terms that is essential to any social archaeology. Potentially important historical contexts for aspects of material culture have been defined (e.g., the link between geometric settlement morphology and Improvement, Gailey 1960:104; 1962a:162–163). However, the fact remains that such work has remained very superficial in terms of writing social history (MacKay 1988:111).

A small minority within the subject has recently begun to address the passive role of archaeology. The two main discussions here are both concerned with assessing the cognitive aspects of past landscapes (see Knapp and Ashmore [eds.] 1999 for a range of similar studies). Donnie MacKay (1988:111–112) outlines this approach as a concern in rural settlement studies. He writes:

> Clearance settlement archaeology, for want of a better title, is about people, and the effect that the various social processes at work in the 17th,

18th and 19th centuries have had. Archaeology should not merely be restricted to classification ... we should elaborate on our evidence to consider
the implications of social and ideological factors in creating our historical
landscapes. ... Field survey ... with the help of documentary and folklore
sources and an awareness of the social processes at work throughout the
period, give us the opportunity to relate archaeology to the ideological and
cultural factors which were transforming the lifestyle of much of the Scottish
Highlands ... (MacKay 1988:111)

The importance of MacKay's approach is its emphasis on considering how people perceived their material surroundings. He outlines
how we might see this perception as mediated through folklore and religious belief, for example (Gazin-Schwartz 2001 is a recent statement
of this sort of analysis and extends the discussion to moveable material
culture).

This approach has its problems in that material culture is separated from transformative ideological and social processes. There is a
danger here, again, of uncritically lifting narratives constructed in the
discipline of documentary history and applying them in archaeological
contexts. Again, history and archaeology are kept separate. In understanding the archaeological data by pasting separately constructed
historical narratives on top of it, the potential of material culture
as a resource in the construction and reconstruction of society is
ignored. Material things are seen to change as a consequence of change
in ideological and cultural factors. There is no scope for seeing the
material environment as active in the creation and maintenance of
social relationships.

This first criticism relates directly to a second. The construction of
cognitive landscapes in the approach outlined by MacKay is the construction of normative and largely static perceptions of landscape. We
are met with statements of how the association of fairies and dwarfs
with landscape features and times of the day impinged on travel, for
example (MacKay 1988:112). The assumption is that everyone held the
same ideas about their material surroundings and this caused everyone to act in the same way. There is no discussion of how such concepts
might be mobilized, questioned, or refuted in different social contexts or
by different people. For MacKay, ideology is apparently directly translatable as belief. There is no social component, in the sense of the dynamics of interpersonal relationships.

Olivia Lelong has put forward a more concrete study of such cognitive landscapes (2000). She discusses the Sutherland Clearances and
the attendant relocation of tenants of the Sutherland estates from the
inland straths to the coastal strip. With this physical dislocation came

a cognitive dislocation. Tenants, their families and others were up-rooted from a landscape they knew intimately and a landscape that structured their understanding of the world. This was a landscape of fields and agriculture, of mountains and rivers, that bore the physical marks of past human activity and within which their daily practices were embedded. Physical relocation to the coast confronted these people with a new landscape dominated by the sea. This was fluid, bearing no physical trace of past activity that they could understand. It was strange. People did not have the necessary experience required to extract a decent living from it. Some learnt to adapt while others protested at this enforced physical and cognitive relocation through emigration.

Lelong's paper is different from MacKay's in that she considers how people interacted with their material environment and how this structured their perception of their world. She is less concerned with symbolism and more interested in daily practice and routine. Her account is to some degree still normative, though, in that different perspectives made possible by those daily routines are not considered. An assessment of differing daily routines within a given settlement or group of settlements in the landscape is of course difficult due to the limited excavation and survey data available. It is vital, therefore, that those recording rural settlements and landscapes in the Highlands take on board the potential contribution of their work to the social history of the region and rethink their fieldwork strategies.

In general, then, some recent studies have begun to question traditional interpretations of recent Highland history, or at least to elaborate new and complementary perspectives. In doing so they have started to redefine the role of archaeology in writing that history. They have underlined the need to "adopt an approach to the past which recognizes the cultural unity of the various sorts of evidence—one which is attentive to the importance of material things" (Driscoll 1984:109).

However, these studies are questionable on theoretical grounds. Both Lelong and MacKays' studies are to different extents normative. Further, MacKay seems to envisage landscape as passive, although Lelong argues that it did play a role in structuring peoples understanding of their world.

AN ACTIVE ARCHAEOLOGY OF IMPROVEMENT

Through this chapter, I have traced the development of historicity and of the modern archaeological approach in rural settlement studies.

These two themes underlie any current study of Highland rural settlement.

The rise of historicity has given the discipline of archaeology a role in writing the history of the Highlands and Islands of Scotland in the historic period. It has become clear that material culture, settlement and landscape were not static prior to the period of agricultural Improvement as had previously been assumed. Some evidence of their changing nature has been documented in recent years. The assumption of stasis had discernable roots in the theoretical assumptions of the *Ethnology* and *Folk Life* approaches. Most notable here is the distinction drawn between traditional and modern society and the characterization of the former as conservative, homogenous and unchanging. For some, these theoretical orientations allowed the assumption that, in the case of traditional societies, the past and the present merge into one and are directly translatable as each other.

It is now recognized that there are fundamental gaps in our knowledge of recent historic society and its material world in the Highlands and Islands. With the introduction of the modern archaeological approach, archaeology as a discipline has given itself a significant role in future research. Currently, this is especially clear in the case of Medieval rural settlement, where archaeological fieldwork is perhaps the best line of approach to the problem (although history and historical geography have also proven the usefulness of a re-assessment of known cartographic and documentary sources).

However, archaeology should not confine itself to filling in gaps left by documentary historians. Some recent studies have sought to develop new approaches that allow archaeologists to say something new about well-documented periods and processes, such as the clearance of the land. In these studies, archaeologists have a basic role in building our understanding of Highland society as we can construct possible routine environments in which people would have learnt and renegotiated their understanding of and role in society. With such different understandings and related social relations in mind, we can engage in discussion of how people in the past may have perceived, approached, instigated, or attempted to reject historical episodes like clearance and processes like Improvement.

The concern with practical understandings of the world, learnt in everyday, routine life, is a strength in archaeology and gives the discipline a significant role in relation to historical periods. However, a re-assessment of the theoretical assumptions of this archaeology of the routine in a Scottish context is needed. The construction of homogenous, normative routine environments, from which all people approach society at large with the same understanding of the world, does not allow for differences, misunderstandings, and conflicts within Highland society. Traditionally, discussion of such difference and conflict has been confined to tenant–landlord relationships (on this tendency see, e.g., Carter 1981; MacDonald 1997:69–75; Macinnes 1998b:180–184; and Chapter 7, this volume). In many historical narratives, a Highland people is described which is a homogenous entity (MacDonald 1997:69–75). Some recent history is challenging this assumption and the received fact that the said Highland people was conservative, traditional and passive with regard to social change (e.g., Devine 1999).

In adopting an active role in the construction of the recent history of Highland and Island society, archaeologists should take account of the increasingly evident complexity and diversity of that society. The archaeological concern with the material and routine provides an opportunity for the consideration of social diversity and the ways in which people constructed, accepted or sought to change their social world. In the next chapter I will discuss in detail how we might understand and analyze society and social change, particularly with reference to the emergence of capitalism, of which Improvement was a part.

Capitalism and Society | 3

Improvement in the Scottish Highlands was a process involving the transformation of social relations, the transformation of the ways in which people related to one another. In undertaking a social analysis of Improvement, that process should be relocated as part of a more general process, the emergence of capitalism. Some consider it settled that the emergence of capitalism is the proper subject of study for archaeologists of the recent past (Leone and Potter 1988:19). Whether or not this is true is irrelevant here, but it is clear that archaeologies of capitalism are an established concern in some parts of the world. The notion of an explicit archaeology of capitalism has recently been introduced to English archaeology (e.g., Johnson 1993a; 1996). The word capitalism denotes a complex process and there are a bewildering variety of ways in which to characterize it and address it from an archaeological perspective (for an introduction see, e.g., Johnson 1996; Leone 1999; Orser 1996:71–81). Capitalism can be seen to relate to architecture, garden design, landscape form, or settlement pattern. It is bound up with the growth of consumerism and the mass-production of ceramics and other goods. It connects the modern factory with a distinct concept of time and with work discipline. It involves a transformation of gender relations. It is at once a local and a global process, transforming relations at a regional level and operating across and between continents. The list goes on. I will not, and could not, attempt to combine all that has been said about the archaeological study of capitalism here. My primary interest is to outline capitalism as a form of society, as a particular way in which people relate to each other. Central to this form of social interaction is a concept of the self as autonomous individual.

Improvement should be understood as a series of social and material transformations brought about by individuals and groups addressing their own interests. These interests were not conceived in abstract terms, but were grounded in the past and in prior experience of the social and physical world. Improvement was also not a homogenous, universal or inevitable phenomenon. UnImproved ways of living, interacting, and thinking were maintained or constructed in opposition. This is not to say that we should oppose different cultural groups within Highland society in the recent past and narrate that past as the history of conflict or conciliation between these different cultures. Rather, we should explore a process of social interaction, which is complex and diverse. The same person could engage with many others in differently structured relationships. This engagement did not involve the free determination of social position and the unhindered manipulation of the material environment, however. While Improvement was a process involving fundamental change to the practice of social interaction, it was also a process inextricably bound up with relations of power.

The points just raised will be considered below in discussing capitalism and its archaeological study. They will then be further refined in a more general discussion of the constitution of society, or how social relations are structured, and the process of social change. The manner in which social structure is constituted, maintained, and transformed can be defined analytically in terms of social practice and ideology. Social practice refers to the interaction of people in different contexts, such as in everyday life around the farm or in more ritualized spaces and during more defined and bounded periods, like at church or during a feast. As social relations have a material component and social change is in part instigated or resisted through the ordering of the material world, archaeology is relevant to any analysis of past society. The maintenance or transformation of relationships between people is connected to the ways in which different physical environments facilitate or obstruct patterns of interaction. Ideology describes explicit statements of how the world is or how it should be. It is not the same as simple belief, but has a social component at its core. Ideological statements aim to justify or question the structure of society.

ARCHAEOLOGY AND CAPITALISM: THE GEORGIAN ORDER

The project of an archaeology of capitalism is frequently traced back to James Deetz' work on the Georgian worldview (e.g., Deetz 1996) and further to Henry Glassie's *Folk Housing in Middle Virginia* (1975). The key characteristic of these works here is that they understand material culture, architecture, and landscape as conditioned by deep-seated worldviews, by structures of cognition, by culture (and they are thus related to the cognitive landscape studies discussed in Chapter 2). They can be labeled structuralist in that they see all objects in a particular culture as equal with respect to the overall organization and coherence of the total structure of that culture (Leone 1982:743).

Glassie (1975) relates a wide variety of changes in building tradition to what he sees as their underlying structure. He sees a series of binary oppositions that, from the eighteenth century, increasingly characterized the thinking behind buildings and that mediated between the builder and occupier and both nature and society. For example, there was increasing emphasis on intellect over emotion in building design, on private space over public space, and on artificial over natural construction materials. For the period from the eighteenth century, Glassie primarily focuses on the opposition of intellect to emotion and private to public in social relations and on the opposition of artificial to natural in ecological relations. Such binary oppositions seemingly relate to more general oppositions, principally the contrast between the internal and the external and between the artificial and the natural. Glassie suggests that there are degrees of internalness and artificiality in both human-to-human and human-to-nature relations.

On the subject of intellect and emotion he says:

> ... the house is an expression of a cultural ideal that valued the intellectual model over emotional need. It is not that the spaces provided by the house for human action were dysfunctional, but that the people were willing to endure chilly corners or rooms that may have felt a bit spacious or cramped in order to live in a house that was a perfect representation of an idea. (Glassie 1975:119)

Giving substance to an idea takes precedence over behavioral need. This was increasingly seen to be the case in Middle Virginian house building from around 1760.

On private or public space:

> This is the relation between inhabitants and visitors—the opposition of internal and external humanity. ... Between the older and the newer houses there was a near volumetric identity ... [b]ut the arrangement of these volumes was dissimilar, and that dissimilarity signals a great change in the desire for privacy. In the new house the most public room was only as accessible as the most private room was in the earlier buildings. (Glassie 1975:120–121)

The increasing need for privacy is to be seen, to give one example, in the fact that the visitor first enters a hallway in the later house. In the older form, they would enter the main room directly, where the family might be eating or chatting by the fire (Glassie 1975:121).

The history of the opposition between artificial substance and natural substance from the first European colonization of the area through to the nineteenth century is seen as diverging from the above trends.

Rather than natural substances increasingly being replaced by artificial ones from the mid-eighteenth century, there was from the start a strong transformation of nature in the Middle Virginian house: "The inferences drawn from old houses . . . indicate that artificiality and internalness were less aggressively mediated in man-to-man relations than in man-to-nature relations" (Glassie 1975:135).

Artificiality is seen here in the transformation of natural substances through such processes as making planks from trees, making bricks from clay or earth and emphasizing geometrical forms (e.g., uniform and straight timber-framing) over forms derived from the properties of the material (e.g., naturally curving crucks). However, despite this long-standing opposition of the man-made and artificial to the natural, from the early nineteenth century on buildings were erected with less and less reference to the local environment (Glassie 1975:136–137), perhaps displaying an increased opposition of artificial to natural in decreased reference to nature.

Glassie sees the increasing lack-of-fit with the local environment as related to the opposition of extensiveness to intensiveness (Glassie 1975:138–140,146–151). Extensive architecture is that which fits best in a hot and wet climate, with the house extended outwards and upwards. The house is lifted from the earth, the ceilings are high and the space contained within the house is expanded by way of extensions to the main fabric. Windows and doors are relatively large and chimneys are exterior to the house. Extensive architecture is complex in comparison to the relative simplicity of intensive architecture. Through time, windows and doors become smaller, chimneys are incorporated into the main fabric and extensions no longer push out from the sides of the house but are tucked round the back.

A shift from extensiveness to intensiveness can also be seen at the landscape level (Glassie 1975:140–141, 143–144). Farms had been dispersed, as had their constituent houses and outbuildings. Stores, schools, post offices, and churches were located at crossroads, but not usually the same ones. Cemeteries were likewise dispersed. Through the nineteenth century, people moved closer to the roads and to one another. Farm outbuildings were increasingly pulled towards the house and linearly arranged. Other oppositions, however, constrict the move to intensiveness at this level, most notably the increased need for privacy.

For Glassie, these varied oppositions—private to public; intellect to emotion; artificial to natural; internal to external; intensive to extensive—are ordered by another, fundamental opposition (Glassie 1975:160). This is the opposition of chaos and control, with increasing emphasis on the latter through time. There is an increasing effort to exercise control over natural substances, over spaces, and over human will and ability (Glassie 1975:162). The bilaterally symmetrical, tripartite design of Georgian architecture "was the perfect end to the builder's search for architectural order" (Glassie 1975:170).

The concept of the Georgian worldview and its defining role in Anglo-American society from the eighteenth century on was picked up in James Deetz' *In Small Things Forgotten* (1996 [1977]). He contrasts the Georgian worldview to the Medieval and concludes:

> Order and control: the eighteenth century is called the age of reason, and it saw the rise of scientific thought in the Western world and the development of Renaissance-derived form, balanced and ordered, in the Anglo-American world. By 1760 significant numbers of American colonists partook of this new worldview. Mechanical where the older was organic, balanced where the older had been asymmetrical, individualized where the older had been corporate, this new way of perceiving the world is the hallmark of...[the period] which lasts to the present and accounts for much of the way in which we ourselves look upon reality. (Deetz 1996:63–64)

Deetz goes on to reference Glassie's work in defining the shift from the Medievally-derived, organic house form to that of the tripartite, bilaterally symmetrical Georgian house (Deetz 1996:66), and his book contains a whole chapter on changing house forms (Deetz 1996: Chapter 5). However, his major contribution is in extending the analysis of the impact of this worldview beyond the province of architecture. For him, the extent to which the Georgian worldview structures a vast array of the material aspects of life in this period "demonstrates the power with which cognition reshaped the Anglo-American material world" (Deetz 1996:67). His focus is the stronger emphasis on the individual with the Georgian worldview, something Glassie had touched on in noticing an increasing need for privacy, for example.

In discussing ceramics, Deetz (1996:Chapter 3) emphasizes their role in the foodways of early America. Foodways are the particular system of food conceptualization, procurement, distribution, preservation, preparation, and consumption. As ceramics play an important role in foodways, changing ceramic form can be tied to changing foodways. Deetz defines three main phases in the changing ceramic assemblages from sites in New England. First come the plain, utility earthenwares, with small quantities of Delft, Rhenish stoneware, and slipware. These come from sites predating the mid seventeenth century. Second come a broad variety of imported wares alongside vast quantities of American-made utility wares dating from the mid seventeenth to the late eighteenth centuries. The third phase is characterized by popular creamwares and pearlwares, dating from the time of the Revolution through the first quarter of the nineteenth century.

The first period is seen to relate to the foodways of English yeomen, as many early American colonists are held to derive from this group. Under this system of foodways, ceramics played a minor role, with food served directly from metal cooking pots and eaten from wooden trenchers. These trenchers were communally used, by two or more trencher mates, as were drinking vessels. Most of the ceramics from these early sites relate to dairying activity.

In the second period, dairying ceramics are joined by a diversity of other forms. In contrast to contemporary England, there is a scarcity of plates and, in America, those that are found were probably used as display items rather than in food consumption. Ceramic cups and mugs do become common after 1660, however, and were probably being integrated into food-consumption alongside the trencher. In this period, there is a steady increase in the use of individualized utensils seen in the increasing numbers of ceramic drinking vessels.

After 1760, there is dramatic change with the preponderance of plates and other items, such as chamber pots. The plates match each other and match the ceramic cups and saucers found. Through ceramics, Deetz argues, we see a shift from a corporate to an individual emphasis in foodways. People come to have their own plate and cup. The one person-one dish relationship is symmetrical in contrast to the corporate way of eating. This individualism is also to be seen in the increase in personal chamber pots. Foodways and ceramics after 1760 display an increased emphasis on order, control, and balance.

Moving to the gravestones of New England, Deetz (1996:Chapter 4) outlines three basic designs used between about 1680 and 1820. The earliest is the death's-head with blank eyes and a grinning visage. Sometime in the eighteenth century, according to location, the winged cherub replaced this design. In turn, towards the end of the eighteenth century, the cherub was replaced by a third basic design of a willow tree overhanging a pedestaled urn. The shift from death's-head to cherub is related to a change from Puritan religious views, where the death's-head as reminder of mortality was appropriate, to the views of the mid eighteenth century religious revival movements known as the Great Awakening.

During the Great Awakening, from the 1720s to 1760s, a doctrine espousing personal involvement of the individual with the supernatural was preached. In this context, cherubs became appropriate. This change is accompanied by a change in inscriptions on gravestones, moving from the "Here lies . . ." formula to that of "Here lies the Body. . . ." The latter group of inscriptions emphasizes the departure of the soul and talk of resurrection and heavenly reward, as opposed to the stress on decay and the brevity of life in the first.

The urn-and-willow style stones bear inscriptions akin to memorials. Deetz suggests that these stones are a depersonalization of burial markers and point to the secularization of religion. The memorial stones of the third period are held to display an increased emphasis on the individual, relating as they do an account of that person's life. This came with an increase in family burial plots towards the end of the eighteenth century, representing a shift from the earlier practice of packing bodies into a finite burial ground. By the early nineteenth century carefully designated lots had appeared and there was only one body per grave pit.

The individualization of the Georgian worldview can be extended beyond gravestones, houses, and ceramics to include many of those other small things forgotten (Deetz 1996:Chapter 6). Cutlery is seen to increase in use with the emphasis on individualized foodways and place settings. Individual chairs become important. Meals are decreasingly of the composite stew-type and increasingly composed of individual portions, ending in the mechanical and tripartite meat, potato and vegetable dish. Deetz sees these changes, and others, as relating to change at a very deep level of the Anglo-American mind, so abstract that it manifests itself in a bewildering variety of ways (Deetz 1996:174).

These two influential, structuralist works have been critically appraised by Mark P. Leone (1982). He defines the two basic assumptions of structuralist archaeology as: first, that all objects in a particular culture are equal with respect to the overall organization and coherence of the total structure of that culture; and, second, that while the details or particulars of a past culture may be lost, the principles of that organization, or structure, may be suggested through what remains (Leone 1982:743). The first assumption can certainly be seen in both Deetz and Glassies' work and Leone considers the linking of a large variety of artifact types under the concept of the Georgian worldview, also known as the Georgian Order, a strength in these analyses. However, it can also constitute a weakness, as the reduction of all artifact forms and uses to one set of guiding structures does not allow us to consider other possible uses and meanings. As Leone notes, there is an assumption that the underlying order—in this case the Georgian Order, emphasizing the individual—can be extended to explain all archaeological assemblages (Leone 1982:744, 746). If material is uncovered that does not seem to conform to Georgian principles of organization then what this means is that the original analysis by Glassie and Deetz is void. In this case, the characteristics of the Georgian Order must be modified or another all-encompassing order has to be discovered. This does not consider the possibility that aspects of material culture primarily associated with the Georgian Order could have been rejected or deliberately misused.

The second assumption of structuralist archaeology, that the structures or organizing principles of past culture can be explicated separately from and despite the absence of the details or particulars of a past society, is Leone's main focus in discussing the weaknesses of the structuralist approach. The problem is that such thinking forsakes context (Leone 1982:745).

Deetz does offer an explanation as to why the Georgian Order arose, emphasizing the secularization of religion and the consequent loss of spiritual comfort and support (Deetz 1996:182–186). This explanation is, however, unsatisfying in that it takes these changes as given and sees the Georgian Order and its material correlates as an adaptation to an almost inevitable force.

Glassie's explanation of the rise of the Georgian Order is similar. He ties its inception to the conflict between the American colonies and England (*sic.*) in the late eighteenth century, the tobacco industry, which went into sharp decline in mid century, recent religious dissent, and unrest amongst Virginia's growing slave population (Glassie 1975:176–193). In the middle of the eighteenth century the Middle Virginian's political and religious traditions were unsteady. The need for order and control were met culturally by the Georgian Order and its varied manifestations. Glassie extends his conception of the Georgian Order as a control mechanism operating in times of increased social stress to Northern Ireland in his analysis of changing house forms there (Glassie 1995 [1982]:Chapter 13). In this case, the rise of privacy and other concepts associated with the Georgian Order are connected to the political turmoil of the first half of the twentieth century. The Georgian Order is picked up late in relation to other areas, as the conflictual conditions underlying the desire for control do not occur until that time.

Glassie and Deetz do discuss historical context in their own way, but as Leone suggests, they see the Georgian Order as an abstract and almost autonomous force. Why were the Georgian mindset and Georgian forms of material culture appropriate means of dealing with perceived social instability at *this* time and in *this* place? How did they act in this social context to maintain social order? As Leone (1988:235–236) asks, why do changes in material culture appear in one place before others? How are changes in material culture, taken by Glassie and

Deetz to reflect changes in ways of thinking, tied to material conditions? What exactly is it that is being controlled?

Leone built on this critique in his analysis of the William Paca garden in Annapolis, Maryland (Leone 1996 [1984]). The garden in question was that constructed in the 1760s by William Paca, a signatory of the Declaration of Independence, to complement his large Georgian mansion, built at the same time (Leone 1996:378–380). The house and garden were designed and laid out professionally after Paca married into wealth. The garden is of a type found elsewhere in the area. In form, such gardens are largely ornamental, although probably also containing kitchen plots. Layout was symmetrical and the garden walled in with built or planted materials. There were often exotic and imported plants and built terraces descended in an even series to a natural or constructed focal point, controlling the view.

In interpreting this garden form Leone stresses the importance of ideology (Leone 1996:372–373). For him, ideology is neither worldview nor belief, but ideas about nature, cause, time, and person, or a society's givens, that serve to naturalize and, thus, mask inequalities in the social order. They make these inequalities appear resident in nature or history, rather than arbitrary.

This concept of ideology is combined with the analysis of eighteenth century Virginian society given by Rhys Isaac in *The Transformation of Virginia 1740–1790* (Isaac 1982; see Leone 1996:372–375). In this, Isaac argues that between 1740 and 1790 in Tidewater Virginia, the social hierarchy became more and more rigid with the planter-gentry increasingly isolating itself "on the top of a pyramid which was becoming ever more shaky" (Leone 1996:373). This came as an attempt by that gentry to construct, with an undetermined degree of consciousness, a local order which allowed them to maintain control over what they possessed in the face of constrictions on wealth and the sources of its prosperity as a result of English control over the colonial economy and the continued long-term decline of tobacco prices. The result was a tight hierarchy with little access to the premier places from below or outside. As the existing hierarchy became more and more threatened, the gentry sought greater and greater control in maintaining their position, expressed as the Georgian Order. The material aspects of the Georgian Order all created the inhibitions, withdrawal, and isolation needed to prevent any attack on the established order. The Georgian Order grew more and more definite as challenges to established hierarchy grew in strength. It came to its fullest expression as the American Revolution approached. When the Revolution was over, and its effects on the mobility and growth of American society were fully felt in the early nineteenth century, and when those planters who had controlled the Revolution died, the Georgian world died also.

Taking this analysis of eighteenth century Virginian society, together with a concept of ideology, Leone understands the William Paca garden as one of those arenas in which the Georgian Order and the values this expressed were naturalized and, thus, legitimated (Leone 1996:380–389). The garden is divided by a central path, which allows descent through five similar terraces that fall away from the house. The principals of bilaterally balanced symmetry govern its layout. Furthermore, the garden was laid out as an exercise in optics. The terraces carry the axis downward to a distant focal point and create a three-dimensional volume out of the flat plan. Parallel lines of vegetation along the line of sight enhance the illusion of distance.

This garden, as garden building manuals of the time and contemporary parallels suggest, would probably have functioned in one role as a scientific observatory on nature. Experiments with nature would have involved the grouping, segmenting, grafting, breeding, and transplanting of flora, linked to observations on sunlight, fire, soil, weather, and water. Paca demonstrated that he understood nature and could control it, through the use of geometry and optics in garden layout and experimentation with plants. Paca can be seen to be placing his position in society (as a wealthy, slave-owning planter) in nature. More generally:

> Perspective allows one to view space and time in measurable interchangeable segments; and this is how universal space and time link Mr. Paca's garden to his law, Annapolis's workers to their hours, capital to interest, ships at sea to weeks traveled and thus to profit and loss. (Leone 1996:387)

Material culture and, specifically, the Georgian Order are linked to the social relations of capitalism as ideology naturalizing those social relations and as aspects of active attempts to impose those relations:

> The formal garden . . . was a place for thinking and for making the observations which were essential to economic and social life. It was not passive; it was very active, for by walking in it, building it, looking at it, admiring and discussing it, and using it in any way, its contemporaries could take themselves and their position as granted and convince others that the way things are is the way they always had been and should remain. (Leone 1996:389)

The key contribution of Leone's analysis of the Paca garden and his criticism of structuralist analyses of the Georgian Order is in providing a link between material culture and the social relations of capitalism. There are, however, specific problems with his account (see, e.g., Hodder 1991 [1986]:67–72). The ideology he outlines appears to be shared by all society, with no indication that the same material culture may have held different meanings for different social groups. Further, the separation of ideology and reality takes no account of the fact that reality is perceived and created by the observer. The ideology in question needs to be situated within routine social practices. If the concept of ideology is going to be of use in discussing the creation and perpetuation of capitalist social relations, it should not be uncritically accepted as the dominant worldview masking real social relations to the benefit of an elite.

Leone has since extended his analysis of the Georgian Order in Annapolis, through the study of archaeologically recovered material culture and the study of probate inventories (Leone 1988). He has asked how capitalism operated in people's daily lives in order to subordinate the working population, thus attempting to counter some of the criticisms put forward by Hodder and others. Against the background of the increasing control of wealth by a small minority in Annapolis from the late seventeenth century, aspects of moveable material culture can be seen as acting to legitimize this minority's position and create capitalist work attitudes necessary in the furtherance of their interests. Between 1710 and 1730, clocks, scientific instruments, and musical instruments were introduced and used to show that newly aggregated wealth was legitimate because its possessors understood natural law through direct observation, justifying both hierarchy and individualism. From about 1730 on, sets of cups, plates, knives, forks were used to define individual place settings and individualized dining practices, and together with many other forms of material culture helped to create work discipline. They helped to create and maintain the internalized set of rules that structured the self-maintaining individual essential in capitalist society. The legitimization of a hierarchy with the planter-gentry at its top was played out through architecture and through landscape from around 1760.

These trends in material culture were aspects of the beginnings of restructured work habits and social relations, with almost all the wealthy and between a fifth and a third of the poorest property owners influenced by the Georgian Order by 1770 (Leone 1988:245–247). The population was largely absorbed by 1830 and completely by 1860 (Leone 1988:247). As Leone suggests, this opens the way for seeing a long period of resistance to capitalist social relations through material culture, though this remains to be demonstrated (Leone 1988:247).

In light of the criticisms considered above, this analysis takes some significant steps, particularly in relating the social relations of capitalism to everyday practice and in allowing consideration of the negotiation of those relations by different individuals and groups. However,

problems remain in that resistance is only allowed for, not demonstrated, and those accepting the Georgian Order into their everyday
existence come across as doing so passively and, eventually, completely.

One approach to the problem of resistance to capitalism and the
Georgian Order, that of Beaudry, Cook and Mrozowski (1991), looks to
the concept of cultural hegemony (see Orser 1996:167–174 for a critique of this approach). Here, different groups can maintain competing ideologies grounded in their own self-perceived interests (Beaudry
et al. 1991:158–159). From this perspective, the relationships between
different classes consist of the negotiation of these ideologies. These
competing ideologies are symbolized in everyday material culture.

Beaudry, Cook and Mrozowski (1991) use the case study of Boott
Cotton Mills, Lowell, Massachusetts, to show that the negotiation of
social relationships involving the creation of competing ideologies can
be seen through everyday objects, like household ceramics, and alcohol
and high-alcohol-content medicine bottles. The owners of Boott Mills
frowned on the consumption of alcohol, yet archaeologists have found
large quantities of alcohol bottles and bottles of medicines that had high
alcohol content. For Beaudry, Cook and Mrozowski, these bottles offer
testimony to small-scale, everyday acts of resistance as the workers established their own leisure behavior (Beaudry et al. 1991:169). Through
drinking, workers not only acted against the wishes of the mill owners,
but also created and maintained a distinct subculture. This suggests
the workers at Boott Mills were not automatons, because even though
they worked all day in oppressive mills, in their spare time they were
free to express themselves (Orser 1996:169). The workers were able
to negotiate the creation of a subculture, and though the owners controlled the day, the workers could control the evening and night (Orser
1996:169).

The household ceramics of the workers at Boott Mills tell another
story (Beaudry et al. 1991:169–174). The supervisory personnel and
their families, who lived in tenements, emulated middle class dining
rituals and adapted their limited ceramic assemblage to form as close
as possible the appropriate table service. Boarding house owners, however, provided only the most basic complement of ceramics for food service and consumption, serving meals on a single plate. In part, this
was perhaps a measure of economy. The tenement dwellers chose their
own ceramics and so could engage in social discourse through them.
They sought to emulate the middle class. Boardinghouse residents, the
workers, did not have the same choice in ceramics and, so, these did not
provide a medium for social discourse.

For Beaudry, Cook and Mrozowski (1991) the study of everyday objects can allow us to consider resistance through the concept of cultural hegemony. The mill owners may have controlled work during the day and may have sought to influence the behavior of the workers through the expression of their own ideology, their contempt for alcohol consumption for example. However, the workers in turn could control their leisure time and in the process they created their own subculture. They were not overwhelmed by the inexorable march of the Georgian Order and of capitalism, but negotiated their relationship with the mill owners in their own self-expression. The supervisory personnel adopted the Georgian Order to align themselves with the mill owners.

BEYOND THE GEORGIAN ORDER: SOCIETY AND THE INDIVIDUAL

The Georgian Order or Georgian worldview has proved a useful construct in relating the material world archaeologists study to thought, ideology, and capitalism, to elite justifications of their position, to the cultural and practical subjugation of other groups, and to the resistance of the subjugated. The concept of the Georgian Order has been refined as its pervasiveness has been questioned and the ability of the subjugated to construct alternatives ways of life and of thought have been explored. In the studies just discussed, the Georgian Order is seen as a sort of cultural package, standardizing the material world and stressing the individual, to be adopted or resisted. The Georgian package is a bounded one and relates in different ways to a series of bounded communities. Such cultural communities, from prehistory to the present, continue as popular units of study for many archaeologists, despite their divergent theoretical backgrounds (see, e.g., papers in Canuto and Yaeger (eds.) 2000).

However, there are many who now question the usefulness of the Georgian Order (Orser 1998:315–316). In considering the possible application of the concept in English archaeology, Matthew Johnson (e.g., 1993a; 1993b; 1996; 1999) has explored the possible genealogies of the cultural and social practices and ideas associated with capitalism. The concept of genealogy as used by Johnson derives from the work of Michel Foucault and involves a move from history as the straightforward search for origins to history as an exploration of the many and various social processes that come together to form a society at any one juncture (see Johnson 1993a:352). In accordance with this concept of the social genealogy, Johnson has argued that capitalism had no simple origin, but was the result of diverse and long-lived material and social changes. Further, it was the conjunction of these genealogies that formed capitalism, which was not a simple cognitive structure powering all social action.

Johnson traces several main genealogies. The first relates to diverse changes in landscape, architecture and much else, and is termed closure (see Johnson 1993b; 1996:Chapter 4, in particular). Here, the material world is re-ordered in that peoples' relationship with their material environment becomes abstracted, or objectified, through the enclosure of fields, the individualization of space within the house, the writing of documents, and the creation of maps and plans. Material culture in all these domains increasingly emphasizes the polite over the vernacular as knowledge is disembedded from the local context. To take one example, there was a transformation in the layout and technical system of traditional houses in England between AD 1400 and AD 1700 (see, above all, Johnson 1993b). Late Medieval houses were dominated by a large, central hall open to the roof, with parlor and service rooms at either end. They came to be transformed as the hall was reduced in size and ceiled in. It became less central to circulation patterns within the house and there was a clearer boundedness and segregation between areas of space. At the same time, houses became more "rational" in building technique and differentiation between social classes in terms of house type became more apparent.

Johnson's second main genealogy traces the increasing imposition of authority at a series of levels (see Johnson 1996:Chapter 5, in particular). State, Church, and even the heads of households are seen to cultivate increasingly elaborate forms of spatial and temporal discipline. The world and the people within it are ordered through documents, through maps, and through space. The discipline and ordering of people is seen most explicitly and in a developed form in nineteenth century prisons, asylums, and other institutions (see Markus [ed.] 1982; 1989 on this process in Scotland).

Thirdly, a commodified mentality and worldview is seen to restructure architecture and the world of objects, amongst other things (see Johnson 1996:192–201, in particular). Commodification as a process was underway long before the consumer revolution of the eighteenth century. Architecture, landscapes, and material culture came to be viewed as abstract things, no longer controlled by custom but subject to untrammeled use rights. The enclosure of fields, for example, was tied to the increasing conception of land as something to be owned outright and exploited in a quite functional way. Landscape became less of an arena for the mapping and practice of social relationships, in open fields for example, as the life of the community was disembedded from land as a commodity.

Matthew Johnson's *An Archaeology of Capitalism* argues:

> ... that the apparent unity of this set of eighteenth-century architecture and material culture [the Georgian Order] is partly due to the perceived nature of its arrival as a 'complete package' in the context of the American colonies. Each element in fact has a genealogy several centuries old, and can be placed in disparate contexts, often within the patriarchal structure of early modern England. (Johnson 1996:206)

Georgian houses, individualized ceramics, rationalized gardens, and much else, are not so much evidence of a unifying order as of the conjunction of distinct, but related, cultural practices. In arguing this, Johnson does not suggest that the archaeology of capitalism should be a collection of fragmented studies of different processes like commodification, closure, or whatever else. For Johnson (1996:17), the essence of an archaeology of capitalism is to understand not so much the changing meanings ascribed to material culture with the emergence of the modern world, as the changing ways in which things come to have meaning. An archaeology of capitalism should concern itself with the changing nature of the subject, with changing notions of the self and how the self relates to others (1999:221, 231).

This is, of course, a subject on which sociologists have something to say. To take a prominent example, Anthony Giddens has outlined how, with capitalism, the manner in which people relate to each other changes so that face-to-face interaction becomes less significant (Giddens 1995).

With capitalism, the economic sphere of life becomes peculiarly significant as a medium of power in social relations (Giddens 1995: 111–112). For Giddens, the threat or use of force normally backs surplus extraction in European Medieval societies. Whether this dictum is universally applicable is questionable. However, the significant point is that in such societies the economic power involved in class relations is rarely achieved or sustained by solely economic means, and this is above all the case with agrarian production. With capitalism, the dominant class acquires its position by virtue of the economic power yielded by the ownership of private property. The dominant class consists of those with access to capital, and the propertyless wage-laborer is rendered dependent by their lack of capital (Giddens 1995:112). The dominant class in capitalism exercises much more control over the processes of production. In many other forms of society, the dominant class does extract a surplus, but they exercise little direct control over the manner in which that surplus is produced.

The restructuring of power in social relations along economic lines is achieved through and results in changes in the manner in which society is integrated (Giddens 1995:114–116). In societies such as those in Medieval Europe, the prevalent modes of social association are composed of face-to-face encounters. Examples of societies that are involved in wide-ranging trade and commerce are no exception as trading relations there are carried on between communities that sustain a high degree of local autonomy. In capitalism, money expresses and makes possible the dismembering of communities founded on frequent physical interaction. The economic foundation of social relations in capitalism allows the extension and integration of these social relations across wide reaches of space and time without the need for physical presence.

Important here is the relation of money to commodity production (Giddens 1995:116–117). Commodity production involves the commensurate exchange of incommensurables (Giddens 1995:116). Goods can have a functional value, a use-value, without being a commodity. What defines a commodity is its exchange-value, and the exchange-values of different commodities only differ from one another quantitatively, money expressing this quantification. The detachment of exchange-values from products, seen in the existence of such exchange-value as money, allows commodities to circulate at an advanced level. The circulation of commodities in capitalism can operate across wide reaches of space and time, without the face-to-face interaction of those involved in exchange.

In capitalism, labor itself becomes a commodity and enters into a transformative relationship with other commodities (Giddens 1995: 118–120). The common existence of both goods and labor as interchangeable commodities is permitted by an underlying constitutive component, time. Every commodity, including labor-power, is the objectification of a given amount of labor-time. For their exchange, commodities must be equated with a common element other than themselves, and that element is the labor-time invested in them.

Pulling together this discussion of how social relations in capitalism are constituted, Giddens suggests that:

> The interlocking of capital and wage-labour in a relation of dependence and interest conflict is the *chief basis of the dialectic of control* in the productive order of the capitalist economy. This is a matter of fundamental importance in separating capitalism from class-divided societies. In the latter it is the resistance of the local community, tradition and kinship circles to the penetration by relations of absence that sustains a definite measure of control of the exploited over their conditions of day-to-day existence. The vast

extension of time-space mediations made structurally possible by the prevalence of money capital, by the commodification of labour and by the trans-
formability of one into the other, undercuts the segregated and autonomous
character of the local community of producers. (Giddens 1995:120–121;
emphasis in original)

In capitalism, the primacy accorded to the economic and the in-
trusion of exploitation and class domination into the heart of the labor
process undermines the effectiveness of local community, tradition, and
kinship as the bases of resistance to outside, absent exploitation. Face-
to-face encounters are generally no longer the basis of effective social
control and social relations operating in absence become more significant than those amongst the local, face-to-face community and kin-
group. Routine experience of social relations with capitalism is an experience of physical and social separation from others. People experience
significant social relationships, in this situation, apart from others in a
physical sense, where many such relationships are mediated at a distance. They also experience their relationships with others as a socially
distinct individual.

To return to the archaeology of capitalism, we can relate the changing sense of the individual and the increasing prominence of relations
of absence to the changing material environment. Individualism, or a
heightened stress on the unified, autonomous individual over the community, is one feature of Georgianization and appears in the work of
Glassie, Deetz and others (Johnson 1993a:336). Some have even attempted to measure the degree to which a material assemblage may be
said to be individualistic, though it is not clear exactly what we should
be measuring in such instances (Johnson 1993a:336). Many have considered that changes in domestic architecture like the multiplication of
rooms and the separation of functional spaces can be explained by their
connection to processes like the rise of privacy or the rise of the individual, where we see a deepening concern for the needs and rights of the
individual over the household and community (Johnson 1993a:339).

The development of capitalism involved more than a simple shift
from the community to the individual, though (Johnson 1993a:341–342;
1993b:106–107). Individuals were recognized in pre-capitalist society.
The difference comes with a change in the way in which one individual was demarcated from another. In the Medieval house, demarcation
took place *within* the hall, a single body of space. Social relations were
played out in terms of asymmetrical face-to-face demonstrations of relative status, such as between master-and-servant, husband-and-wife,
and parent-and-child. Relations of status were created and maintained
in face-to-face contexts at the everyday level and depended on notions
of difference and deference. With capitalism, people are segregated in

space. There is a shift of everyday social life away from the articulation of status to the articulation of the relations of class. The relations of class depend not just on objective socio-economic relationships, but also on the development of subjective class-consciousness and the development of separate spheres of interaction, of meaning, and of worldview. They come with the breakdown of the day-to-day interdependence of the patriarchal community as different social groups come to be marked by different patterns and rhythms of social life (Johnson 1993b:137, 149). The shift from status to class depends on a heightened perception of the individual as distinct from the community (however defined), as a unified, cohesive whole, and, as an autonomous and active being (Johnson 1993a:348). The capitalist individual is not the passive bearer of statuses and roles moving within the Medieval community.

Johnson's analytically distinct genealogies of closure, commodification, and discipline are connected through this analysis of the changing articulation of the self. Closure itself is the material form in which changing attitudes to the individual, family, household, and wider community were played out (Johnson 1993b:175). Walls were erected between people and fields enclosed as those people less and less defined themselves in communal space.

With the shift from status to class, difference came to be defined much more by wealth as reflected in moveable goods and different classes had access to different kinds of goods (Johnson 1993b:150). There was a move from social interaction within a customary and accepted frame of reference towards social interaction within a richer and more varied material environment, but one where the value and the meaning of things were more freely changed (Johnson 1993b:176).

Discipline over oneself came to be related to the creation and maintenance of sharper material and symbolic boundaries with external society and with the natural world. Discipline and observation depended on a spatial and social separation between the observer and the observed (Johnson 1993b:175). So, disciplinary society, reaching its most overt material expression in institutions like the modern prison, but also seen in the daily life of the household, relies on the creation of autonomous individuals who can be defined and isolated, and thus categorized apart and studied.

Others, notably Charles E Orser, have also questioned the validity of the bounded cultural package of the Georgian Order (e.g., 1996; 1998). Despite linking the Georgian Order to capitalism, Orser says, historical archaeologists after Deetz and Glassie could not make a serious break from the culturalist position (Orser 1998:313–312). They chose to define capitalism as a culture and sought to maintain a coherent cognitive and structuralist interpretation of its material component. People in the past grew up with the culture of capitalism, learnt it, and passed it on to subsequent generations.

From the cultural perspective, our culture makes us do what we do and think like we think, and the world consists of a mosaic of distinct cultural groups defined in space, with some hybridization at the edges where these groups meet (Orser 1998:312). Culture provides a convenient final explanation for all that happened in the past (Orser 1998:312). Even archaeologies focusing on social resistance and cultural hegemony, as in Beaudry, Cook and Mrozowski's account of Boot Cotton Mills discussed above, subscribe in some way to this perspective (see Orser 1996:167–174). At Boott Mills, the culture of the mill owners, the Georgian Order, can apparently be placed in opposition to the distinct and separate culture of the workers.

One significant problem with such interpretations of the past is that they skirt round the issue of social power (Orser 1996:173–174). They imply that people, whoever they are, have the ability to freely create an identity through their actions, attitudes, and material culture. They are free to choose how they express their identity. It is not that such analyses are simply wrong or that they do not acknowledge social power at all. Rather, relations of power remain largely silent and the focus is almost exclusively on the creation of working class culture, which becomes by default freely constituted. Orser (1996:173) agrees that people do act to transform the meanings of the material world around them. However, they are constrained by the objects and material available to them and by what they can afford to buy. In both regards, they are subject to some extent to the will of their employer, who controls their wages and, in the case of Boott Mills, the things they can spend their wages on.

Orser (1996) suggests that there is another way to interpret the past, one that is more relevant to our understanding of the modern world, and this is based in a consideration of social relations. It is not that culture does not exist, but that the concept of culture as it has been used is unhelpful (Orser 1998:313–314). People may have acted within culturally prescribed parameters, but they constructed their daily lives around a series of shifting, changing interpersonal connections.

To take an example, Orser (1998:313–314) gives an account of an estate in the rural midlands of Ireland in the nineteenth century. The landowner there lived in a Georgian mansion, a fine example of Palladian architecture. He was of English descent. The Georgian Order could be said to be present in this case, but, Orser asks, where is its relevance to the cottiers who formed the bulk of the Irish population?

Life went on for them in a decidedly non-Georgian, albeit non-Medieval, manner. Still, they cannot be studied in isolation from their landlords.

In seeking to overcome the culturalist perspective, Orser (Orser 1996; 1998:316–317) turns in particular to the work of cultural anthropologist Michael Carrithers (see Carrithers 1992), who considers the relationships of interacting people to have primary significance in-group dynamics. People act and react in relation to one another rather than in direct response to some hazy, cultural abstraction. People do not do things because of their culture, as the culturist perspective implies. Rather, people do things with, to, and in respect of each other. We may describe the means with which they act as cultural, if we wish. People produce culture and create history in the relations they invent, and such relations are constantly changing. These relationships occur on both small and large scales—between two individuals or between two continents, for example—and relationships at each scale rely on the other (Orser 1996:55).

Again, as an example, I will take Orser's (1996:144–158; 1998:317–320) account of the Irish Midlands, and in particular its landscapes. With the culturalist perspective, cultural landscapes are created as people transform a given terrain to fit pre-conceived cultural ideas. For Orser, landscape construction is not such a determined and inward looking process. Landscapes are constituted with reference to the networks of relations people maintain between one another and between themselves and the natural world.

The Georgian mansion of the landlord, with its large demesne and walled garden, could not have existed except for the rents of the cottiers. The cottiers certainly lived in a different landscape, but this was as connected to their landlord's as his was to theirs. When the landlord entered the world outside his mansion and its policies he entered a world he controlled only tenuously, yet without him the cottiers could have constructed an agricultural system built solely around subsistence and their own needs. The impact of the cottiers on the landlord's landscape is at first less obvious, but when he built a high wall round his demesne he was to some extent protecting himself and his family from the alien space outside (Orser 1996:155). Each landscape was part of the other and both were inexorably tied together by social relations (Orser 1998:320). Here we do not see two distinct spaces, one English and one Irish, but one Anglo-Irish place created in the practice of social relations.

Other relationships are evident in this case. The form of the mansion and demesne proclaimed the landlord's membership of the Protestant Ascendancy, the ruling class (Orser 1996:146–149). The gate to the grounds of the mansion was directly linked by a road to the local

Protestant church (Orser 1996:148). This configuration of the landscape shows that the estate's owners were part of a network that extended beyond their immediate surroundings, throughout Ireland, into England, and across the Atlantic to America (Orser 1996:149–151). All the same, the landscape immediate to the landlord's house did not exist in isolation as some abstract and perfect expression of a wider ideal. It was designed with reference to those in the surrounding countryside and paid for by their labor.

The give-and-take witnessed in the creation of these different landscapes was connected, but it was not equal (Orser 1996:156–157). Both the landlord and the peasantry created space, but the fact that the landlords were, in the end, more powerful in this regard is to be seen in his clearance of people, houses, and peasant landscape at the time of the Great Irish Famine in the mid nineteenth century:

> Remnants of folk landscapes do exist throughout Ireland. But at the rural townlands themselves... it is the landlord's improving hand that is most obvious. The net that landlords threw over the land was powerful and permanent. It was made of brick walls, massive mansions, and granite archways. The peasants, with their single-room mud cabins and their lazybed fields were erasable. (Orser 1996:157)

They were not entirely erasable, though, as the survival of remains of those very cabins and fields shows (Orser 1996:157). To relate the above to Boott Mills, it can be argued that Beaudry, Cook and Mrozowski played down the voice of the elites in attempting to give a voice to the workers (Orser 1996:177). They subtracted the oppressive, paternalist situation from their analysis and discredited those cases when the owners spoke with an indisputably clear and loud voice. However, while the owners at Boott Mills could suppress the workers, they could not erase them.

Orser (1996:178–179) makes clear that he does not consider the subjugated in history to be unimportant. On the contrary, he sees giving a voice to the otherwise voiceless as the rightful destiny of historical archaeology. However, this goal cannot properly be achieved by diluting the oppressive force exerted by the superordinate.

THE CONSTITUTION OF SOCIETY
AND SOCIAL CHANGE

Above, several salient characteristics of daily social life under capitalism have been outlined. Capitalism is not a culture. It is a form of society and archaeologies of capitalism study how people relate to each other and how they relate to the physical world. Important is the increased emphasis on the autonomous individual. This is fundamental to how people see themselves and relate to others. However, capitalism is not all pervasive. Many choose not to conduct all their relationships simply as autonomous individuals or to submit fully to the power-relations that capitalism creates and is created by. This is not to say that they live their lives entirely as they choose or that they can construct distinct and bounded subcultures. Rather, they are constrained and empowered by their relationships with others and by the past. It remains to discuss the question of the origins of capitalism, raised at points above, and the mechanisms of social constitution in more detail.

Deetz and Glassie, as Leone (1982) argues, had real problems explaining the emergence of the Georgian Order. Their works portrayed it as an abstraction, unrelated to specific historical circumstances. Leone (1988; 1996 [1984]) argued that the Georgian Order should be seen as an ideology naturalizing the position of an elite and cultivating subordination in society at large. Here, the Georgian Order is actively created to justify and extend the asymmetrical relations existing with capitalism. The explicit link between the material world, ideology, power, and capitalism is an important one and all of these themes remain central to archaeologies of the modern world. Central to Leone's contribution is the idea that real people actively used and created their material surroundings in relating to others. However, the distinction between capitalism as a form of social relationship and the Georgian Order as an ideology justifying its existence presents the archaeologist with a problem in accounting for origins. In studying the Georgian Order in this way, we are not answering the question of how capitalism came to be.

To get at this question of origins, it is necessary to study the changing relations between people themselves. In tracing the genealogies of capitalism, Matthew Johnson, as outlined above, considers how the way in which people related to each other changed. Charles E Orser has also placed a strong emphasis on social relations, on the way in which people acted with reference to others.

When studying specific categories of architecture, landscape, or material culture change within controlled geographical and temporal boundaries, on the small scale, Johnson has seen capitalism as actively created by individuals and groups in specific historical circumstances (e.g., Johnson 1989; 1993a; 1993b). He has studied the origins of capitalism through the concepts of agency and structure, of which more below. There are, of course, similarities to Leone's perspective here. However, as we have seen, Johnson is also concerned with the large scale, with the myriad genealogies of capitalism that stretch back through the centuries and are grounded in a huge variety of historical and social contexts. There are problems in narrating origins here and, certainly, the concept of a single, definable genesis is inappropriate. It is in keeping with Johnson's perspective that he does not attempt to reduce the origins of capitalism in its wider form to a single motivation, circumstance, or social dynamic (see, above all else, Johnson 1996).

There is a tension, then, in explaining the origins of capitalism. Many archaeologists have confined themselves to small-scale social interactions and, there, the concepts of agency, structure, power, and ideology have proved significant in understanding social change. Explaining the origins of capitalism on a larger scale is a quite different exercise and will involve quite different structures of thought. In the rest of this book I will not attempt to address the latter problem. This is because this book deals with one of those small-scale moments in the emergence of capitalism. This is not to downplay the significance of the changes to be studied or the actions of the people involved. This was a small-scale moment in a wider change, but I hope to show that it was a crucial one nonetheless. It is also not to deny the connections between the people involved in this moment and those outside of their time and immediate locality. Some of these connections will be highlighted. This time and this place were not bounded and isolated. The separation is an analytical one.

As just suggested, agency, structure, power, and ideology have all been powerful concepts in understanding social change and social constitution with capitalism. One of the achievements of early postprocessual archaeology was an emphasis on agency and meaning in archaeological explanation, in reaction to the passive individual of processual analysis. This to some extent mirrors early criticism of the structuralist approach to the Georgian worldview (e.g., Leone 1982; 1996 [1984]). Ian Hodder argued that people actively use material culture in the creation of society:

> We are not simply pawns in a game, determined by a system—rather, we use a myriad of means, including material culture symbolism, to create new roles, to redefine existing ones and to deny the existence of others. (Hodder 1991:6 and 8; emphasis in original)

In this, continuity and change in social relations are not conceived as entirely determined by the free will of the individual. Rather, some importance is accorded to structure, which can act to define the purposes, meanings and intentions of that individual (Hodder 1991:9). Meaning is not purely subjective as it is referent to the human situation and to consciousness, and consciousness is not idealized but practical (Kus 1984:103).

However, the dialectic between agency and structure is not fully considered, and analyses carried out from this perspective tend to over-emphasize the individual as autonomous. Again, there are parallels to be drawn here with discussions of the archaeology of capitalism (e.g., see the previous discussion of Beaudry et al. 1991). Some more recent work has focused in greater detail on the relationship between agency and structure (e.g., Barrett 1988, 1994, 2001; Johnson 1989):

> In his own attempt to escape functionalist explanations Hodder has shifted the attention of archaeology towards considering the intentions and motivations of human agents. He seems to suggest that through a detailed analysis of the patterns preserved in the material record it should be possible to re-cover something of the ideas in people's heads. Even if this were possible, and published examples of this kind of reasoning are far from convincing, we are simply moved from a position where social structures govern human behaviour to one which reasserts the primacy of the individual. (Barrett 1988:7–8)

The starting point for John Barrett's reassessment of the structure-agency dialectic is Giddens' conceptualization of *Praxis* (Barrett 1988:8; see Barrett 2001 for a recent discussion). Giddens says:

> To speak of human social activity as *Praxis* is to reject every conception of human beings as 'determined objects' or as unambiguously 'free subjects'. All human action is carried on by knowledgeable agents who both construct the social world through their action, but yet whose action is also conditioned or constrained by the very world of their creation. (Giddens 1995:53–54; see also Giddens 1979)

The relationship of agency and structure is a reflexive one. The actions of an individual structure and restructure their social world, but that world acts back to structure human action in an ongoing re-flexive process. In this process, knowledge extends beyond a discursive understanding of the world to include practical knowledge, which is in turn distinguished from unconscious sources of cognition and motivation (Giddens 1984:7). In this, practical consciousness, or "knowing how to go on" (Giddens 1995:27), is rediscovered and reproduced in action and discourse.

So, practical action in the world serves to define human consciousness in part, which consciousness acts back to structure people's actions. In this way structure interacts with agency. Taking up this concern with the relation between structure and agency Randall McGuire suggests that Giddens' notion of structure and the individual is flawed in the separation of the two into distinct entities:

Human action should not be opposed to social structure because human action and social structure form a unity. The existence of one necessarily requires the prior existence of the other. Humans make history as social beings, and they do so as members of social groups.... Just as the individual cannot exist in the absence of society, so too society cannot exist in the absence of individuals. Social structures have no existence independent of the people who form them. These structures are not things but instead are sets of relationships that link individuals. Because society is a relational network of differences, that is, a network of contradictions that define individuals in definite ways... conflict is built into these unities.... People take on certain social characteristics and consciousness as a result of their position *vis a vis* others in these sets of relationships and, for this reason, people make history as members of social groups. (McGuire 1992:134 and 136)

McGuire seems to slightly overstep the mark. The whole idea of practical consciousness, of knowing how to go on, is that people produce a knowledge of how to act through their experience of social relationships. However, McGuire is right to underline the fact that social structure is not something separate from social beings.

It is people as active social beings who create society and bring about change. They do not, however, do so with absolute freedom. They are both constrained and empowered by their knowledge of how to act and, referring back to above discussion, by their relative position within social relations of power. These relations of power are not only central to our understanding of the limitations of action, but also inform our understanding of the triggers of and motivations for change. In the above quotation from McGuire, society is conceived of as a network of contradictions that necessarily embody conflict. Society is structured by a network of internal relations that are made up of contradictions binding together individuals and groups with opposing and conflicting interests (McGuire 1992:12). For example:

This logic shows two opposed social categories, master and slave, to form a unity. That is, they are the observable manifestations of a single underlying relation of slavery. The existence of one necessarily entails the existence of the other, yet they are opposites and, as such, potentially in conflict. (McGuire 1992:96)

In such contradictions, which exist in all human relations with each other and with the natural world, we find the dynamics of change (McGuire 1992:15). This is as society is always in flux as small changes in any part thereof will alter the structure of relations (McGuire 1992:12). So, a series of small quantitative changes in a relationship, such as between master and slave, can lead to a qualitative change involving the transformation of the relations that constitute the social structure (McGuire 1992:97). Importantly:

> Not all conflicts within social forms result from contradictions.... But only
> those conflicts that result from relational contradictions, that are necessary
> for the existence of particular processes and entities, will lead to a trans-
> formation of the social form. Such relations hold within them their own
> negation, the contradiction that will make the relation into something else;
> likewise, these relations are themselves the negation of a prior relation or set
> of relations. The negation of the negation thus refers to the process whereby
> the negation inherent within a relational contradiction transforms the re-
> lation or set of relations into another form—something different. (McGuire
> 1992:97–98)

Contradiction inherent in the web of social relations does not always result in change; rather quantitative changes in everyday life can
heighten that into conflict, resulting in qualitative change (McGuire
1992:150). For example, increased hardship in the daily life of a slave
can lead to the conflict inherent in their relationship with the master
being highlighted and could thus lead to expressed discontent. As a result, the master might step up punitive measures for objection to the
current form of the relation that, in turn, might lead to revolt and the
negation of that relation.

Giddens' discusses contradiction in more generalized terms:

> ...societal totalities are *structured in contradiction*, involving the fusion
> and exclusion of opposites. In other words, the operation of one structural
> principle in the reproduction of a societal system presumes that of another
> which tends to undermine it. This view supposes that...there is one prin-
> cipal axis of contradiction, which I shall call the *primary contradiction* of
> that type of society. (Giddens 1995:231–232, emphasis in original)

In European feudal society, for example, Giddens considers the
primary contradiction to be located in the city–countryside relation:
"Agrarian states involve an antagonistic fusion of two modes of social
organization, the rural community on the one hand, and the city based
institutions on the other" (Giddens 1995:237).

While the kind of contradiction outlined by Giddens' can exist, the
notion of a primary contradiction detracts from the fluid nature of social
interaction and draws attention away from the variety of social relationships that people enter into. While it is important to study and clarify
one social contradiction, that between the master and slave or between
rural and urban society, the interaction between different social relations and social contradictions can be equally enlightening. One contradictory relationship impacts on another. To take McGuire's example of
the master and the slave, we might envisage that conflict and change
resulting from that contradiction could create new tensions between,
for example, the master and their peers or between one ex-slave and

another. Equally, existing contradictions within each peer group might become exposed or amplified as the master–slave relationship dissolves and recedes as the site of conflict. Also, the contradiction inherent in the master–slave relationship might become explicit and become a site of conflict as a result of contradictions existing in other relationships. For example, and hypothetically, the identity of an individual British plantation owner as a slave owner might have become problematic where they operated within a commercial metropolitan community where relationships were increasingly between distinct individuals theoretically freely entering into labor contracts. In such a case, slavery might be seen as something of an anathema to the advancement of capitalist society. The connection between such diverse relationships spanning wide reaches of time and space is of course not simple. For example, it is clear that, in some contexts, the nature of British capitalist enterprise borrowed heavily from the plantation system (see, for example, Blackburn 1998, 565; Macinnes 1998a). The point is that one contradictory social relationship did not exist in isolation from others.

Scottish Highland society was constituted in the antagonistic fusion of such contradictory relationships. In the case of Kintyre, later I will explore the important contradiction resulting from the fusion of kin-based and legalistic principles of territorial and social organization. Society was structured according to the landlord–tenant–sub-tenant relationship *and* that of clan gentry–clan at one and the same time. There were of course other dimensions to Highland social structure, but this set of contradictions is fundamental to an understanding of in the instigation of Improvement in Kintyre. The landlord–tenant–sub-tenant relationship became the site of conflict when changes in landholding meant that the person of the landlord was separated from the person of the clan chief. The contradictions inherent in the landlord–tenant–subtenant relationship and between the clan–clan gentry and landlord–tenant–sub-tenant relationships were exposed and this proved to be a catalyst for change.

For Kilfinan, I will argue that Improvement was in part a strategy in landowners' maintenance of their position within the urban-based middle class, emergent from the late eighteenth century. Giddens' emphasis on the city–countryside relationship could be considered as significant here. The Kilfinan case study will also underline the importance of qualitative changes in distant social contexts, such as the Lowland burghs, in understanding change near at hand, in the rural Highlands. Improvement in Kilfinan in no small part stemmed from the tensions arising from the various attempts of landlords to interact with different people in different contexts. It stems from the proximity of diverse social relations. The exploitative nature of the landlord–tenant–sub-tenant relationship was increasingly exposed as the landowners engaged in commercially orientated, capitalist society. As such, their involvement with the middle class required a restructuring of rural society in Kilfinan both to maintain their position within that middle class and to address the exposed contradiction of their position as landlords who exploited the profits of an estate through the labor of others. Improvement, for them, addressed their interests with regard to several different, but intertwined social relationships.

The concept of social contradiction does not allow us to predict from the nature of any given contradiction what path change will take. Contradiction is a starting point. In order to study why a particular change took the form it did we must return to structure and agency. We should not only look at previous relations in order to understand where the conflict leading to change could have come from, but also to understand how the characteristics of previous relations enabled various courses of action. In Chapters 5 and 6, I will argue that the connections some landlords had with English and Lowland Scottish society structured their approach in resolving the contradictions mentioned above. I will refer to Scottish Enlightenment thought, to settlement patterns, landscape form, and domestic space, and to the practice of day-to-day social relations. These connections with the Lowlands and beyond are also part responsible for the contradictions at the root of change themselves.

However, to describe the actions of landlords and to concentrate on their world alone is to ignore the rest of the rural population and render them entirely passive. According to what has been said above, we should accord all individuals or groups the ability to actively engage with and influence their social and material environment. Social change should not be conceived of as a one-way process dictated by an elite. It should also be remembered at this point, though, that there is and was an asymmetry to social relations. We must be careful not to render all people autonomous and free to act as they will.

Recent archaeological understandings of how people actively negotiate their position in social relations, under the constraints of structure, have proceeded from a consideration of the concepts of power and ideology.

Power is not just a negative, repressive force, a quantity held by some, an elite (see McGuire 1992:132; Miller and Tilley 1984:5). Power is present in all social relations, not just those between an elite and a subject population (see Miller and Tilley 1984:5). Power is a universal ability of individuals or groups to act to change their conditions of existence. This is not to deny that power does not have a negative or repressive aspect. Rather it is to distinguish that aspect as one form of power and thus allow all people in the past participation in the creation of their social world. In this, power should not be conceived of as a distinct entity (McGuire 1992:132). Power only exists in the web of relations between people, so that to possess wealth, for example, does not necessarily imply to possess power over others. The power that wealth might give will depend on particular historical conditions.

So, to think of power is to think of an aspect of all social relations that is not just associated with repressive actions, but also with resistive actions. The compliance of one person with another's wishes is always at question, making power exercise the result of the interplay of domination and resistance (Paynter and McGuire 1991:5).

The interplay of domination and resistance, or the negotiation of social conditions, can be carried out through a number of means, such as physical force, but perhaps most effectively ideology:

> The ideal situation for the As in the dyadic relationship of power is for the Bs to be inclined to follow the As' requests, nay, even anticipate the needs of A and provide without request. One way for this to happen is when the Bs consider the As' requests as legitimate.... The optimal order, from the point of view of the As, is one in which the Bs participate in their own oppression. (Paynter and McGuire 1991:8)

Ideology, then, can be an effective means of creating or maintaining dominance by legitimating the interests of the dominant. Ideology, for Miller and Tilley (1984:13) is the representation of sectional interests in the creation of the cultural world. Such representations tend to exhibit certain properties that serve to legitimate those sectional interests: they tend to represent as universal that which may be partial; they tend to represent as coherent that which may be in conflict; they tend to represent as permanent that which may be in flux; and, they tend to represent as natural that which may be cultural (Miller and Tilley 1984:14).

Ideology can serve to legitimate elite interests, but to consider ideology simply in this fashion is to subscribe to the dominant ideology thesis (see Abercrombie et al. 1980). It can be countered that ideology is not solely the resource of an elite and that ideologies of the elite need not necessarily pervade all sections of society, in the same form:

> ...[the dominant ideology thesis] denies subordinate groups the ability to formulate their own ideologies and has been found to be subject to many exceptions when measured against historical situations...(Beaudry et al. 1991:157)

All groups in society are capable of formulating ideologies counter to those put forward by so-called elites. In a given society, a whole range of ideologies can coexist alongside an apparent dominant ideology, serving to limit the assumed pervasive nature of that ideology, if not overthrowing it (Miller 1989:73). As we shall see below, dominant ideologies can be exposed as false if they do not accord with routine conditions of existence.

We should be careful, however, not to see opposition to a dominant ideology in terms of simple bipolar opposition. As will be argued in chapter seven, the farming population did not simply accept or resist Improvement. Rather, action was contingent on circumstance and could be ambiguous. What I will define as external Improvement (to landscape organization, settlement pattern, and morphology) might be accepted, while internal Improvement (to domestic space) was shunned. The former was public and visible, while the latter was more private. Response also varied within the tenant and sub-tenant population. Response to Improvement will be understood as structured by a previous concern for continued occupancy of the land. It was contingent on the implications of Improvement for the various tenurially defined sub-groups, with reference to that occupancy, to the question of land rights.

As seen above, we should also be careful not to separate ideology and social relations, and thus see people as belonging to bounded cultures. People didn't simply create, accept, or reject an ideology. They sought to maintain or transform their relationships with others. They did so in the Highlands, in no small part, with reference to their perceived right to land. They did not negotiate this right by simply opposing differing statements of their legitimacy to that land. This did happen, but it was connected to attempts to maintain or change the ways people interacted in practice in different places, in the house, in the fields, and elsewhere.

IDEOLOGY, MATERIAL CULTURE, AND ROUTINE PRACTICE

It is the relationships between people that matter, not those between competing ideologies or cultures. I will conclude my discussion of social constitution and change with reference the concept that anthropologists and social theorists have variously referred to as *habitus*, practical consciousness, or practical cognition, already introduced.

The starting point I will take is anthropologist Maurice Bloch's discussion of cognition (1989:Chapter 5). Bloch outlines how social structure is learnt, distinguishing two different processes of cognition. The first of these he refers to as non-ideological cognition, which derives from practical experience of the social and material environment. The second is ideology, which is, for Bloch, most notably learnt through ritual practice.

Bloch begins discussion of non-ideological cognition (similarly known as practical cognition, practical consciousness, or *habitus*) with reference to the work of Pierre Bourdieu. Bourdieu's *Outline of a Theory of Practice* has as its aim the study of practical apprehension of the familiar world and the construction of a theory of practice and of practical knowledge (Bourdieu 1977:4). In this, social actions, such as gift exchange, are not subject to strict rules of behavior, but rather should be conceived of as dialectical strategies where the response is not mechanistic (Bourdieu 1977:3–9):

> ... practical knowledge, based on the continuous decoding of the perceived—but not consciously noticed—indices of the welcome given to actions already accomplished, continuously carries out the checks and corrections intended to ensure the adjustment of practices and expressions to the reactions and expectations of the other agents. (Bourdieu 1977:10)

Action is regulated improvisation. Practical consciousness does not consist of rules, but of more general resources for action. In gift exchange, Bourdieu defines a *sense* of honor on which people draw to guide their actions (Bourdieu 1977:10–15). I will draw on this concept of sense later, defining particular *senses of the community, of the family,* and *of the individual* in discussing the Highlands. These dispositions were central to the successful construction and destruction of the social relations of clanship, and significant in structuring changing concepts of occupancy of the land.

So, people's actions are generated with reference to learnt dispositions. Bourdieu refers to systems of such dispositions as *habitus*:

> The structures constitutive of a particular type of environment... produce *habitus*, systems of durable, transposable *dispositions*, structured structures predisposed to function as structuring structures, that is, as principles of the generation and structuring of practices and representations which can be objectively "regulated" and "regular" without in any way being the product of obedience to rules... (Bourdieu 1977:72, emphasis in original)

Habitus enables some forms of action and excludes others, but is not the sole principle of practice. Some areas of social practice are freely given over to the regulated improvisations of *habitus*, while others are more strictly regulated by cultural norms upheld by social sanctions (Bourdieu 1977:21). This is something to which we will return below.

The dispositions to act that are *habitus* are, from the above discussion, the result of experience of past social encounters. They come from experiencing the many ways in which individuals relate in given circumstances. Importantly for the archaeologist:

> In a social formulation in which the absence of the symbolic-product-conserving techniques associated with literacy retards the objectification of symbolic and particularly cultural capital, inhabited space—and above all the house—is the principal locus for the objectification of the generative schemes . . . (Bourdieu 1977:89)

Bourdieu places an emphasis upon the particular material conditions in which social practices are situated, something extended by John Barrett:

> The material world, permanent and decaying, constructed and demolished, exchanged and accumulated, is a potentially powerful system of signification. It is inhabited by actors whose practical understanding of their daily routines is constructed with reference to a material architecture and their temporal movement through those spaces and across their boundaries. (Barrett 1988:9)

People's experiences of social encounters and of their relationship to the physical world have a material component. Architecture, for example, facilitates some lines of movement and of sight, but constricts others. How an individual in a given building will be positioned towards others, in both a physical and a social sense, is partly a function of the organization of that building as a material space. Similarly, moveable objects might be deployed in social practice, whether in ritualized contexts such as gift exchange or in the mundane as an everyday meal. Practical knowledge that informs action comes in no small part from experiences of inhabited space. It is for this reason that the archaeologist can begin to understand the nature of past societies:

> An archaeological engagement with the past now becomes an attempt to understand how, under given historical and material conditions, it may have been possible to speak and act in certain ways and not in others, and by so doing to have carried certain programmes of knowledge and expectation forward in time. (Barrett 1994:5)

In this sense, the material world is active in structuring people's social practice. However, as we have seen, people are not determined, they can act to change their world. As such, material culture can be manipulated in practice to alter the conditions of existence. The conditions for the generation of *habitus* can be altered.

According to the view formulated by Bourdieu, and adopted by some archaeologists, cognition is built from experience of an environment that is historically specific. Bloch has rightly suggested that Bourdieu's concept of *habitus* as a form of practical consciousness does not explain how experience of the environment leads to the elaborate and arbitrary schemes described by anthropologists, and referred to as ideology by Bourdieu (Bloch 1989:118–119). Bourdieu was able to link elements of the material environment to elements of discursive ideology, but could not show how that link was constructed.

Bloch suggests that we can overcome this problem by conceiving of cognition as the result of more than one process, where practical cognition is differentiated from ideological cognition (Bloch 1989:120–136). In this, ideology is not simply a discursive rendering of, equivalent for, or distillation of non-ideological cognition. These forms of cognition should not be seen as segments of a unitary system. We should see knowledge as the momentary crystallization of different processes that interact with each other. Analysis should focus on the processes of formation of cognition and their interaction, not on a finished product.

The formation of practical cognition, or *habitus*, has already been discussed. For Bloch, the major process of the formation of ideology is ritual practice, although he does not consider this exclusive. Discussion, and disagreement, over cosmological principles can and does take place in daily life. However, such discussion is to be distinguished from the formation and transmission of ideology, which is related to institutional hierarchy.

Different ritual practices have in common the fact that they move the participants from non-ideological to ideological cognition. The social structure of practical cognition is refuted and an alternative view of the cosmos is constructed. This ideological cognition is usually vague. It does not specify who should act in what way, when and where. Rather it constructs a general hierarchy in social relations. Ultimately, ideological cognition is related to the non-ideological. However, one is not the distillation of the other. Rather, ideology is the transformation of practical cognition, and the latter in many ways negates the former.

Bloch's emphasis on ritual practice as the major process of the formation of ideology is only of partial use. The community of the clan, for example and as will be seen in Chapter 6, *was* maintained and justified in part through ritual feasting and feuding. Ideological statements were not confined to such moments of ritual practice, however. They could be expressed in the names people took or the leases they signed. Leases could reify and naturalize an asymmetrical relationship between two individuals and were an expression of the fact that those people related as individuals. I have found it more useful, therefore, to think of ideological cognition as involving explicit, often codified statements on the proper constitution of society. The expression of such statements need not be confined to ritual practice, especially in a society where they can be enshrined in documents.

This discussion of different forms of cognition is directly relevant to archaeological considerations of ideology and the constitution of social relations. Meaning of whatever type is not simply encoded in material culture. Rather, there is a more complex relationship between the material environment and cognition. John Barrett's *Fragments From Antiquity* (1994) is such an exploration of the interplay of practical and ideological consciousness in relation to material culture, with reference to the southern British Neolithic and Bronze Age. In discussing ritual practice throughout the period in question he argues:

> ... we must isolate the principles which structured the biographical relation-
> ship between the participant and the metaphysical values of the ritual itself.
> Each biography could be lived because it carried the agent forward in such
> a way that the various structuring principles were recognizably reproduced
> in other, diverse areas of social practice. (Barrett 1994:136)

Barrett argues that we can trace a transformation between two concepts of temporality in the period in question (Barrett 1994: 136–153 and *passim*). With the first concept, human existence was a process of becoming, where life might be seen as an ephemeral journey towards a future state. This future state may have been the community of the ancestors, reached on death. This belief belonged to the third millennium B.C., with a history stretching back into the fourth and fifth.

The ritual monuments of this period were typically places, or nodes, on a network of paths. This is particularly evident at Stonehenge and Avebury where avenues defined by banks and standing stones define processional routes leading up to the enclosures themselves. These sites lie at the end of one path and beginning of others.

Movement along paths also structured daily life. The gatherer-hunter communities of the fifth millennium would have regularly moved to exploit locally and seasonally available resources, like flint sources, animals, and edible vegetation. This situation need not have changed with the introduction of farming at the end of the fifth millennium. Pastoralism and long-fallow systems of agriculture easily accord with patterns of seasonal migration. Access to land under these systems would have been claimed as generalized rights arising from alliances between the members of a wider community. The community held the land in trust and individuals had no claim to a particular portion of that land.

In this situation both everyday experience of the world and ritual practice emphasized place, path, and the identity of the community:

> All the participants [in ritual] will . . . have understood something of the fundamental structure of the ritual code as being a recognizable transformation of their own diverse and routine experiences. . . . These monuments were the theatres of transitory experience, where the passage of an individual's life could touch upon the presence of the ancestors and gods. (Barrett 1994:146)

Ritual practice ideologically naturalized the claims of an elite to authority as that ideological practice accorded with everyday experience. An ideology that portrayed human life as transitory movement towards the community of the ancestors was knowable because people's daily experience of life was of migration along paths to places of communal activity.

However, in the second millennium the organization of agriculture was transformed. Short fallow systems emerged, where land was used more intensively. This is evidenced archaeologically by colluvial soil deposits that are the result of a process of erosion. The important point about this shift in agricultural practice is that a particular area of land came to be maintained by a particular portion of the community. The daily experience of a landscape of paths and places was replaced by that of a landscape viewed from the center of a domain and where that domain was distinct from similar neighboring domains. The enclosure of fields and settlements became common at this time.

Now people experienced vertical social divisions in their daily routine, contrasting with the ideological propositions encountered in ancestral ritual. It comes as no surprise, then, that ritual practice also changed dramatically in the second millennium. The chambers of tombs were sealed, gradually in cases. Burial now took place under tumuli that blocked access to the interred remains:

> . . . the early barrow cemeteries were instrumental in allowing a different history to be read, a reading which helped to make possible the gradual changes in control over the natural resources to be understood and given voice. The significance of these material conditions therefore lay in their interpretation. Agents could no longer recognize their identity in the more general community. The chains of metaphorical association by which the agent moved between routine and ritual practices and back, now fixed them in time and spoke to them as members of a differently constituted and more restricted community. The burial mounds, for example, were no longer constructed as a consequence of a burial ritual but had now become a focus of veneration . . . (Barrett 1994:151)

Ritual and its material aspects now emphasized the history of a lineage with reference to a monument specific to the lineage.

Considering the time scale involved here, we should not conceive of change in ideological and practical consciousness as related in a simple cause and effect relationship. We should not conceive of ideology as a superstructure adapting to changes in a material base. Rather, the relationship should be seen as reflexive. What is most important about Barrett's work here is his exploration of the possible subjectivities created in the interaction of both realms of consciousness. Through a consideration of routine practice and experience of a daily environment we can construct generalized contexts from which to assess possible readings of a given ideological statement.

The point I want to emphasize is that ideological statements about the world, such as "I have a hereditary right to this land," are assessed from a background of experience in the world. This statement might make sense, it might appear as common sense, because it accords with someone's experience of how they relate to other people and to the physical world. This statement is more likely to make sense in a world where day-to-day experience of the world is structured through the lineage than in one where people relate to each other as seemingly autonomous individuals, whose rights are those of an individual and based on their personal qualities, or lack thereof.

However, society is not simply constituted in the conjunction of one form of social relationship and attendant ideologies. We cannot simply state that an asymmetrical relationship existed between tenant and landlord and this was justified or disputed in different readings or assertions of ideology. Society consists of diverse relationships. For example, the landlord-tenant-sub-tenant relationship can in part be justified, rendered natural, if it accords with the structuring of relationships within the home, between parent and child for example.

Ideological statements can naturalize or refute social relations and the structure of social relations can act back to make ideological statements appear as right or wrong. At the same time, social relations at one level, in the house for example, can form the basis of an assessment of the legitimacy of social relations at another level, in the community of the farming township or between the tenant and landlord. There is an inter-connectedness between the diverse relations people have with others and between those relations and practical and explicit forms of consciousness. For this reason, society cannot be seen as simply constituted of competing ideologies or distinct cultures because different ideologies, different cultural practices, and different forms of social relations underpin and undermine each other and are inextricably related. As Orser and Johnson have suggested, and as discussed above, an archaeology of capitalism is an archaeology of the changing and diverse ways in which people related to each other and the connections between these relations, concepts of the self, ideology, and power.

CAPITALISM, CAPITALIST SOCIETY, AND ARCHAEOLOGY

In the following chapters of this book, capitalism will be understood as a form of social relations. Central to capitalism is the way in which people relate to others as autonomous individuals. Relations of absence are more common than previously and face-to-face interaction less significant.

The origins of capitalism, in general terms, are complex in the extreme. Here, I will focus on the rise to prominence of capitalism in one place and time, the southern Scottish Highlands in the eighteenth and nineteenth centuries. This place and time did not exist in isolation, as will be clear from the fact that I will step outwith their boundaries on a number of occasions. The concepts of agency, structure, and power are fundamental to an understanding of social change and the emergence of capitalism. It was people who brought about change and they did so actively. They did not do so freely, however. The possibilities for change were both constricted and enabled by existing social practice, by structure. The exercise of control over the conditions of existence was also conditioned by relations of power. People are influenced and restricted by those with whom they interact, positively or negatively. The character and extent of this influence and restriction are dependent on a person's position within an asymmetrical network of social relations. The need for change is often grounded in social conflict resulting from contradictions and asymmetries within the social structure, in the ways in which people relate to one another.

The manner in which society is constituted and in which social structure is maintained or altered can be defined analytically in terms of social practice and ideology. People form a practical understanding of the world and their place in it from their everyday experience. This practical knowledge forms a basis for assessing ideological claims, making them appear as common sense or nonsense. The same goes for the connection between different relationships within a social network. The relationship of a tenant and landlord will be justifiable or disputable from their experience of other relationships, in the home for example. Different forms of social interaction can be in conflict. The same person may have to maintain a variety of relations with others and to engage with them in quite different ways. Conflict arises with a need to reconcile these differences. We can, therefore, see ideology and different sets of social relations as existing in a complex web of interaction. The former does not simply change in reaction to the latter, or vice versa, and potentially conflicting ideologies and social relationships can be maintained by the same person. People can seek to indoctrinate others in their ideology to influence the way those others engage in social activity, they can attempt to alter the way in which people relate to others to influence the way they explicitly conceive the world, and they can try to alter the basis of one social relationship to affect the practice of another. People act in complex ways to address their own interests, which are rooted in the past and constructed with reference to others. The distinction of ideology and social relations and the separation of different forms of social relation are abstractions of this process.

The role of archaeology in studying this process comes from the fact that social relations have a material component. People are situated with respect to others in part through the physical environment they inhabit, whether that refers to architecture, field boundaries, the plates on the table, or something else. The maintenance or transformation of the relationship between one person and the next relates in no small part to the way in which the environment facilitates or denies certain patterns of movement or action, lines of sight, and much else.

With Improvement, for some, Highland landscapes, settlement, and domestic architecture were restructured in order to privilege absence over presence as primary in social relations. Everyday experience of the local environment increasingly undermined the communities that formed the basis of the clan, and increasingly privileged the individual. Likewise, the reordering of the house played a significant role in undermining hereditary, kin-based notions of tenure and likewise privileged the individual. All of this occurred with the increasing control of the landlord over the productive process and over the construction of the material environment. Economic relationships became primary in the structuring of society, where those of community and kin had predominated before. All of this made concepts of private property and individualism knowable, common sense.

However, to study Improvement is not to narrate the progress of a universal process. Rather, I wish to discuss the active creation of capitalism through the interplay of material culture, social practice, and ideology in several localized contexts. In Chapter 7 in particular, I will argue that social relations within Highland society in the eighteenth and nineteenth centuries did not solely come to be structured in terms of capitalism. Capitalism, in this instance, should be reserved as a term to describe certain social relationships or aspects of those relationships that existed alongside other relationships and other understandings of the world. Capitalist society in a broad sense can incorporate both capitalism and social relations structured in quite different ways at one and the same time. That such a society can still be called capitalist, though, underlines the significance of asymmetrical relations of power in all social interaction. Alternative ways of living, thinking, and relating to others were possible and significant, but they were not easily or freely created and maintained and they could not exist in isolation.

The Changing Material and Routine Environment | 4

A consideration of routine practice and the material environments that structure and are structured by that practice is basic to our understanding of society. An archaeological consideration of routine is fundamental in assessing the potential penetration of the ideology of the individual, and the associated concept of private property, into different historical contexts. This is because routine practice forms the conditions from which the ideology of capitalism is knowable. Routine practice and its associated physical environment are also essential to a consideration of how everyday relationships connected with other social relations, such as those between tenant and landlord and clan and clan gentry. In this chapter, I will consider how routine practice and its environment were transformed in eighteenth and nineteenth century Kintyre and Kilfinan through the process of Improvement.

In those areas and at that time, the ways in which people lived and worked did change in such a way as to inculcate a *sense of the individual*, as experience of the world was increasingly understood from the position of the individual. This understanding came in place of one where experience of the world was as part of a community or a family, with a related *sense of community* and *sense of the family*. In these latter situations, the individual was not absent, but articulated within the community or family. I will also suggest below, and discuss in more detail in Chapter 7, that the Improvement of routine practice and its physical environment was not universal or uniform. The ideology of capitalism would have been understood, and evaluated, in fundamentally differing ways by different groups of people and people within those groups would have understood that ideology differently in various social circumstances. Furthermore, the fact that Improvement was not monolithic suggests that the connections between different relationships would have been varied and diverse. In this, the different structuring of family life will have impacted on the relationship between the farmer and the laborer, as it would on that between the tenant or subtenant and the landowner. The same would be true in reverse, though not necessarily equally so.

I have divided this chapter into three main sections. The first considers the material environment of the pre-Improvement period, between the late Middle Ages and the eighteenth and nineteenth centuries. The second considers changes to the material environment with Improvement. This process begins substantively in Kintyre in the late eighteenth century, but not until the first half of the nineteenth century in Kilfinan. The third section relates these different environments to changing routine practice. Discussion in all three sections has been arranged in relation to three themes: settlement pattern and morphology; the wider landscape; and, the organization of domestic space.

THE PRE-IMPROVEMENT MATERIAL ENVIRONMENT

A useful starting point in understanding the pre-Improvement material environment in the southern Highlands is the Military Survey of Scotland, otherwise known as the Roy Map, surveyed on behalf of the British government in the wake of the Jacobite Rebellion of 1745 (see, e.g., O'Dell 1953; Skelton 1967a, 1967b; Whittington 1986a, 1986b, 1986c). This is the earliest map to give any reliable detail on settlement and landscape form, which are depicted at a time prior to intensive Improvement. There are earlier maps, like those of Timothy Pont, but their usefulness here is limited (see Findlay 1978; Moir and Skelton 1968; Morris 1986; Stone 1968, 1991).

Survey of Scotland north of the rivers Forth and Clyde for the Roy Map was completed between 1747 and 1752 (Whittington 1986b:18). William Roy, who was principally responsible for the execution of the survey, described the result as "rather . . . a magnificent military sketch, than a very accurate map of a country" (quoted in Skelton 1967b:11). The military agenda of the survey and the nature of the instruments used have been discussed by some in order to define the accuracy of the map (Skelton 1967b:7–9, 11–12).

The survey was carried out using a chain of about 14 or 15 meters length to measure distance and a circumferentor (a graduated circle with compass and alidade) for measuring angle (Skelton 1967b:8, 11, 16 n.10). Such equipment would have itself led to significant errors (Skelton 1967b:11). However, Skelton (1967b:12) has argued that the military nature of the map means that it probably gives a fairly correct impression of relief, routes of communication, and other information pertaining to the movement of troops and supplies, such as the limits of cultivation and waste, of enclosed and unenclosed and of drained and undrained land, and of woodland and open country. While some such features may have been accurately surveyed, others were filled in by eye (Skelton 1967b:8).

On the other hand, some have suggested that the accuracy of the Roy Map should not be overstated. In contrast to the above, it has been argued for areas of Fife that the limits of cultivation and other areas of land use are not accurately depicted and that the appearance of cultivated land is symbolic, with lines of rig cultivation drawn at random (Whittington 1986b:25–27). The representation of settlement has also been seen as symbolic and, thus, unreliable for detailed study of settlement morphology, although the depiction of the larger towns may be representative (Whittington 1986b:20–25; 1986c:71).

The sections of the Roy Map for Kintyre and Kilfinan, as will be seen, carry both representative and symbolic depiction. On the whole, settlement form, land use, and what little enclosure is shown do appear to be stylized in form. However, in some areas enclosure in particular seems to be representatively recorded, as is the layout of Campbeltown, the only sizeable town in the area. Further, the nature of the stylized depiction of settlement and landscape does vary and seems to do so in a meaningful and locally sensitive fashion. The Roy Map therefore gives a good and varied general picture of settlement and landscape form with some limited information on specific areas of enclosure.

The Roy Map is of use as a general source on the character of pre-Improvement settlement and landscape. There is some limited archaeological data from the study areas with which to compare it (the archaeology of the period of Improvement is much more extensive.) There are also other relevant cartographic sources, consisting of a group of eighteenth century estate surveys. These are more representative than the Roy Map, but their geographical coverage is less extensive. To these sources, we can add relevant archaeological sites and landscapes from outwith the study areas.

Settlement

Settlement form on the Roy Map appears very similar for Kintyre and Kilfinan. Settlements are generally shown as small amorphous clusters of three to six structures in Kintyre and three to five in Kilfinan. Settlement is amorphous in Alan Gailey's terms in that there is:

> ...no clear indication of logical layout; the group of dwellings and associated out-buildings are amorphous, although individual structures within

the group may show a preferred orientation in one of two directions at right-angles to each other. This latter feature appears to be related to slope. (Gailey 1960:104)

The important defining elements of this form are conformity as best can to the immediate topography of a specific site, taking into account such factors as slope and drainage, and the gradual growth of the settlement over time, to no consciously predetermined plan.

Structures are shown as solid and largely undifferentiated rectangles. The settlements themselves are unenclosed, but are frequently associated with small rectilinear enclosures. These are probably kailyards (garden plots), small livestock pens, or stackyards for the harvested corn stacks (Fairhurst 1960:68; Dixon 1994:34). While some have referred to this form of settlement as the *clachan* (e.g., Fairhurst 1960; Gailey 1962a), I agree with others that this term refers specifically to settlement associated with a church (Laing 1969:73). Here, I will use the more general term for a farming township, *baile* (Gaelic, pl. *bailtean*). The term *baile* as used here carries the connotation that the settlement in question was organized as a joint-tenancy farm.

The uniform size of the *bailtean* depicted, together with the conclusions of the detailed studies of the Roy Map discussed above, suggest that these amorphous clusters are symbolic representations. Work on the Argyll sections of the Roy Map has suggested, however, that the survey was at least sensitive to regional variation in settlement size (Gailey 1961:258; 1962a:159–160). There is a general increase in settlement size from southern to northern Argyll related to the spread of Improvement from south to north, allowing a greater increase of population in the north before Improvement (Gailey 1962a:158–159).

The morphology of settlement on the Roy Map, and the few distinctive features depicted, like kailyards, are probably reliable in giving a general impression of the nature of the *bailtean*. Such settlements that survive, all of which are deserted, are few in the study areas, but compare well with the map. The oldest of these archaeological examples probably dates to the mid-eighteenth century at earliest. However, comparison with the archaeology of the surrounding area and with other cartographic data suggests that these surviving *bailtean* are of a type that was common in the region, probably from the late Medieval period.

Archaeological remains of the *bailtean* depicted on the Roy Map are almost non-existent in Kintyre. This is probably largely the result of later intensive farming practices, the re-use of stone from the settlements in dyke construction, and forestry plantation. There is only one site that can be assigned to this group with any degree of confidence, and one other probable, both of which are to be found on the Mull of

Kintyre in the far south west of the peninsula. The latter of the two sites is Feorlan, where a series of structures survive as low turf and stone banks. These structures form an amorphous cluster. The other site, Balmavicar (see RCAHMS 1971:192–196), is better preserved and, as such, I will focus on it here (see Figure 4).

Balmavicar is one of a group referred to by Gailey as the *Innean* settlements (Gailey 1961:85). His term derives from a Gaelic place name element common to many of the group and meaning cleft, as in *Innean Còig Cailleiche* ("Cleft of the five old women," Gailey 1960:102). These deserted settlements are to be found along the west coast of the Mull of Kintyre, situated in the occasional large hollows that cut into the high moor ground along that coast and overlooking the Atlantic cliffs of the Mull. The settlements and their immediate environs are thus in the few sheltered locations within an exposed landscape.

At Balmavicar, discounting structures A and B, which are almost certainly of later construction than the rest or at least heavily modified, there are eight surviving structures that probably belong to the pre-Improvement *baile*. The largest buildings, G and O, are 10.7m by 6.7m and 12m by 5.5m respectively, sub-oval, and have opposed entrances. The opposed doors, allowing a through draft, suggest that these were threshing barns. That O was a barn is suggested by the presence of a corn-drying kiln in its western end. It is possible that G was a dwelling, with a byre outshot to the west. Structure F is the remains of a horizontal mill. Traces of the lade can still be seen leading up to the structure. The uses of structures C, D, H, L, and M are less clear, with no diagnostic features. Some at least must have been dwellings and others were possibly outhouses. The Royal Commission have suggested that C, D, and H were outbuildings, although their reasons for saying so have not been given (RCAHMS 1971:194).

Associated with the buildings are several small enclosures, C_1, D_1, J, K, and M_1, whose use is unclear. Presumably they were kailyards, stock enclosures, or stack yards, as suggested for those depicted on the Roy Map.

The arrangement of the buildings and small enclosures at Balmavicar is random in terms of the plan view. They are placed in accordance with the topography of the site, on some of the few level or near level areas in the restricted space of the steep-sided cleft. The area over which the buildings are spread is some 95m by 50m. They are closely, but not restrictively situated.

The structures and enclosures at Balmavicar probably date to the late pre-Improvement period in this particular area of Kintyre. Their abandonment in the late-eighteenth and early-nineteenth centuries is

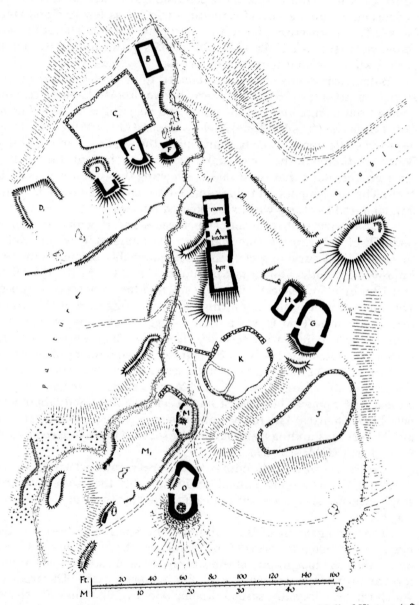

Figure 4. The *baile* and later farmstead at Balmavicar on the Mull of Kintyre (after RCAHMS 1971:figure 182; crown copyright: RCAHMS).

fairly certain. Some of the *Innean* settlements appear as occupied on the Roy Map, but are omitted from censuses of the Argyll Estates (on which they stood) in 1779 and 1792 (Gailey 1960:104). Others that survived into the nineteenth century were abandoned as permanent sites in 1816, and had disappeared by 1818, with the conversion of the Mull into a permanent, large sheep-walk (Gailey 1961:85). Balmavicar itself is listed as uninhabited on the 1779 census, and so was presumably out of use as a township by that time (Cregeen 1963:115). This means that the pre-Improvement structures at Balmavicar are probably contemporary with the Roy Map.

The general type of settlement found at Balmavicar, amorphous and clustered, is found elsewhere in the Highlands, as the excavated sites of Easter Raitts, in Badenoch (Lelong and Wood 2000), and Rosal, Strathnaver (Fairhurst 1968), show. Archaeological remains at these sites have been dated to the period immediately before the townships they represent were cleared for Improvement.

While surviving examples of this type of settlement in Kintyre may be few, the widespread distribution of *bailtean* suggested by the Roy Map is confirmed by a series of estate plans. Most useful of the available estate surveys for the area are a series of plans by George and Alex Langlands surveyed between 1777 and 1806. These plans depict settlement and landscape on several of the small Kintyre estates that bordered the Duke of Argyll's lands. Undoubtedly, suitable plans of the Argyll Estates exist within their archives, but access to those archives is limited and was not permitted for this study.

George Langlands surveyed Knocknahall, adjacent to the house and policies of Charles McNeill of Kilchrist, its proprietor, in 1777 (ABDA DR3/21; ownership information from Timperley [ed.] 1976:30). The plan shows eleven separate structures in an amorphous cluster (see Figure 5). One of these is indicated as a mill, the uses of the others are unknown. The relatively large size of this settlement may be connected to its close proximity to McNeill's house and its presumed function as the mains farm. The structures at Kilchrist are associated with a series of small enclosures, and are situated amongst a system of much larger enclosed fields forming the estate policies. Other similar settlements are shown on the plans of the Largie estate surveyed by George Langlands in 1790 (ABDA DR4/9/109). The *bailtean* depicted there vary in size from three to six structures and are almost without exception associated with the type of small enclosure depicted on the Roy Map and seen at Balmavicar.

On these plans, we are seeing settlement at a time when Improvement was already substantially underway. Nearly all the settlements

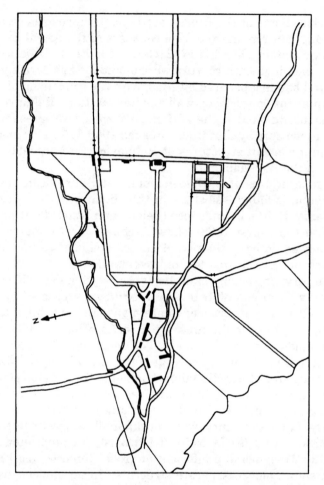

Figure 5. The house and policies of Kilchrist with the township of Knocknahall as surveyed by George Langlands in 1777 (redrawn from ABDA DR3/21).

shown are situated within systems of enclosed fields and appear to exist alongside Improved forms of settlement (see below). However, it is reasonable to suggest that the settlements shown represent an originally pre-Improvement form, which with hindsight was on its way out at the time of the surveys. Some of these *bailtean* seem already to have been deserted by the time of survey, depicted as they are in outline and not as solid rectangles (e.g., Culfuar and Laigh Runaheuran on the Largie Estate, ABDA DR4/4/8).

No pre-Improvement *bailtean* have yet been identified in Kilfinan, but settlements similar to Balmavicar and comparable with the Roy

Map do exist in wider Cowal. To take an example, Strone Point on the Colintraive peninsula is a *baile* probably abandoned in the late eighteenth century (RCAHMS 1992:478). The hearth-tax assessment of 1693 names three tenants, and the surviving buildings can be divided into three groups. Two groups are of two buildings, probably a dwelling and barn pair in each case. The third is composed of two large buildings and a further two smaller ones. The *baile* is bounded to the north by a massive turf-and-stone dyke.

Kilfinan does boast a number of Improvement period amorphous settlement sites, with examples at Ardgaddan South, Ardgaddan North, Ascog and Craignafeoch (see Figures 15 and 16). The greater survival of this settlement form in Kilfinan is related to their later date of use, with structures in all the examples named above shown as roofed (that is, as solid rectangles) on the first edition Ordnance Survey (OS) maps of the mid-nineteenth century. These sites formed part of an Improved landscape and farming regime, as will be seen in detail in chapter seven. In terms of routine practice they should be distinguished from the *bailtean*, but the distinction is a blurred one.

The settlements shown on the Kintyre estate plans, as discussed above, also belong to a landscape in part Improved. However, it is clear that intensive Improvement was a recent phenomenon. Whether the amorphous settlements shown on these estate plans were joint-tenancy farms is unclear. However, this is possible for the Kintyre plans, where it was certainly not the case for the surviving Kilfinan settlements (see Chapter 7).

The distinction to be drawn here is one between the different routine practices associated with these settlements, and, as such, I will hold back detailed discussion of the Kilfinan amorphous settlements for now. It is enough here to suggest that the existence of amorphous settlement in this later context makes it likely, taken with the diagrammatic depictions of settlement on the Roy map, that this was the usual pre-Improvement settlement form in Kilfinan.

The antiquity of the *baile* in the Highlands is uncertain, which is unsurprising considering the dearth of knowledge on Medieval settlement as a whole (see Chapter 2). However, some recent work allows a late Medieval date of origin to be suggested. Several contrasting and recently surveyed and excavated sites are relevant here, primarily those of Finlaggan on Islay, a large island close by to the west of Kintyre, and Craigs, in County Antrim in the north of Ireland (Caldwell and Ewart 1993; Caldwell et al. 2000; Williams 1988). The late Medieval settlement excavated on Gunna (James 1998) has been omitted here because its full extent is as yet unclear.

The island of Finlaggan, with its hall, chapel, and neighboring Council Island, is famous for its association with the Lords of the Isles and has been described as the center of the Lordship (Caldwell and Ewart 1993:146). Its interest here, however, is in the fact that the island was colonized by more mundane settlement after the fall of the Lordship in the late fifteenth century (see chapter 6 below for a more detailed account of the Lordship).

A substantial township inhabited the island in the sixteenth century (Caldwell and Ewart 1993:155–156). This township consisted of a series of house and barn units, each comprised of two separate adjacent structures, alongside other individual structures. This is a situation also found at Balmavicar, where house and barn pairs (H with G, and perhaps M with O) sit alongside other structures. The *baile* on Finlaggan was also accompanied by one small enclosure, which appears to have contained cultivation (Caldwell et al. 2000:65).

The contemporary situation at Craigs (Williams 1988) contrasts markedly with that at Finlaggan. The relevance of this site is clear if we consider the geographical proximity, and strong social and political connections in the period of the Lordship of the Isles and later, between the west Highlands and Islands and the north of Ireland (see Chapter 6). At Craigs, an isolated sub-rectangular structure was found upon excavation to have been a sixteenth-century dwelling (Williams 1988:94–95, 97–99). This structure was associated with a series of enclosed fields, to which we will return.

In the sixteenth century, then, in two areas close not only in geographical but also in political and social terms we have two significantly contrasting forms of settlement. What is of interest is the possibility that the type of isolated settlement found at Craigs was once widespread in the Highlands and Islands of Scotland, and that the *baile* form of settlement found at Finlaggan was relatively new at the time.

Robert Dodgshon has recently questioned the assumption that the origins of the *baile* lay beyond the Medieval period, in late prehistory (Dodgshon 1993a). Focusing on Lewis and Skye in particular, Dodgshon argues that nucleated *bailtean* were preceded by more dispersed forms of settlement, the shift between the two probably taking place at some time from the late Medieval period, between the thirteenth and fifteenth centuries (Dodgshon 1993a:424–435).

Dodgshon looks in detail at the settlements of North and South Bragar on Lewis (Dodgshon 1993a:424–428). Prior to the reorganization of these settlements into crofts, a nineteenth century plan suggests that neither of these two townships had a single settlement nucleus. In fact, several individual foci were recognized on the first edition OS map of the area as having their own names. This, together with some rental data, suggests that the dispersal of settlement had organizational meaning. The townships of North and South Bragar, therefore, are taken to be the consolidation of several isolated and separate units.

This last point is expanded in relation to data from Skye (Dodgshon 1993a:428–434). A series of eighteenth century plans there detail fairly conventional *bailtean*, with settlement clustered in a single nucleus. However, these plans also show a number of small shaded areas scattered across the arable of the townships. These shaded areas, when examined in the field, were not found to refer to rock outcrops or areas of broken ground. Rather, Dodgshon suggests, they represent areas of former settlement where wall footings and the like could still be traced at the time of survey for the plans. This is also suggested by aerial photography of some of the sites. These plans, then, hint at a chronology of change from dispersed to nucleated settlement, perhaps seen in process at Bragar.

An archaeological example of the pre-*baile* dispersed form of settlement is to be found at Borrafiach, Vaternish, Skye (Dodgshon 1993a:431–434). There are no signs of nucleated settlement there. Rather, there are as many as fifteen small settlement sites scattered across an area of 600m by 500m. Two of these sites may be late eighteenth or nineteenth century in date, but the rest appear to be of the early eighteenth century or earlier. When it is added that these dispersed settlement foci occur in association with an enclosed field system, the similarity to Craigs is obvious.

The *baile*, then, may have its origins in the late medieval period in the west Highlands and Islands and may have replaced a pattern of dispersed settlement as the dominant (though not universal) settlement form. Admittedly the evidence for this process is as yet limited, but it is suggestive. Hopefully, detailed fieldwork currently exploring this problem will prove successful (e.g., Banks and Atkinson 2000).

In summary, a general impression of the character of pre-Improvement settlement in Kintyre and Kilfinan can be drawn from the variety of sources outlined above. The type of settlement shown can be called the *baile*, amorphous and consisting of several types of structure, most notably dwellings and barns along with occasional mills and other buildings. The presence of a church is what defines a *clachan*. The buildings of the *baile* are frequently associated with small enclosures, probably relating to the domestic economies of individual households (kailyards, stackyards, or stock enclosures).

The origins of the *baile* as a settlement form probably lie somewhere in the late Medieval period. It may have come to replace small, dispersed farms of the Medieval period. At Bragar, traces of this dispersed settlement pattern survived until Improvement in the nineteenth century. Dispersed settlement foci within a single farm also seem to have been evident elsewhere in the Highlands, representing a similarly incomplete adjustment to the *baile* form as in the Isles, some would argue (Dodgshon 1993a:424). Rather than an incomplete adjustment, the presence of dispersed settlement foci within the lands of a single *baile* could relate to the social structure of that *baile*. In Waternish, Skye, isolated structures have been identified on the outskirts of the arable land of certain farms with larger clusters of settlement at their core (RCAHMS 1993; other farms in the survey area are more tightly clustered). These isolated structures could be the houses of the farm's sub-tenantry, with the tenants inhabiting the nucleated settlement within the arable land (RCAHMS 1993, 9).

In reality, there were probably several different forms to the *baile* (Dodgshon 1998a). A single named unit of assessment in a rental could represent a township with discrete clusters of settlement, but which operated as one farming unit, or a township with discrete clusters of settlement that were operationally more distinct, or several distinct townships who were jointly responsible for the rent (Dodgshon 1998a:53–54). Also, the different forms of township clustering and association were not static. They were constantly changing through aggregation and dis-aggregation (Dodgshon 1998a:55). Many *bailtean* were in part formed into distinct crofts separate from the main part of the township (Dodgshon 1998a:56). Much work remains to be done on the organization of the pre-Improvement *baile*. The point I would make here is that, while in many *bailtean* there were clearly distinct individual units, we can still see a degree of communal organization. Here, in terms discussed in chapter three, we see something of the articulation of the individual as part of the community.

Landscape

As already outlined, the depiction of landscape on the Roy Map is similarly diagrammatic to the depiction of settlement. The direction of rigs (cultivation ridges) and the precise extent of cultivated land may be questioned, for example. As with settlement, however, the map does give a good general impression of some aspects of the pre-Improvement landscape conforming to surviving archaeological data from the study areas and neighboring regions. In some instances, the Roy Map seems to depict a pattern of incipient enclosure in Kintyre that may be taken as representative, conforming as it does to the pattern of landownership associated with early Improvement. The Roy Map may, in such cases, be a valuable source in understanding the *specific* dynamics of Improvement in one of the case study areas. By contrast, the Map seems to completely ignore the pattern of shieling (transhumance settlement) that we know from other sources to have existed in the areas in question. Its usefulness seems to be confined to low-lying areas of settlement and agriculture.

On the Roy Map, the landscape immediate to the *bailtean* in both Kintyre and Kilfinan is characterized by a pattern of unenclosed cultivated fields. These are indicated with parallel hatching running in different directions, with adjacent patches often running at right angles. This hatching is presumably a diagrammatic depiction of rig cultivation. These areas of cultivation focus on the *bailtean*, although they are often interrupted by what appear to be boggy areas. In places, the boggy zone can be extensive. Above the boggy and cultivated areas the hillsides appear as completely open.

Archaeological indications of the openfield system suggested on the Roy Map are limited in the study areas. Again widespread forestry and more recent and intensive farming practices are probably the major factors. Most of the relevant archaeological landscapes are confined to now marginal areas, such as the Mull of Kintyre.

On the Mull, stretches of earthen dyke run above known or probable settlement sites, notably at Balmavicar, Creagan Fithich, Innean Coig Cailleiche, Ballygroggan, and along either side of Borgadale Glen. I will argue below that some later enclosed field systems in both Kilfinan and Kintyre reused these earlier dykes, one further significant reason why pre-Improvement landscapes are not readily archaeologically visible.

These earthen boundaries are usually referred to as head dykes (e.g., Dixon 1994:34–35). The contemporary use of this term and the widespread existence of the boundary form is confirmed for Kintyre by an Act of Bailyierie of 1672 where the "eating of moor grass without the head dyiks" was not to be covered by a penalty extracted for one township's livestock eating the grass of another township (Act reproduced in Stewart 1992:220). Although these head dykes are generally not indicated on the relevant portions of the Roy Map, they do demonstrate the existence of the basic two-fold division of the landscape suggested there. The head dyke separates a zone immediate to the *baile* from the wider expanse of the hillside. The head dyke divided the bulk of the arable from the pasture land (Gailey 1963:107), a division suggested in broad terms by the zoning of arable around the *bailtean* on the Roy Map. In the southern and central Highlands in this period, most farms also practiced less intensive cultivation on the outfield (Dodgshon

1993b:685–688). Outfield arable may have been contained below the head dyke, or spread above it (Gailey 1963:107–108). In cases, multiple parallel head dykes can be found where arable has at some time extended uphill (Gailey 1963:107–108; examples of this are to be found on the Mull of Kintyre).

Occasionally, the patchy remains of unenclosed rig and furrow cultivation do survive, providing further indication of arable farming (as on the steep-sided southwest slopes of The Doune in the south of Kintyre).

There was one other form of linear boundary, the march dyke, common to the pre-Improvement landscape of the area. For the Argyll Estates in Kintyre at least, such physical boundaries between the lands of different townships seem to have been in place in the seventeenth century (Stewart 1992:216, 220). However, march dykes between neighboring farms were not universal until about 1800, when enclosure was well underway anyway (Gailey 1963:107). Certainly, the marches of a farm might be defined in a variety of ways. In seventeenth century Kintyre for example, it was ordained that "march dykes be digged in all touns quhair it may be done and that march stones sheuchs and ditches be made and sett doun be the tenants" (Act of Bailyierie 1672, reproduced in Stewart 1992:220).

Head and march dykes, while forming significant boundaries within the pre-Improvement landscape and enclosing the arable of the farm, were associated with quite different routine practices from the enclosures proper of Improvement. These practices are something to which we will return below. The limited beginnings of the enclosure of fields, however, were taking place in the seventeenth and early eighteenth centuries.

The Roy Map shows enclosure to be of limited extent and concentrated in the policies of the houses of landowners. Later estate plans also show enclosed policies as developed, sometimes forming a grid pattern of fields, as with the grounds of Kilchrist, mentioned above (ABDA DR3/21). Interestingly, the sheets of the Roy Map covering the southern Highlands show a concentration of estate policies in Cowal, not least in the parish of Kilfinan (Gailey 1963:110–112). This may be related to the strong commercial links between that area and the Clyde burghs (Gailey 1963:110–112), something that will be explored in greater detail in Chapter 6.

The early development of the Cowal policies, and something of their character, can be seen from a near contemporary account of Campbell–Lamont conflict during the Civil Wars of the mid-seventeenth century. At that time, Campbell of Achavoulin and Campbell of Evanachan "did cut doune and destroy the wholl planting in and about ... [the Lamont] hous of Towart, orchzairds, parkis, and walkis thereof" (quoted in McKechnie 1938:195). To a large extent, then, these policies consisted of ornamental enclosure (Gailey 1963:112). As such, they can be distinguished to some extent from enclosure in the wider farming landscape.

The Roy Map does also suggest, though, that limited enclosure was evident in parts of the wider landscape. Examples are confined to Kintyre and take two forms. First, on some farms there seems to be a greater elaboration of the small yards already discussed. Second, in one small area in the north of Kintyre we can see the extension of enclosure into the fields of the farm in a pattern that has lasted into the present.

Concentrated along the west coast of Kintyre and inland in the area from the Laggan south, the Roy Map depicts what appear to be small tree-lined enclosures associated with many settlements. These are rectangular in form, number one per settlement where shown and appear to be not much bigger in size than the usual yards. The distribution of these tree-lined enclosures stops in the north in the vicinity of Largie and, concentrating as it does on the west coast and in the south they probably equate with the extent of the Duke of Argyll's lands in Kintyre (see Timperley [ed.] 1976:29–30, 35, 37–38, 42–43 for data on landholding in Kintyre contemporary with the Roy Map). This is interesting considering the coincidence of other early Improvements and the Argyll Estates (see below).

These tree-lined enclosures perhaps date as early as the seventeenth century. Certainly, an Act of Neighbourhood of 1653 suggests so (reproduced in Stewart 1992:216–219). The purpose of the Act is laid out as a preamble. It was drawn up at Lochheid (later Campbeltown) on the tenth of June, 1653:

> The quhilk day the Right honorable My lord Marqueis of Argyll, Earle of Kintyire Lord Campbell and Lorne and Lord Neill Campbell chalmerlane of Kintyire his lordships sonne, with ane certain number both of Lowland and hieland gentlemen of the countery Being mett; for the better settleing the conditioun of the countery; and for keiping good nybourhood among the severall inhabitants thereof doeth with mutuall consent aggrie to the particullars efterspecifiet. (reproduced in Stewart 1992:216, see Chapter 6 for an account of the presence of Lowland farmers in Kintyre)

Among the "particullars efterspecifiet":

> It is . . . with mutuall consent aggried that at everie dwellinghouse ther sall be a kaillyaird and that the kaillyaird dyike sall be planted with trees round about at an equall distance, and that the samen sufficientlie hayned with libertie alwayes to the planters of the said kaillyairds and tries to cutt for the wse of building and labouring within the ground such trees as sall be

wsefull for that effect; provyding they immediatlie plant thrie trees for ilk
tree cutted. (reproduced in Stewart 1992:218)

What we are seeing here, it seems, is the elaboration of the kailyard
with planted trees, one major purpose of which is the provision of timber
for building and for "labouring within the ground" (for making ploughs
or spades?). These enclosures, as such, represent the continuation and
elaboration of an existing practice, rather than the initiation of a new
pattern of land use. Their existence does not suggest a widespread and
fundamental break in the use of land.

There seems to be only one case where this fundamental break may
have occurred by the time of the Roy Map. Around the village of Whitehouse in the north west of Kintyre, a pattern of enclosure had developed
by the time of the Roy Map closely resembling the pattern of enclosed
fields shown both on the first edition and current OS maps of the locality. This pattern of fields is grid-like, but the nature of construction
of the eighteenth century boundaries is unknown. The farms border-
ing this enclosed land at the time of the Roy Map were on the estate
of Archibald Campbell of Stonefield (Timperley [ed.] 1976:35). Again,
along with the Dukes of Argyll, the Campbells of Stonefield were known
early Improvers (Gailey 1962a:162–163).

The depiction of the pre-Improvement landscape immediately adjacent to areas of settlement on the Roy Map is, as for settlement, useful
in gaining a general impression. Existing major physical boundaries do
seem to have been omitted, however. Further, despite its usefulness
in discussing the landscape immediate to areas of settlement, the Roy
Map's worth as a source is questionable when we move to consider the
landscape beyond the head dyke. The Map shows the hills as devoid of
contemporary anthropogenic features, when there is much evidence to
suggest that this was not in fact the case.

Most significant here are the shielings. These were the summer
hill pastures of the *bailtean* (see Gailey 1963:106–107; and, in general,
Bil 1990). These pastures are indicated today by their associated settlement remains and greener surrounding vegetation, presumably a
result of the concentration of livestock there over the years. They are
associated with watercourses in upland locations, which in Kintyre and
Kilfinan means inland from the coast. Many of the extant shieling sites
are within 1.5km of the nearest probable contemporary settlement locations, while some may have been 3km or more distant. In Kintyre
in particular the distance from settlement to shieling is limited by the
fact that the area is a narrow peninsula, reducing the distance that
can be traveled into the upland. The survival of shieling settlements in

Kilfinan is limited. In Kintyre, they are more widespread and can be on a larger scale (e.g., Cressey 1996; Graham 1919:82–98, 1920; Hood 1996; RCAHMS 1971:197–200; SRC SMR 1993:72).

Typically, shieling settlements are amorphous clusters echoing the morphology of the *bailtean* (Gailey 1963:107). These clusters can be small, with nine structures at Gartavaich in Kintyre for example, or much larger, as at Talatoll, Kintyre, where there are some forty-three (RCAHMS 1971:197, 200, respectively; see Figure 6). The shape, size and construction of the different structures can vary widely. Many are single-celled and constructed of stone and turf, while some might be of stone entirely or have more than one room (e.g., RCAHMS 1971:197, 200). The differing form and construction of the individual buildings may relate to functional and chronological difference (Atkinson 2000:155). The dates of most of the structures at sites like Gartavaich and Talatoll are uncertain. One oval turf and stone structure at Gartavaich was excavated in the early twentieth century and found to be associated with pottery of red fabric and green glaze (Graham 1920:201). This description is reminiscent of Medieval wares dating from the thirteenth to late fifteenth centuries (see, e.g., Hall 2000:173–174). A date at the end of that period would concur with the results of recent excavations on Lochtayside where shieling occupation has been dated to between the fifteenth and nineteenth centuries (Atkinson 2000:157). In Argyll in general, and perhaps most notably in Kintyre, shieling settlements were probably falling into disuse in the eighteenth century (Gailey 1963:107).

At some sites, small enclosures are associated with the shieling structures. At Talatoll, for example, a small circular hut is incorporated in the bank of a large penannular circular enclosure, but this arrangement is exceptional for the site (RCAHMS 1971:200). On the whole, shieling settlements are associated with expanses of unenclosed pasture.

The antiquity of shieling settlement in the area is unknown. Taking the early excavations at Gartavaich together with those on Lochtayside, it could date back at least into the late Medieval period, and may be older (see Gailey 1963:107). The dating of the openfields surrounding the *bailtean* as a form probably also extends back into the late Medieval period. It is in that period that openfields in the west Highlands seem to have originated, along with the *baile*.

We saw above that the sixteenth century settlement at Craigs, County Antrim, and the similar dispersed settlement at Borrafiach, Vaternish, Skye, were associated with enclosed field systems, and there are other cases we might add to these (Dodgshon 1993a; 1994; Williams

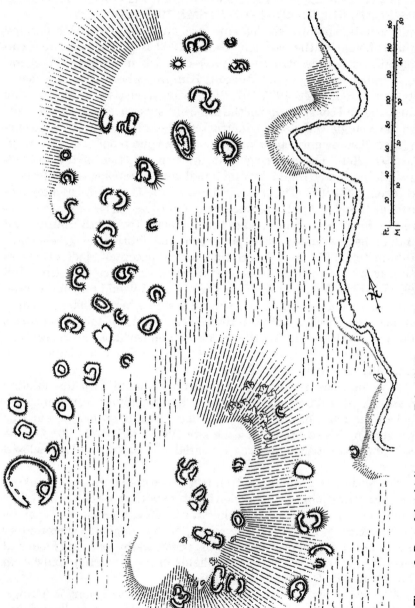

Figure 6. Part of the shieling group at Talatoll, Kintyre (after RCAHMS 1971:figure 190; crown copyright: RCAHMS).

1988). Earth and stone banks, which may originally have been planted with hedges, enclosed the sub-rectangular fields at Craigs (Williams 1988:91–94, 97). The areas enclosed were as much as 100m by 100m or 150m and in cases contained the remains of cultivation ridges. These fields are broadly similar in size and shape to those at Borrafiach (see Dodgshon 1993a:433, illus. 6). There is no direct evidence of such field systems in Kintyre or Kilfinan. However, it seems reasonable to extend the tentative conclusion from the neighboring areas discussed that a pattern of small, enclosed fields may have existed prior to that of the openfields. The sequence of changing field types may not be straight-forward, however. When Improvers of the eighteenth and nineteenth centuries described an open landscape in need of enclosure, they may have been providing an over-simplified account of a landscape that was not absolutely enclosed, in their terms (Smout 1996a). There is some evidence from Lochtayside, again ambiguous and tentative, that the agricultural lands of some Highland townships were divided by low stone dykes, not entirely stock-proof and created through the consump-tion of stones cleared from ploughed land (Smout 1996a).

The pre-Improvement farming landscape, then, consisted of a pat-tern of open fields surrounding the *baile*. This type of field system may have origins in the late Medieval period and may have been preceded by a pattern of enclosed fields and some form of enclosure may have been evident through to the period of Improvement. However, any enclosure in the centuries prior to Improvement seems to have been limited. The inner agricultural zone of open fields was separated from hill pasture, and perhaps some further cultivated land, by one or more head dykes. The marches of a particular farm may have been similarly physically defined by dykes, or otherwise. The hill pastures bore shieling settle-ments, occupied during the summer months in a system of transhu-mance. The antiquity of shieling is unknown, but certainly stretched back into the fifteenth century.

Domestic Space

The Roy Map may be of use as a source in considering some as-pects of pre-Improvement landscape and settlement, but it has little or nothing to say about building construction or the use of domestic space. This is also true of the majority of estate plans. These carto-graphic sources are simply at too small a scale to give much detail on individual structures. I will argue here, with reference to other sources, that the structures at Balmavicar, the best-preserved pre-Improvement settlement, are probably generally representative.

At Balmavicar, as discussed, there are some eight pre-Improvement structures, discounting A and B as later. All are of drystone or stone-and-clay construction, with walls in the region of 1m thick (RCAHMS 1971:194). These structures are of varying types. G and O are the largest, although L may also be of similar size. G and O are both 10 to 12m long and 6 to 7m wide and have opposing entrances in their long walls. Both are sub-oval, with markedly rounded corners suggesting a hipped roof. The opposed doorways, and the internal kiln in O, suggest that these structures were threshing barns.

Structures C, D, H, and M also seem to be similar to each other. All seem to have a single entrance in one of their long sides, although this is less clear for M. C and D have one rounded and one straight gable. H has two straight gables, but with slightly rounded corners. M is more properly oval. All are of similar size, being roughly 6 or 7m by 4 or 5m. Some of these structures must have been dwellings, most likely H and M. It is possible they all were, although there are no diagnostic internal features visible. The Royal Commission has suggested that C and D were outbuildings, despite their similarity to H and M (RCAHMS 1971:194). The eighth structure, F, was a horizontal mill.

H and G and M and O seem to be arranged as pairs, being closely situated. Yards K and J may be associated with structures H and G, and M_1 with M and O. Structure L is perhaps earlier, being more denuded. C and D, with C_1 and D_1, may form a further grouping. It is also possible that C and D, with their respective enclosures, formed two separate units.

Alan Gailey (1962b) has argued that the round ended, and thus hip-roofed, house was typical of the southwest Highlands prior to Improvement, and perhaps a common form in the Medieval period. Even if such long continuity in the basic form of the house can be demonstrated, construction methods seem to have changed significantly about the middle of the eighteenth century (Gailey 1962b:234–239). Relying largely on documentary data, Gailey suggests that prior to that time organic construction materials like turf and wattle were preferred to stone. This is perhaps one reason why Medieval settlement sites remain elusive, structures of materials like turf being less visible archaeologically (see, e.g., Dodgshon 1993a:421–424). The use of organic materials need not have been ubiquitous prior to the eighteenth century, however (see below).

Despite this major change in building construction, which remains to be understood, the basic form taken by the Balmavicar structures seems on comparison with those at Finlaggan and on Gunna, already mentioned, and at MacEwen's Castle, Cowal (Marshall 1983), to have been current from at least the late Medieval period. The excavated sites of Finlaggan, Gunna, and MacEwen's Castle also allow us to shed some light on the possible organization of space within the pre-Improvement house.

The most substantial building of the sixteenth century *baile* at Finlaggan was a rectangular, lime-mortared, two-storey dwelling, probably once inhabited by a tacksman (Caldwell and Ewart 1993:155–156). This dwelling is exceptional amongst the surviving sixteenth century structures. The typical structure is oval or sub-rectangular in form, of drystone or turf construction, though perhaps occasionally lime-mortared (Caldwell et al. 2000:62–64). These buildings rarely exceed 10m by 7m and in most cases have opposed entrances. The walls of the lime-mortared structures may have been load bearing and there is no evidence for cruck trusses to take the weight of the roof, although the walls often do not survive to a height that would make this certain. This form of structure has been found elsewhere on Islay, and beyond.

Such structures would have served many purposes (Caldwell et al. 2000:62). One of the Finlaggan buildings has been interpreted as a byre, and others may have been barns with their opposed entrances allowing a through draft for winnowing. However, most have been found on excavation to have been dwellings, as they had hearths, placed centrally. Interestingly, some structures at Finlaggan appear to have formed house and barn units (Caldwell and Ewart 1993:156). This was an arrangement suggested above for some of the structures at Balmavicar.

On Gunna, similar late Medieval structures have been found underlying later settlement. One structure there consists of the footings of an oval building whose walls have a double stone skin filled with a core of sand (James 1998:23). One entrance survives, though the structural remains are fragmentary, and there is evidence of a hearth sitting centrally in the floor. Three other structures there, though more fragmentary, probably represent similar dwellings (James 1998:25–26, 28). These late Medieval structures in cases replaced earlier timber and turf ones (James 1998:15). They were succeeded by substantial post-Medieval (eighteenth century?) buildings (James 1998:16–19, 29). In many ways these structures are similar to those at Balmavicar and Finlaggan, being sub-rectangular in shape with opposed doorways, and with hearths placed centrally in the floor.

To the structures on Gunna and at Finlaggan may be added those at MacEwen's Castle. The late Medieval buildings at this site, in Kilfinan parish, probably formed the residence of a member of the Campbell clan gentry (Marshall 1983:132–133). However, in terms of form and spatial organization they should not be set apart from the dwellings on Gunna and at Finlaggan.

MacEwen's castle is an Iron Age dun that was subsequently re-used in the Medieval period. It is the remains of this later phase of activity that are of interest here. Two structures there, named Site A and Site D by the excavator, were both found to be oval or sub-rectangular buildings, although D had one squared end (see Marshall 1983:137–139). Site A measures roughly 10m by 8m and Site D 6m by 4m. Site A had turf walls and opposed entrances. Internally, there was a central hearth placed on the floor. Turf benches seem to have abutted the walls in the north, west, and east of the interior. The floor was of compacted earth, with occasional patches of cobbles. Site D had walls of turf and stone and two not quite opposing entrances, one of which had at some point been blocked. Again there is evidence of a central hearth set in the cobbled floor, the fuel for which came from a peat stack found outside the northeast wall. A turf bench possibly sat to the north west of the hearth.

One further site is worth brief mention here, that excavated at Ardnadam in Cowal, and is probably of Medieval date (Rennie 1984:35–36). The structure in question had stone footings and turf walls, with the roof supported on timber uprights. There was a central hearth and a peat stack outside the building. The whole structure measured 11m by 7.5m. This area was divided into two by a cross wall and the area with the hearth measured some 7.5m by 5.5m. This building may have been associated with industrial activity, and is thus perhaps not typical farming settlement. However, I mention it here to demonstrate that some of the features found at MacEwen's Castle were not exclusive to elite sites in Cowal. The area with the hearth in the Ardnadam structure is similar in size to site D at MacEwen's Castle.

A picture of the likely typical pre-Improvement dwelling in Kintyre and Kilfinan can be constructed by comparing all of the sites mentioned above. The house was probably oval or sub-rectangular, perhaps measuring 6 to 12m by 4 to 8m. The walls could have been constructed in a variety of materials, from turf, turf and stone, unmortared stone, or stone bonded with lime mortar. The roofs of such houses were probably of thatch (see, e.g., Gailey 1963:229–230). With the lime-mortared structure at Finlaggan, this roof may have sat on the wallheads, which would have been strong enough to support the weight. It is more likely, considering the widespread use of turf and of turf and stone, that the roof usually sat on cruck trusses carrying its weight down to the lower wall or even floor level. The lack of evidence for such crucks in the excavated structures perhaps suggests that they sat within the fabric of the wall. The rounded corners of the walls suggest that these buildings had hip-ended roofs.

Many of these houses had opposed entrances, although this was not universally the case. People passing through these entrances entered a single, undivided space. There is little evidence for partition at excavated sites. The focus of this space was a hearth set centrally in or on the floor. Aside from the late Medieval examples quoted, central hearths were found in an excavated structure of possible eighteenth century date at MacEwen's Castle (Site B) and in a similar structure of uncertain date at nearby Auchategan, Glendaruel (Marshall 1983:138–139; Marshall 1978:66–68, respectively). The central hearth might be accompanied by one or more turf benches, which could have served a multitude of purposes including sleeping, working, or sitting. Little evidence of other forms of fixed furniture has been found.

In cases, barns, sometimes with their own kiln for drying the crop, accompanied these dwellings. The presence of byres is more problematic. It is traditionally assumed that the longhouse, with dwelling and byre under the same roof, was common throughout the Highlands and Islands in the pre-Improvement period (e.g., Fairhurst 1960:68; Gailey 1963:235). This assumption has recently been questioned (Branigan and Merrony 2000). This revision of the accepted view is based on the survey and excavation of a number of blackhouse sites on Barra, where the buildings are characterized by thick double skinned stone walls with an earth core (see Branigan and Foster 1995).

Survey found that most Barra blackhouses were under 12m in length, making them in general shorter than their counterparts on Lewis, Harris, and South Uist (Branigan and Merrony 2000:4). The internal area of these houses is also smaller than their northern counterparts, and the Barra houses display less internal division of space (Branigan and Merrony 2000:4–5). Considering that the average family size on Barra was probably similar to that on the islands to the north, if cattle were housed in the Barra blackhouses, living space would be greatly reduced (Branigan and Merrony 2000:5–6).

That cattle were probably not housed in these structures is suggested by the survey and excavation data (Branigan and Merrony 2000:6–8). In contrast to houses on the islands to the north, which have off-center doorways, Barra blackhouses have entrances central to one of their long walls. The northern houses also frequently have two opposed entrances, one presumably for cattle and the other for humans, while those on Barra usually only have one. All of this is taken by Branigan and Merrony to suggest that the use of space within the Barra houses was different from that in those to the north, with the Barra blackhouses lacking a byre (Branigan and Merrony 2000:8–9).

Excavated blackhouses on Barra and South Uist confirm this difference in the use of space (Branigan and Merrony 2000:9–13). The lack of cobbling and lack of disturbance of the floor deposits in the Barra houses suggest that cattle were absent. Indeed, in one such house the hearth and dresser were placed in such a way as to preclude the presence of cattle within the house. On Barra, the cattle seem to have been housed in separate structures, either tacked onto the end of the dwelling, but not intercommunicating with it, or entirely freestanding (Branigan and Merrony 2000:8).

Turning to the south west Highland mainland, Alan Gailey has claimed that "[o]lder houses were always byre-dwellings, even well into the nineteenth century, and in as progressive an area as Kintyre, where, in 1843, they were being reported as common in the parish of Killean and Kilchenzie" (Gailey 1962b:235). Gailey's source here is The New Statistical Account of Scotland, wherein the Reverend MacDonald, minister for Killean and Kilchenzie parish in the north of Kintyre, says that the cottagers and laborers of the area "live in wretched hovels, rudely constructed without any mortar, one division of which is occupied by the family, and the other converted into a kind of byre, and often no partition in the hut to separate the human from the brute creation" (MacDonald 1845:387).

This is a clear description of a longhouse and we might assume from it that the communal housing of humans and cattle was the norm in Kintyre and the surrounding area, as Gailey did. How much faith should we place in this single statement, though? The minister in question clearly had a pejorative attitude towards the dwellings of the poor families in question, those wretched hovels, rudely constructed. These dwellings stood in contrast, for him, to those of the tenant farmers: "The farmers, with a few exceptions, enjoy, in a reasonable degree, the comforts and advantages of society. They are, upon the whole, comfortably enough lodged, and well fed with wholesome and substantial food" (MacDonald 1845:386). It is worth asking what experience these generalizations were based upon. How many of each of these types of dwelling is MacDonald likely to have visited? Could he be generalizing from one or two examples for the sake of effect in contrasting the civilized dwellings of the better off tenants with those of the smallholders and landless?

We might consider the agenda behind descriptions of the longhouse in sources such as The New Statistical Account and question the widespread applicability of statements like MacDonald's. However, this does not establish whether the longhouse was widespread or not in the pre-Improvement southwest Highlands. I will consider the question further by comparing the buildings of Balmavicar and the late Medieval structures at Finlaggan and the other sites discussed above with those on Barra. The widespread existence of the longhouse in Kintyre, Kilfinan, and the surrounding area is at least questionable.

As has already been mentioned, the size range of the various structures at Balmavicar, Finlaggan, and those other sites discussed was roughly 6 to 12m by 4 to 8m. This is a similar size range to the Barra blackhouses discussed above. Further, while the position of the hearth in many of the houses is towards one end of the structure, allowing for the differential use of space, there is nothing to suggest that the opposite end was for cattle. No drains seem to have been found and there is a general lack of cobbling, yet no major disturbance of the floor deposits is reported. Indeed, one of the Finlaggan structures has been interpreted as a byre in its own right (Caldwell et al. 2000:62), suggesting that if the cattle were housed at all, they were housed in separate buildings.

Of the excavated structures in Cowal, the two that show a marked division in the use of space within the dwelling, at Ardnadam and Auchategan, seem to be associated with industrial activity (Marshall 1978:67–68; Rennie 1984:35). Further, in two of the MacEwen's castle structures the hearth was placed in the center of the house and close by the entrance, suggesting that cattle were not meant to come in.

It seems likely from all of this that the longhouse was probably not common in the extreme south of the Highlands and the adjacent islands. This is not to say that, in cases, the longhouse was necessarily unknown. Many of the houses discussed had opposed doorways, a feature that Branigan and Merrony suggest is associated with the byre-dwelling. However, upon excavation, in most cases and as we have already seen, this entrance arrangement was not found to be associated with other diagnostic evidence for a longhouse.

Site A at MacEwen's castle is one possible exception, where the opposed entrances were of different sizes. Perhaps one *was* meant for humans and the other for cattle. The excavator did argue for a division of the use of space within the house (Marshall 1983:137–138). This was based on artifact distribution within the house and the difference in floor deposits between the hearth end and the other end. At the end without the hearth there was some evidence of cobbling.

THE MATERIAL ENVIRONMENT OF IMPROVEMENT

Settlement

With Improvement, the *bailtean* came, on the whole, to be replaced by dispersed settlement. This consisted largely of isolated farmsteads, with the dwelling and outbuildings of the farm grouped together in linear ranges or rectangular courtyards (see Gailey 1961:269–274 for a variety of examples). Occasionally, we also find linear ranges of cottages, those of the farm laborers. Broadly, then, Improved settlement forms can be divided into three categories: the range farmstead, described first below; the cottage range; and, the courtyard farmstead.

The change in settlement pattern and morphology with Improvement is quite obvious on the Mull of Kintyre. Returning to Balmavicar, it will be remembered that structures A and B were set aside from the rest. B has been substantially rebuilt in recent years (RCAHMS 1971:194), perhaps as some form of shelter. It may originally have been similar to C and D. Structure A, on the other hand, stands apart in character from the other buildings at the site. In contrast to those other buildings, it is a long tripartite structure, 19.2m by 5.3m (RCAHMS 1971:194). The Royal Commission interpret the most westerly subdivision of the structure, probably the first built as the others appear to be tacked on to it, as a byre. It has a single entrance and few other distinctive features. There is no internal communication between this and the other apartments, which appear to be domestic spaces. Adjacent to the byre, to the east, is the kitchen. This apartment has opposed entrance-doorways and a window. There is a fireplace built into the partition wall that separates the kitchen from the next apartment to the east, of a type variously referred to as the room or spence. This inner room can only be reached through a door from the kitchen. The uses of these various domestic spaces will be returned to below. It is enough here to note that structure A seems to represent the grouping of previously commonly disparate elements of the farm, byre and dwelling, in one linear range. Further, structure A stands in isolation. Where there had previously been several dwellings with their associated outbuildings on the site, now there was one. Some of the surviving pre-Improvement structures may have been reused as outbuildings.

To the northwest of Balmavicar, perhaps no more than 100m away, is a large rectangular drystone sheepfold. This is probably contemporary with Structure A as together they resemble a pattern of association found in other places up the west coast of the Mull. An example is Currach Mor, which lies about 500m south of the current mapped position of the place name Innean Coig Cailleiche, a settlement marked on the Roy Map, and may represent the successor of that settlement. The lack of pre-Improvement settlement remains in the immediate area may be the result of the robbing of stone to build the extant structures, of which there are two at Currach Mor. One is a simple rectangular structure, reduced to turf covered foundations, measuring some 4m by

6m. The other is a larger, tripartite structure measuring 18m by 5m and aligned east to west. This structure survives to wallhead height in places. The western space has opposed doorways. There are no diagnostic internal features, although a knocking stone is still to be seen sitting on the floor. This is a large stone with its center hollowed to create a mortar in which grain was dehusked by being beaten with a pounder or mallet (see Fenton 1999:103–104). The middle space of the building, probably the domestic space or kitchen, can only be entered from the room with the knocking stone. This middle space has what appears to be a fireplace in its southern long wall. The final space, to the east, does not communicate with the other two, having its own external door facing into a yard. It could be a byre, or a store, although there is nothing to suggest its use. There is a kiln to the west of this structure.

These structures at Currach Mor are associated with three small enclosures. The easternmost division of the tripartite structure is only accessible from one of these yards, the enclosure walls of which are tacked onto the building. Another enclosure, this time a sheepfold, is to be found about 400m to the north. Currach Mor was probably, therefore, associated with sheep farming. The knocking stone, kiln and small enclosures associated with the settlement suggest that some crop production was also taking place, perhaps at subsistence level.

There are several other sites along the western and southern coasts of the Mull of Kintyre that should probably be associated with sheep farms like Balmavicar and Currach Mor. There are several sheepfolds, which are usually fairly simple drystone enclosures, such as those found in Borgadale Glen. Occasionally, these sheepfolds are associated with one or two small, single cell structures, perhaps only measuring 2m by 3m internally. Such structures are found associated with sheepfolds in isolated stretches of the coastline and are probably shepherd's bothies. Massive, naturally occurring boulders have been joined with sections of drystone walling, in places, to create shelters, this time probably for the sheep.

Associated as all these sites are with sheep farming, they must date to the period when the Mull of Kintyre was converted to a sheep walk, by 1818 (Gailey 1961:85). As we saw above, Balmavicar is listed as uninhabited on the 1779 census, and so presumably out of use as by that time (Cregeen 1963:115). Range farmsteads and their associated features on the Mull can therefore be dated in general to the last quarter of the eighteenth and first quarter of the nineteenth century.

These range farmsteads are not confined in distribution to the Mull of Kintyre, but can be found throughout the peninsula. The association with sheep farming is less prevalent away from the high ground,

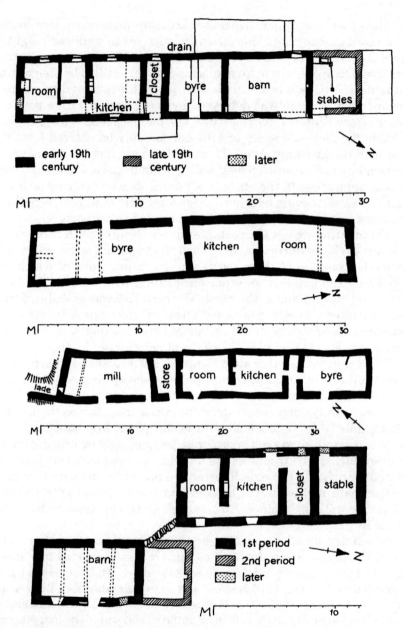

Figure 7. Range farmsteads from Kintyre: A) Keremenach; B) Drumgarve; C) Farmstead with mill at Drumgarve; and, D) Garvoine (after RCAHMS 1971:figures 184, 185, 187, and 189; crown copyright: RCAHMS).

however, and many examples outside of the Mull should be associated with mixed farming regimes (see Kelly 1845:432–433; MacDonald 1845:387–390; Stark 1845:367). Some farms in Kintyre were increasingly associated with commercial dairy farming through the nineteenth century (MacNeilage 1912:290; McClement 1927:23).

Range farmsteads in other areas of Kintyre are similar to those on the Mull, although they can be larger and often exhibit greater internal subdivision (see Figure 7). Two such ranges at Drumgarve, situated some 200m from each other, illustrate this (see RCAHMS 1971:196–197). The first resembles structure A at Balmavicar, being a tripartite structure, measuring 33m by 6m. In this case, the presence of the byre is certain, being evidenced by a central drain. The second structure at Drumgarve, although of similar dimensions to the first, displays greater subdivision. Separating the byre from the kitchen this time is a small lobby, about 1.5m wide. Beside the kitchen, and separated from it by a partition wall containing a hearth, is the spence. Beyond the spence, though not communicating with it, is a small store. Adjacent to the store is a mill. The greater subdivision of this structure is, therefore, to be associated with its part function as a mill.

Other range farmsteads in Kintyre are likewise highly subdivided (e.g., Keremenach, RCAHMS 1971:200). However, the reasons for greater internal subdivision at these sites is often unclear as a result of the dilapidated nature of the buildings, or seems to be unrelated to the presence of such specialized elements as a mill.

The examples discussed above appear to be the working farmhouses of a single family. That is, the individual divisions of the range add up to the different functional spaces of a single farm. There is *one* living space (kitchen), *one* spence, *one* byre, and so on. However, there are linear ranges elsewhere in Kintyre and in Kilfinan that appear to be the congregation of several spatial units of the same type. The provision of several large windows in more than one of the divisions of the longest range at Low Stillaig, Kilfinan, indicates that this structure was primarily an agglomeration of dwellings (see Figures 8 and 9). A second structure at Stillaig (S2) may be an isolated laborer's cottage, and has an attached outhouse and one other adjoining space. Meall Darroch is an example in Kintyre (see MacDonald [ed.] 1992). That such single structures are actually several combined dwellings is underlined by the fact that the individual divisions do not intercommunicate as do those of the range farmsteads. The individual dwellings of the cottage ranges typically consist of a single undivided space, entered through a door placed centrally in one long side of the house.

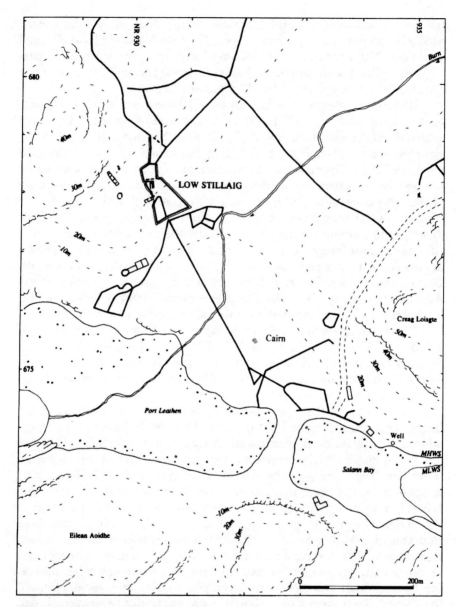

Figure 8. Settlement at Low Stillaig, Kilfinan. Structure S1 is a cottage range and the beginnings of an amorphous field system can be seen running off the top of the page (copyright University of Glasgow).

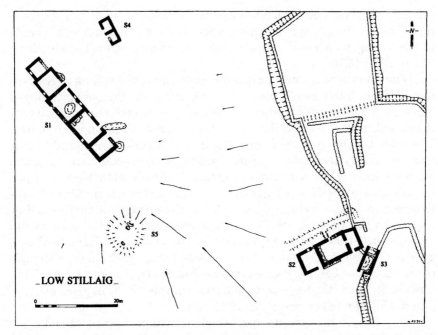

Figure 9. Buildings at Low Stillaig, Kilfinan (copyright University of Glasgow).

The occurrence of these two different forms of linear range in Kintyre and Kilfinan can be explained by the social dynamics of Improvement in those areas (see Chapter 7 below). It is enough to note here that the cottage ranges probably represent the houses of farm laborers. The site of Low Stillaig, for example, is shown as inhabited on the first edition OS map of the area (1863), when it must have been on the lands of the single or double tenancy farm of Stillaig (see Chapter 7).

So, the cottage ranges of Kilfinan were certainly in use by the mid-nineteenth century. When they were first built is unclear, but if they do represent the laborers' cottages of the large tenant farm then they may only predate the first edition OS maps by a few years (see below). In Kintyre, in association with the other linear ranges and the large tenant farms, the cottage ranges may be as early as the first years of the nineteenth century, or perhaps slightly earlier.

The laborers' dwellings represented by cottage ranges like Low Stillaig should not be viewed in isolation from the contemporary houses of the large tenant farmers, on whose farms they stood. The dwellings of these larger tenants have been described by some as the Lowland-type steading (Gailey 1960:104–105), and are referred to here as courtyard farmsteads. In describing just such a steading, the minister for Southend parish noted with pride in 1843 that "[t]here has ... been lately a farm-steading erected on the Duke of Argyle's lands of Machribeg, which will compete with most in any part of the kingdom" (Kelly 1845:433).

The courtyard farmstead is the prevalent farm dwelling in Kintyre and Kilfinan today (see Gailey 1961:94). It was first widely introduced to the Argyll Estates in Kintyre in the early years of the nineteenth century (Gailey 1961:94). Its date of introduction in Kilfinan is unknown. The minister for the parish in 1843, Joseph Stark, considered that it was "necessary that suitable farm-buildings be erected instead of the old black huts which are now on the farms" (Stark 1845:368). If we are to take him literally, then the courtyard farmstead had still to be introduced in 1843. Certainly, examples of the form, that survive today, appear on the first edition OS maps of the parish (1863), such as the example at Stillaig already discussed. The courtyard farmstead was possibly introduced, then, in the 1840s or 1850s in Kilfinan, although there may have been earlier examples that Stark chose to ignore. This conclusion fits with the observation that Improvement in general came late to Kilfinan (Atkinson et al. 1993:7).

However, in Kintyre at least, the courtyard farmstead had a longer history. Limecraigs House, now within Campbeltown, but previously standing within its own policies in the countryside, has been described as having a layout typical of that adopted for the small laird's house of the early eighteenth century (RCAHMS 1971:190; see Figure 10). The Duchess of Argyll occupied it as a dower-house and died there in 1735 (RCAHMS 1971:190). In some ways, Limecraigs is very similar to nearby tacksmens' dwellings of the same period. Cara House, on the small island of that name off the west coast of Kintyre, was probably built in 1733 (RCAHMS 1971:189). Like Limecraigs, it is of two storeys and internally highly subdivided. Although these buildings are exceptional in being the dwellings of the local gentry, they can in many ways be considered as of one class with the courtyard farmstead. Limecraigs was certainly a working farm in the mid-eighteenth century, to judge from its outbuildings. The substantial farmers who inhabited the later courtyard farmsteads were in many ways successors to the tacksmen.

Like the range farmstead discussed above, the courtyard farmstead is an isolated dwelling with appended outbuildings. In the more fertile areas of Kintyre, only 0.5 or 1km may separate such farmsteads. In other areas, a separation of 1.5km is common and in the more upland regions 2 to 3km is not unusual. Throughout Kilfinan, courtyard farmsteads are fairly regularly dispersed, with intervening distances of around 1km, although they can be separated by 2 to 3km.

Figure 10. The early eighteenth century dower house and farmstead of Limecraigs, Kintyre. The dwelling, now within a residential area of Campbeltown, has two main storeys and a garret floor. Two chimneys are situated either side of the central hall (National Monuments Record of Scotland reference AG2358; crown copyright: RCAHMS).

In contrast to the range farmstead, the dwelling of the courtyard farmstead is often of two-storeys and highly subdivided internally. Such dwellings often form one side of a three-sided courtyard, together with outbuildings that are often substantial structures in themselves. A stable, byre, and barn are common separate elements. A plan of Limecraigs House drawn in 1757 shows in addition to these elements a calf-house, coalhouse, bakery, and what are probably laborers or servants cottages (RCAHMS 1971:plate 81a). In cases, the courtyard stands apart from the dwelling, as at Corra in Kilfinan. There, in addition to the usual elements we find a mill. A separate courtyard is also to be found at Saddell

Castle, where farm outbuildings laid out from the 1770s by Campbell of Glensaddell fill the courtyard of a late Medieval castle (RCAHMS 1971:161–165). These offices were probably built when the castle was abandoned as the principal family residence, and at the time of building of the adjacent Saddell House (RCAHMS 1971:191).

The courtyard and the range farmstead will be returned to in more detail below. The important point to note here is the dispersal and isolation of settlement with Improvement. The range and courtyard farmsteads represent, on the whole, the house and associated outbuildings of one farming family, with occasional provision for servants in some courtyard farmsteads. More families may have lived side by side in the cottage ranges. In general, however, with Improvement we see the fragmentation of the *baile*. The cottage range and courtyard farmstead often represent the dispersal of the population of a single large farm throughout its territory, being the dwellings of the farm laborer and tenant, respectively. The range farmstead is the single isolated dwelling of a smaller farm. It was noted above that there is evidence from some areas of the Highlands for pre-Improvement settlements that were not nucleated in a straightforward way, with dispersed settlement foci within a single farm and isolated structures on the fringes of the arable. The possibility remains that some *bailtean* in Kintyre were like this, although the paucity of known pre-Improvement settlement remains there makes it difficult to assess if this was indeed the case. However, even in this instance, a distinction can still be maintained between pre-Improvement and Improvement settlement. The houses and other buildings of the inhabitants of those *bailtean* with plural settlement foci were still more tightly gathered than was the case with Improved farms. Frequently, pre-Improvement tenants still lived in a clustered settlement at the core of the arable. With Improvement, the houses of neighboring tenants were separated by much larger distances, perhaps kilometers.

In some cases, the settlement pattern became more dispersed in a second phase of Improvement. Several small Improved farms could subsequently be amalgamated into one large one, resulting in the presence today of a number of deserted range farmsteads near to a courtyard farmstead. Such is the case at Glenahervie in southern Kintyre, where several deserted ranges occur on the lands of a single sheep farm created in 1853 (Gailey 1961:101–102). These range farmsteads appear as unroofed on the first edition OS map of the area, suggesting they probably went out of use prior to this amalgamation. The existence of significant numbers of deserted range farmsteads throughout Kintyre suggests that this was a widespread process. In both Kintyre and Kilfinan, the courtyard farmstead is the prevalent farm dwelling today. However, the introduction of the courtyard farmstead in the early nineteenth century, and in cases before, means that in many areas it would have been contemporary with the range farmstead, as the large and smaller farms to which these buildings belonged were contemporary.

As noted earlier, there are exceptions to the process of settlement fragmentation with Improvement. In Kilfinan, though not in Kintyre, there are several nucleated settlements generally reminiscent of the earlier *bailtean* in form, notably Ardgaddan North and South, Ascog, and Craignafeoch. However, I will leave discussion of these settlements for now, and they will be considered in greater detail in chapter seven.

The only other notable nucleation of settlement in the study area is in the few villages and the burgh of Campbeltown. Both should be considered quite different in character from the *bailtean*. Kilfinan village had a post office, church (also housing a school), and inn in the first half of the nineteenth century, but seemingly little else (Stark 1845:366, 369–370, 372). This village seems to have been the only one of its type in the parish at the time. Inns and churches may have formed similar settlement foci in Kintyre. The name of the present village of Clachan certainly suggests a settlement focused on a church. The fishing village of Tarbert seems to have been fairly sizeable by the mid-nineteenth century (McArthur 1845:411; see also RCAHMS 1971:191), by which time there were also significant service centers at Machrimore and Rhunahaorine (Martin 1987:5).

The village of Southend is of a slightly different character, being laid out as a planned settlement around 1800, rather than developing more organically around a church or similar focus (see Lockhart 1997). The Duke of Argyll founded Southend, or Moneroy as it was originally known, in 1797 (Lockhart 1997:16). By 1851, it housed eleven agricultural laborers and the same number again of tradespeople, including one each of a road laborer, weaver, grocer, shoemaker, coalwright, innkeeper, schoolmistress, midwife, and seamstress (Lockhart 1997:17). Some of these residents also worked their own small patches of land part-time. Such planned villages, and, in this period, established villages like Kilfinan, were distinct from the *bailtean* and should be associated with Improvement. They provided services and a market for the isolated farms and resettlement and employment for those dispossessed by Improvement (Lockhart 1996:31–32; Smout 1996b:75–81).

Campbeltown, founded in 1609 by the seventh Earl of Argyll, had become a substantial settlement in Kintyre long before Southend was conceived (see RCAHMS 1971:184–187). The role of the town in the local economy, and beyond, is suggested in the New Statistical Account.

Listed for the Parish of Campbelton at that time, apart from some 390 people involved in agriculture, are 100 "proprietors, wholesale merchants, ship-owners, capitalists, bankers, and professional men," 520 "masters and workmen employed in manufactures and making machinery, shopkeepers and dealers," and an unascertainable number of "sailors, fishermen, and jobbers" (Anon. 1845:463). Also listed are a number of artisans, colliers, and miners, some of who may have lived in the burgh, but most of who probably resided elsewhere in the parish. At this time, Campbeltown had its own town council, court, and customhouse (Anon. 1845:465). The burgh, then, served as the main market for the peninsula, and presumably a wider area, even providing access to international trading networks. It also presumably provided services, employment, and resettlement for the rural population of the area (see Martin 1987:5 on these last two points), as the other villages did on a much smaller scale.

Landscape

The landscape also underwent fundamental change with Improvement. The country around the *bailtean* was largely open, the only widespread boundaries being the head dyke and march dyke. There was, however, limited enclosure of sorts. There were the yards associated with the houses of the *baile*, which had in cases been planted with trees; the enclosures in the policies surrounding landowners houses; and, the area around Whitehouse in the north of Kintyre where an enclosed field system on a grid pattern had already been laid out by the time of the Roy Map. Above the head dyke the landscape was almost completely open, consisting largely of moorland and of hill pasture, with associated shieling settlement.

With Improvement, low-lying areas of farmland were transformed as the openfield landscape was more systematically enclosed. On higher ground, the shielings fell out of use and the hillsides were turned over to other uses, such as large-scale sheep grazing or, eventually, sports like hunting.

The head dykes and unenclosed areas of rig and furrow cultivation that represent the openfield system rarely survive in Kintyre and Kilfinan. There are probably many reasons for this. However, the main one is that the openfields were engulfed by enclosures in the period of Improvement and subject to intensive farming. As we shall see, this does not mean that all the head dykes or areas of rig were obliterated, as many have probably been preserved in the pattern of enclosed fields.

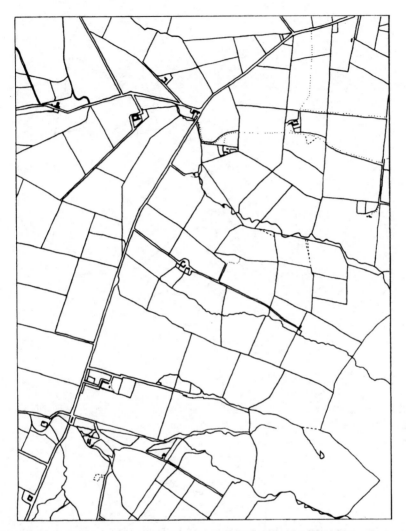

Figure 11. Grid-like enclosures in Kintyre as depicted on the first edition Ordnance Survey map surveyed in 1866 (redrawn from Argyllshire sheet 262).

On the ground today, two distinct patterns of enclosed fields can be discerned. In many areas this was the case by the time of the first OS maps of the mid-nineteenth century. On the lower and more level ground the common form of enclosure consists of large rectilinear fields in a grid-like pattern (see Figure 11). Wire fences now frequently define these, although these fences do preserve the line of earlier boundaries of drystone and hedge. On the fringes of this grid pattern of fields, a system

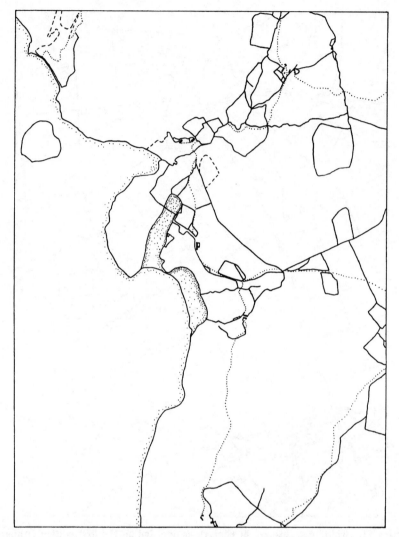

Figure 12. Amorphous enclosures in Kilfinan as depicted on the first edition Ordnance Survey map of 1870 (redrawn from Argyllshire sheet 202).

of irregular enclosures, frequently defined by turf dykes, inhabits the lower slopes of the hills (see Figure 12).

Examples of this irregular form of enclosure can be found on the fringes of the grid system throughout the study areas. There are particular concentrations, though, in Glen Breakerie in the south of Kintyre and in the area of the village of Kilfinan. In the latter area, the irregular enclosures cluster on Ardgaddan Barr, along Strone Burn, and around Kilfinan Burn. These enclosures are typically defined by curvilinear turf dykes, but in cases, as at Low Stillaig, can include sections of drystone wall. They are sometimes sub-rectangular or trapezoidal in shape, although there are many forms, and are commonly between 50m to 250m across. Such enclosures can exist in isolation, but are usually linked in groups.

In areas, the upper edge of these irregular enclosures runs along the contour of the slope at a level that suggests it might represent the fossilization of a head dyke, or system of head dykes. Similarly, Piers Dixon (1994:34) has suggested, for Scotland as a whole, that such irregular boundaries represent the piecemeal enclosure of open areas of rig as a first step of Improvement. His assertion (Dixon 1994:34) that such enclosures were subsequently abandoned holds for Kintyre and Kilfinan, where they largely form relict features today.

In contrast to these irregular enclosures are the areas of grid-pattern fields. These grids occur on lower and more level ground. These are the areas where the Improvers would have had more of a free hand with regard to form, the topography forming less of a constraint. In Kintyre, the grid enclosures concentrate on the west coast and, principally, in the area from the Laggan south, except on the Mull of Kintyre and other high ground. An estate plan of the Pennyland Estate, surveyed in 1806 by Alex. Langlands, shows such grid-pattern enclosure well (ABDA DR4/4/8; see Figure 13). This estate, the property of William MacDonald of Ballishare, may have been enclosed not long prior to the survey as field boundaries can be seen overlying a kailyard attached to one of the depicted settlements. Alternatively, this survey represents intended rather than existing enclosure.

The Laggan in particular saw extensive draining in the period of Improvement, providing an expanse of fairly level ground for enclosure. A large part of that area was shown as bog on the Roy Map, but by the first edition OS map it had been drained and enclosed almost to its present state. In Kilfinan, the main concentration of grid enclosures is on Ardlamont point, though there are smaller patches around Kilfinan village and Otter Ferry, all on the coast.

Where the irregular fields are curvilinear, the grid-like fields are rectilinear, with sharp changes of direction at the junction of boundaries. The shapes of the fields vary. Many are rectangular, either close to square, elongated, or trapezoidal. Occasionally other forms are found, like kites and triangles, filling the gaps between rectangular and trapezoidal fields. The size of these fields also varies. Most fall within the

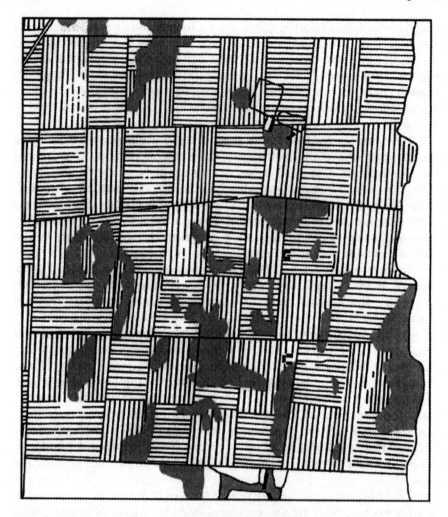

Figure 13. Part of the Pennyland Estate, Kintyre, as surveyed by Alex Langlands in 1806. The plan shows two courtyard farmsteads and two other farmsteads of two buildings each, set amongst a system of regular enclosures. The shaded patches may represent boggy or broken ground (redrawn from ABDA DR4/9/109).

same size range as the irregular fields, although the average size of grid-like fields is larger, with many falling at the top of that range. Some grid-like fields are even larger, being between 250m and 500m across.

Such rectilinear enclosure has been seen by some as the successor to irregular enclosure (Dixon 1994:34). However, the history of enclosure in Kintyre and Kilfinan seems to have been more complex. As has been discussed, irregular fields can be associated with an early phase of Improvement, and subsequently went out of use. The date at which they began to be constructed is unknown. However, they are often found close by deserted range farmsteads, and may therefore date to the late eighteenth or early nineteenth centuries.

Rectilinear fields were, as we have also seen, in limited use at the time of the Roy Map. Soon after, they were becoming more widespread. Argyll Estates leases in Kintyre in the late eighteenth century contained a clause binding tenants to plant and preserve thorn hedges, used to define roadsides, enclose gardens, and line the embankments of march and drainage ditches (Martin 1987:14). The association of these hedges with drainage, roadways, and gardens might suggest that they were being planted in the low-lying areas, and are thus to be associated with grid-like enclosures. Certainly, grid-like enclosure systems appear on estate plans of the period (e.g., ABDA DR4/4/8). It is unclear whether the enclosures depicted on these plans were a physical reality, or just proposed. However, the plans show that grid-like systems of enclosure were recognized at the time.

So, irregular and grid-like patterns of enclosure, close but often inhabiting different zones within the landscape, may be contemporary in origin. By the mid-nineteenth century, according to the first OS maps, the grid pattern of enclosure had evolved almost to its present state. In comparing the first edition maps with the corresponding modern 1:10,000 OS maps (published in 1981), there is a good correspondence between many of the mid-nineteenth century field boundaries and their present counterparts, with some minor differences. In some areas, an extension of the grid system onto previously unenclosed or partially enclosed land has taken place. In others, some boundaries integral to the nineteenth century enclosure pattern have gone out of use. Some field boundaries now in use are not shown on the earlier maps. However, these seem on the whole to be subdivisions of existing fields, not alterations to the overall pattern of enclosure. Interestingly, many of the relict irregular enclosures shown on present maps are omitted from the first edition OS maps, confirming that they had gone out of use by that time. Other relict features, like amorphous settlements and head dykes on the Mull, are also not shown even though some survive today as ruinous structures and landscapes.

So, although the grid and irregular patterns of enclosure were largely contemporary in origin, the former seems largely to have superseded the latter by the mid-nineteenth century. This seems to be reflected in several comments by the minister for Southend parish in the New Statistical Account of 1845. He says: "The earlier cultivation of the soil seems to have occupied solely the higher parts of the ridges, and in almost every hill top in the eastern portion, at least the furrows and enclosures of fields, are easily traced in the old sward" (Kelly 1845:419); and, "Of late years, the spirit of agricultural improvement has carried the cultivator into the low rich lands of the valleys; and draining has enabled him to reap the reward of his enterprise" (Kelly 1845:420).

The landscape beyond the area of enclosure also saw fundamental change of use with Improvement. As enclosure became established, the shieling system declined (Martin 1987:15). With Improvement, the common grazings of the shieling were parceled out to individual farms and tenants, and largely converted to sheep grazings (Gailey 1961:90, 104; Martin 1987:15; Stark 1845:367). The Mull of Kintyre was a single sheep walk by 1843, supporting some six thousand sheep (Kelly 1845:435). The landscape beyond the enclosed fields, and previously above the head dyke, has on the whole remained open. This and the use of the hills as rough grazing demonstrate some continuity between the pre- and post-Improvement eras. The fundamental break was in the way these grazings were organized and managed and in the concomitant abandonment of shieling settlement. By the mid-nineteenth century, in certain areas of Kilfinan at least, the hill ground was seeing increasing use for sport, with a number of areas described as shootings in a Valuation Roll of 1860/1861 (ABDA 1/73/13:52–54; see Chapter 6). Again, this meant that the hillside remained largely open, although going through another change of use.

Domestic Space

Improvement was not confined to the provinces of settlement and landscape, but also entered the home, where the organization of domestic space was significantly altered. Increasing subdivision of space within the house and decreasing emphasis on the hearth as a focus of domestic life were the two main elements of Improvement within the home. However, this transformation of domestic space was not a simple process and, just as there are several different forms of settlement associated with Improvement, there is variation in the character and pervasiveness of Improved domestic space.

Pre-Improvement dwellings were characterized by a lack of internal division. All activities, whether cooking, eating, sleeping, or whatever, took place within a single space. With the courtyard steading there is an obvious transformation of the use of space within the house. The dwellings of these later steadings are highly subdivided.

As we have seen, the houses of courtyard farmsteads are generally of two storeys. This in itself provides a basic division between upper and lower floors. An early example of the type was Limecraigs (a dower house of the Duchess of Argyll, but a working farm all the same). This house has two rooms to the storey, of which there are two with a garret floor, divided by a central stairwell. On a plan of the house, drawn in 1757, the two ground floor rooms are described as a dining room and a hall. The upper rooms are not labeled. Some at least must have been bedrooms. A kitchen and bake-house were situated in two detached buildings to the sides of the main dwelling.

Although the precise arrangement of rooms in courtyard farmsteads throughout Kintyre and Kilfinan varies, all have as a common defining feature this elaborate subdivision of internal space. Many have facades similarly symmetrical to that at Limecraigs, suggesting a similar arrangement of rooms either side of a central hallway. Others have asymmetrical facades suggesting a different arrangement of rooms, but no less internal subdivision.

Range farmsteads also exhibit a subdivision of domestic space. Typically this subdivision is limited to the two rooms of the kitchen and the spence. In many examples, a fireplace sits in one of the end walls of the kitchen, although the spence often also has a fireplace of its own (e.g., RCAHMS 1971:197, 200). In some surviving abandoned range farmsteads, like Keremenach and Garvoine in Kintyre (RCAHMS 1971:197, 200), there is another small room, which has been labeled a closet. Some range farmsteads may have had a useable loft space, probably entered via a wooden stair in the entrance vestibule (RCAHMS 1971:200). Our knowledge of the use of such lofts is limited, but they certainly could have provided additional sleeping space as well as storage. That this may have been the case is suggested by a recommendation in the *General View of the Agriculture of the County of Argyll* (Smith 1798:18) that tenants should be encouraged to live in houses with a kitchen at one end, a family room at the other, and garrets for keeping and sleeping places, accessed by a stair opposite the door.

The subdivision of the dwelling of the range farmstead is more limited than that within the courtyard steading. Most daily domestic activity within the range farmstead would have taken place within the kitchen space, something to which we will return. However, the range farmstead still shows marked subdivision in comparison with the typical pre-Improvement dwelling.

With the cottage range internal subdivision is more limited again. The cottages making up such ranges show no evidence of internal subdivision. These spaces could have been divided by box beds, or by other impermanent means. However, the fact that they are fairly small suggests that this was not the case in many instances. At Low Stillaig, the individual cottages are 7m by 5m internally. At Meall Darroch in Kintyre they range from 4 to 10m long by 2.5 to 4.5m wide (see MacDonald [ed.] 1992). Most of the dwellings at Meall Darroch are therefore of similar size to those at Low Stillaig, although at least one is substantially longer.

The other main element of pre-Improvement domestic space was the centrally located hearth, sitting on or in the floor. Again, with Improvement, this arrangement changed as the hearth was moved to the edge of the floor, usually by an end wall. As with the subdivision of domestic space, though, the history of change in the position of the hearth cannot be understood in a simple linear fashion.

In the courtyard farmstead, hearths are found in many of the rooms within the dwelling, and are situated against the walls of those rooms and not centrally in the floor. This is clear from the position of the chimneys of the house. At Machribeg in southern Kintyre, for example, the main dwelling house has two chimneys, one in each of its end walls. These chimneys are positioned in such a way as to service most of the rooms of the house with fireplaces in their end walls. Limecraigs has a slightly different arrangement, with two chimneystacks situated either side of the central hallway. However, this arrangement still services most of the rooms with end wall fireplaces.

In some range farmsteads there is evidence of a similar movement of the hearth. The kitchen in Structure A at Balmavicar has a fireplace built into the wall separating it from the spence (RCAHMS 1971:194). At Garvoine, both structures at Drumgarve, and at Keremenach, both the kitchen and spence have their own fireplaces built into their end walls.

The movement of the hearth to an end wall was not universal with Improvement. The hearth sat in the center of the floor of some houses in Kintyre visited in the mid nineteenth century by the English traveler Edward Bradley (*alias* Cuthbert Bede) (Bede 1861, volume 2:135–137). Bradley connects this use of space with that described for Highland houses by earlier travelers, such as Dr. Johnson (Bede 1861, volume 2:107, 135–137). He quotes Lord Teignmouth's 1836 description of Kintyre houses as still being relevant in his own time (Bede 1861 volume 2:107). Teignmouth said:

> The farm-houses are generally, throughout Cantyre, old and poor habitations, far behind the general improvement visible in this part of the country ... the fire is placed in the middle of the floor, contained in a grate, either square or shaped like a bowl, and raised a little above the ground, a custom

peculiar to Cantyre. . . . There are some few farm-houses in the modern style,
indicating the slow growth of Improvement. (Teignmouth 1836:388)

The situation described in these texts is similar to that found in excavations at East Lix, Perthshire (Fairhurst 1969). There, the deserted
houses and outbuildings were arranged on a roughly rectilinear pattern, with the structures sometimes forming several sides of a courtyard (Fairhurst 1969:166). The general pre-excavation assessment of
Lix, therefore, was that the majority of visible remains related to the
period of Improvement. This stands in contrast to the excavated plans
of several of the structures. The plan of one excavated structure suggests a longhouse (Fairhurst 1969:181–185). A single entrance in the
south wall leads into a largely unpartitioned space. This door leads into
the western, byre end of the building, identifiable through its central
drain. Turning right would take you into the eastern, dwelling end,
with a hearth placed in the center of the earthen floor.

A second excavated structure followed a similar pattern (Fairhurst
1969:186–187). In this case, the southern end of a long structure was
probably used initially as a byre, subsequently converted to a threshing barn. There was some uncertain evidence of an internal partition
between this section of the structure and that to the north, which had
a hearth placed centrally in an earthen floor. To the south of this structure was another containing a byre drain and central hearth (Fairhurst
1969:187–188).

I will argue in chapter seven that in Kintyre and Kilfinan, where we
see continued use of the central hearth in the period of Improvement,
we are looking at the dwellings of smallholders and farm laborers.

CHANGING ROUTINE PRACTICE WITH
IMPROVEMENT

Through the eighteenth and nineteenth centuries, the environment
familiar to the population of Kintyre and Kilfinan went through a series
of fundamental changes. I have outlined these changes in terms of their
impact on landscape, settlement, and domestic space, and they can also
be related to changes in routine practice. Discussion of the relationship
between routine practice and material environment here is introductory and will be expanded in later chapters. As noted in general terms
in chapter three, routine practice and material culture are intimately
related, each structured by the other. At this stage, I want underline the
increasing emphasis on the autonomous individual in routine practice

with Improvement. As also seen in chapter three above, this emphasis on the individual is commensurate with the emergence of capitalism. However, change to the material environment with Improvement was significantly varied. This clearly has implications for a discussion of changing routine practice and is something I shall return to in more detail in chapter seven.

Pre-Improvement routine practice was communal and familial. By this I mean, specifically, that the individual experienced everyday activity as a member of the community of the *baile* or of several *bailtean*, or as a member of a family. The communal aspects of routine life are most obvious at the settlement and landscape scales of the material environment. Familial aspects are most obviously to be associated with domestic space. The distinction is, of course, not an absolute one.

It was through daily or cyclical communal activity that the community, of the *baile* or of several neighboring *bailtean*, was constituted. Cultivation, often using a plough that required the draft-livestock of several tenants, was communally organized (Fairhurst 1960:69; Grant 1995:44). Individually owned livestock were also periodically communally maintained. The cattle and other livestock of the whole farm or even several neighboring farms were taken to and kept at the shieling as a unit (see Bil 1990). Where, in other situations, a herd was employed, this was the responsibility of the tenants as a group (e.g., Stewart 1992:216). Other tasks, such as the cutting of peat for fuel, were also communal (Grant 1995:199). The inhabitants of a township, or even of several townships, could be jointly responsible for paying the rent (Dodgshon 1998a). Many decisions on the organization of farming practices were discussed and ruled upon in community meetings (see, e.g., Stewart 1992).

Pre-Improvement landscape and settlement both played a part in structuring such communal activity. Shieling and herding made sense in a landscape that was largely unenclosed and where cattle might otherwise freely wander amongst the crops. The intermixture of tenants' strips of arable under the open-field system made communal ploughing sensible and the lack of enclosure of individual portions of arable made such communal ploughing easier. Many *bailtean* were nucleated and, there, the inhabitants of the farm would have been in close daily proximity and in close contact, and they were already gathered for communal activity. In other cases, the *baile* may have had several discernible foci, and even tightly nucleated examples can have distinct groupings of structures. Tenants and sub-tenants may have been separating themselves from each other in space. However, they were still relatively close together and were constantly brought together in communal work. While they lived in separate houses, perhaps a little distance from their neighbors, the individuality this afforded them was an individuality articulated within the township community.

The typical pre-Improvement dwelling was a single unpartitioned space with a central hearth. Thus, all daily activity within the house took place in the presence of other members of the family. Sleeping, cooking, and eating would have all happened in this way. The position of the hearth in the center of the floor meant that all those activities associated with it literally took center stage. This could include some household industries, such as spinning, weaving, or the firing of pottery (Mitchell 1880:27–28). Those facing the fire would direct their attention to others sitting around it. In some of the sites discussed above, turf benches were positioned round the hearth, thus directing attention inward towards the fire and those surrounding it. The hearth provided a focus for story telling or other aspects of the *ceilidh* (Grant 1995:162), an impromptu gathering that could involve music, discussion, and food. This multi-variant use of space is to be seen in Dorothy Wordsworth's description of the kitchen of an early nineteenth century Highland inn:

> About seven or eight travellers, probably drovers, with as many dogs, were sitting in a complete circle round a large peat-fire in the middle of the floor, each with a mess of porridge, in a wooden vessel, upon his knee; a pot, suspended from one of the black beams, was boiling on the fire; two or three women pursuing their household business, children playing on the floor. (Wordsworth, in Thin [ed.] 1981:183)

Material change with Improvement undermined the pre-Improvement structuring of family and community. Settlement was dispersed, consisting of isolated farmhouses grouped together with their associated outbuildings in a courtyard or linear range. The settlement pattern of Improvement represented the fragmentation of the *baile*. There may have been some dispersal already evident in the pre-Improvement settlement pattern, but it was on a much smaller scale and associated with a quite different network of social practices. With Improvement, people would have had less opportunity to spend time together as part of their daily routine. Furthermore, when occasional visits did occur, the arrangement of space within the house to some extent distanced the visitors from the host family. The use of the spence of the range farmstead or parlor, dining room, or other similar room in the courtyard farmstead separated the visit from other activities within the house. Cooking, sleeping, and other areas were avoided, showing the visitor only a fragment of the daily environment of their hosts.

The growth or creation of towns like Southend, Campbeltown and Kilfinan was no exception to the process of the fragmentation of community. These nucleations of settlement consisted of the homes and workplaces of merchants, craftspeople and others who were not engaged in communal routine in the way that the farming population of the *bailtean* had been. Internal subdivision of the houses in such towns was also increasingly common (e.g., RCAHMS 1971:184–187). Indeed, several villas in Campbeltown, dating to the early nineteenth century, have an internal arrangement of space very similar to that of the dwelling within a courtyard farmstead (e.g., RCAHMS 1971:185–186).

The coherence of the community of the *baile*, as routinely structured, was also undermined at the landscape level. The enclosure of fields dispensed with the need for herds or for shieling, as livestock were separated from crops and each other by field boundaries. Enclosures were considered necessary by some for just this reason. Enclosures, we are told, saved the expense of herding and allowed the cattle to graze freely, without being teased by herds and dogs, as well as providing clean grass and a change of pasture when required (Smith 1798:62). Some form of enclosure, consisting of low stone dykes constituted in field clearance, may have existed in the period immediately prior to improvement. However, these dykes were not intended to enclose land in the sense that Improved fields were. They were not stock-proof, for example (Smout 1996a:55).

Shieling settlements were abandoned at this time as the hill ground was turned over to sheep, and eventually sport. On this higher ground, the sheep would still require herding. However, this was the task of shepherds, perhaps living in isolated dwellings like those on the Mull of Kintyre. The gathering of a large part of the township population and their livestock, as a group, at the shieling grounds, although related functionally to herding, was quite a different process in social terms.

The pre-Improvement routine structuring of the family was also undermined with Improvement, and again the material environment had a key role to play in this process. Internal subdivision, most visible in the courtyard farmstead, was associated with an increasing separation and segregation of daily tasks. In the courtyard farmstead, there was (and is) a kitchen for cooking, a dining room for eating, a parlor for entertaining, and several separate bedrooms for sleeping, and these are just the common elements. Of course, other activities could take place in these spaces and it is often wrong to separate some, like eating and entertaining for example. It remains true, however, that the family living in such a house experienced much more of their daily routine apart from each other.

The history of the hearth with Improvement also suggests the same shift in emphasis in daily routine away from the family to the individual. In the courtyard farmstead and the range farmstead, there were several hearths servicing several different rooms. The central hearth therefore no longer provided a single focus for daily activity. The position of the hearth within the room also changed as it was repositioned against a wall, again detracting from its potential to act as a focus for routine tasks.

In the home and beyond, then, people came to experience their daily routine more and more apart from the wider community and from their family. However, we cannot draw a straightforward linear evolution from the community and the family to the individual as foremost in routine practice. Differences in the chronology of Improvement between Kintyre and Kilfinan, and the varied penetration of Improved orderings of space and practice within those areas are clearly significant considering the arguments advanced in chapter three.

The next three chapters will explore the reasons behind these variations. Variation in the general chronology of Improvement will be argued to relate in part to the varied biographies of individual landowners in Kilfinan and Kintyre. Improvement, for these landowners, related to the conception of society embodied in Enlightenment thought. The connection between Improvement and Enlightenment is explored in the next chapter. The landowners in question were not simply passively influenced by Enlightenment philosophy, but instigated Improvement in order to address certain social contradictions specific to their personal biographies or family histories. Kintyre is used in Chapter 6 to investigate Improvement as a solution to long-seated conflict arising from a peculiarity of Highland society under the clan system. This peculiarity was that members of the farming population were at once members of the community of the clan and tenants of a landlord, and therefore potentially held conflicting obligations, rights, and responsibilities. For Kilfinan, I will consider Improvement in the context of the conflict between the position of landowners as members of the emergent middle class and as proprietors of traditional Highland estates.

The history of Improvement in the study areas is not just the history of innovating landlords. Above, we have seen significant variation in terms of material change with Improvement. Improvement of the landscape, most importantly involving enclosure and the decline of shieling, was dramatic and widespread. However, internal subdivision of domestic space and the social defocusing of the hearth, though still hugely significant, formed less of a blanket transformation. The presence of amorphous nucleated settlements in Kilfinan, within an otherwise Improved landscape, may also be significant.

In Chapter 7, the significance of variation in the progress of Improvement will be understood as varied response to Improvement on the part of the resident farming population. Improvement and capitalism were accepted, rejected, or more ambiguously received through the cessation or continuation of different aspects of pre-Improvement practice. The nature of the response of the farming population to Improvement and capitalism will be seen to revolve, above all, around the question of land rights. This response was also conditioned by the position of a given person in relation to others, by the power of others over them.

Improvement and Enlightenment | 5

There is a general connection between Improvement and Enlightenment at an intellectual level. Enlightenment thought encapsulated an understanding of society commensurate with the social restructuring that was Improvement. Beyond this general link, the landowners of Kilfinan and Kintyre can be shown to have been sympathetic to the main tenets of Enlightenment, which they encountered in specific contexts. The Improving Dukes of Argyll had direct links with the Scottish Enlightenment, in particular through their relationship with David Hume. It is possible that they discussed Enlightenment social theory directly with such members of the *literati*, and several of the eighteenth and nineteenth century Dukes certainly read major Enlightenment works. Improving landowners in Kilfinan, in general, came to the Enlightenment rather later and less directly. For most of this group, their contact with Enlightenment was through their membership of the urban-based middle class, emergent from the late eighteenth century.

Several key aspects of Scottish Enlightenment social theory are emphasized below in relation to Improvement. Enlightenment historiography understood the past as stadial. The history of all societies was narrated as their progression in stages to the Commercial Age. This progression was universal and inevitable as its driving force was the innate desire in all people to improve their condition, an aspect of human nature. Importantly, the Commercial Age was considered to be that stage of society already attained in England and to which the Scottish Lowlands were at least in transition. Scottish Enlightenment thought can be seen to have imbued a distinct form of cultural inferiorism. The Scottish Enlightenment also preached the cultivation of a disposition of independence. This disposition was characterized by a belief that people were free to alter the conditions of their existence.

These key aspects of Enlightenment thought combined to provide Highland landowners with an explicit framework for Improvement. It gave them a means of expression for the desired large-scale alteration of their material and social environment and allowed them to relate this change to English and Lowland Scottish exemplars. Significant aspects of Highland Improvement had a prior history in England and the Lowlands, including enclosure, the decline of shieling, the dispersal of settlement, the subdivision of domestic space, and the spatial and social decentralization of the hearth.

In common with the previous chapter, discussion of the relevant aspects of the English and Lowland material environment is structured below in terms of settlement, landscape, and domestic space. Also as previously, this changing environment is related to changing routine practice.

I should make clear that Enlightenment does not represent a culture or abstract cognitive structure. On the one hand, Enlightenment thought influenced how people explicitly expressed their view of the world and it pointed to Lowland and England exemplars for change. On the other hand, it was attendant on the introduction of the social relations of capitalism to the Highlands. Enlightenment thought was not created or adopted in a vacuum, but conditioned by past social relations. In one sense, the farming population of the Highlands were partly responsible for the popularity of Enlightenment thought among their landlords as this thought represents a sophisticated ideology justifying the social changes that were Improvement. Whether this justification seemed reasonable to different individuals or groups will be discussed in subsequent chapters. The point to remember here is that Enlightenment and other, different, contemporary, and explicit discussions of Improvement cannot be separated from the social relations from which they sprang and to which they related.

IMPROVEMENT AND THE SCOTTISH ENLIGHTENMENT

A general link between the Scottish Enlightenment and agricultural Improvement has been noted before:

> These were the years of overpowering intellectual vitality in Scotland that we know as the Scottish Enlightenment . . . [and] the Agricultural Revolution was a facet of the intellectual whirlwind that swept across the land. Man had come to believe that the new science made all things possible. (Adams 1980:173–174)

Improvement, as Berry (1997:11–12) notes, was far from something that happened behind the backs of the Enlightenment *literati*. Henry Home, Lord Kames, one Enlightenment scholar, was himself an Improver and even wrote a handbook on the subject entitled *The*

Gentleman Farmer: Being an attempt to improve Agriculture, by sub-jecting it to the Test of Rational Principles (1776). The work most associated with the Improving movement, the *Statistical Account*, has itself been described as *the* distinctive product of the Scottish Enlightenment (Mitchison 1962:124). Elements of the social theory of the Scottish Enlightenment, discussed below, were almost ready-made to explain differences between Highland and Lowland or English agriculture (Berry 1997:12).

The link between Improvement and Enlightenment is not just general. It can be demonstrated that all the landowners concerned in the case studies of this book had different kinds of connection to the Scottish Enlightenment. The connection is direct in the case of the Dukes of Argyll. David Hume, described by some as the central figure of the Scottish Enlightenment and primarily known for his philosophical and historical works (Broadie [ed.] 1997:799), was an admirer and protégé of Archibald, the third Duke (1743–1761) (Lindsay and Cosh 1973:193). Hume also spent some time at Rosneath, an Argyll seat on the Gareloch, in 1769 when John was fourth Duke (1761–1770) (Greig [ed.] 1932b:207). Further, he was amongst the large retinue that accompanied John, the fifth Duke (1770–1806), on his first visit to Inverary since receiving that title (Lindsay and Cosh 1973:193). Recently prior to this visit to Inverary, Hume had been appointed an Under-Secretary of State by Duke John's brother-in-law General Henry Seymour Conway (Lindsay and Cosh 1973:193).

It is probable that the fifth Duke, one of the noted Improvers of the family, and Hume discussed topical issues, including perhaps agricultural Improvement and Enlightenment philosophy. Certainly, Hume's published letters suggest discussion of the latter, if not the former, with Archibald, third Duke, also a noted Improver. In a letter of February 13th 1748 addressed to Lord Tinwald, Hume asks for several of his essays to be forwarded by the addressee to Duke Archibald, whom he describes as "undoubtedly a Man of Sense & Learning" (Greig [ed.] 1932a:113). Duke Archibald's opinion is clearly valued by Hume who says in a letter of April 12th 1759, this time addressed to Adam Smith, philosopher and economist (see Broadie [ed.] 1997:804 for a biographical sketch):

> I give thanks for the agreeable present of your *Theory* [*Theory of Moral Sentiments*, Smith's first book, just published]. Wedderburn and I made presents of our copies to such of our acquintances as we thought good judges, and proper to spread the reputation of the book. I sent one to the Duke of Argyle...(Greig [ed.] 1932a:303)

Argyll's praise of the book is mentioned later in the same letter, although Hume suggests Smith's usefulness in the Glasgow elections as a subtext to this (Greig [ed.] 1932a:305).

Direct connections with prominent Enlightenment figures aside, the appreciation of Scottish Enlightenment thought by the Dukes of Argyll is evident in other contexts. The eighth Duke (1847–1900), born too late to have met the likes of Hume, says in his autobiography that he read the works of Hume and William Robertson, Moderator of the General Assembly of the Church of Scotland and noted for his historical works, with pleasure and that he was extremely interested in the work of Dugald Stewart, mathematician and moral philosopher (Campbell 1906:84, 224; see Broadie [ed.] 1997:802–803, 805–806 for biographical sketches). This Duke, George, was a prolific author and one of his major works (Campbell 1887), which discusses pre- and post-Improvement Scottish society, is a good example of the progressive, stadial type of history that emerged in Scotland with the Enlightenment, and to which we shall return.

The connection between the House of Argyll and the Scottish Enlightenment is fairly direct. For the Improving landowners of Kilfinan the Scottish Enlightenment also provided a conceptual counterpart to Improvement. It is certainly possible that some or all of the landowners in question read Enlightenment works, though had they not there is still a demonstrable and less overt connection to be found between them and the Enlightenment. As will be seen in the next chapter, and in one way or another, most of these landowners were part of the emergent middle class, who increasingly professed views in line with Enlightenment reason.

Nenadic (1988:111) defines the Scottish middle class, emergent from the late eighteenth century, as consisting of four broad groupings. The largest, around eighty percent in late eighteenth century Glasgow and Edinburgh, and more in the smaller towns, consisted of businessmen. This group was made up of the makers and sellers of goods and services, such as merchants, manufacturers, shopkeepers, craftsmen, bankers, and distributors. The second largest group were professionals, dominated by the ancient professions of law and the church and the more modern medical professions. The other two groups were employees (tax, customs and excise, and local government officials, or business and law clerks) and the leisured (mostly independent women and retired men) (Nenadic 1988:112). It was in the large towns of Edinburgh and Glasgow that the middle class was large and prosperous, although ports like Greenock and Port Glasgow also had substantial middle class populations (Nenadic 1988:112).

Between the last decades of the eighteenth century and the 1830s, an explicit and distinct middle class consciousness emerged (Nenadic 1988:118,120). The professed sense of identity and collective solidarity that evolved in this period can be discussed with reference to a number of themes outside of the basic fact of geographical proximity provided by town life (Nenadic 1988:120–122). Of the themes discussed be Nenadic, I have highlighted those pertinent here.

First, within the context of the towns, ideas, knowledge, and an awareness of common interests or grievances was articulated widely. A sense of intellectual proximity was linked to geographical proximity. By the later eighteenth century a new intellectual movement was based in the thought of the Enlightenment, both in its refined academic and more popular forms.

Also contributing to the formation of middle class identity in this context were the connected themes of consumerism and the re-ordering of space. The display of material goods, centered in the towns on the elaboration of the home, combined with the increasing physical separation of the domestic and work spheres of life, allowed the middle class to distance themselves from the rest of urban society. A new type of home, and the social activities and relationships that home allowed, were central to the development of distinct ways of living. The re-ordering of space went further than this, however:

> The development of the 'new town' in the later eighteenth century—
> Edinburgh was the British exemplar, though there were lesser versions in
> most towns—is vital to an understanding of the Middle Class. New town
> design, symmetrical and grid-like, articulated the desire for a new sort of
> orderliness to replace existing patterns of incoherent urban growth; it was
> a powerful metaphor for social order and control. (Nenadic 1988:121)

Added to a new conception of ordered space, consumerism and a flourishing new intellectual culture born of the Scottish Enlightenment was the desire for cultural assimilation with England. Indeed, I will argue below that this last factor itself cannot be separated from Enlightenment ideas of progress and of stadial history. Part of the middle class identity that was increasingly practiced was a disdain for Scotticisms and the pursuit of the English idiom in speech and literature (see, in general, Basker 1991), or a conscious revision of aspects of the Scottish past, such as Jacobitism, in a romantic and non-threatening form.

Directly or indirectly, then, the Improving landowners of Kintyre and Kilfinan adopted the tenets of Scottish Enlightenment thought. The social theory of the Scottish Enlightenment, often expressed in discourses on history and historiography and on human nature, will be seen below to have provided an explicit program of reform for the Improving movement. Scottish Enlightenment philosophy could not only be held to justify and naturalize Improvement, but to suggest where exemplars for Improved houses, settlements, and landscapes were to be found. This intimate link between Improvement and Enlightenment points to one aspect of an explanation for the chronological discrepancy of Improvement between Kintyre and Kilfinan. The Dukes of Argyll came into direct contact with Enlightenment thought during the *floruit* of the Scottish Enlightenment itself, in the mid to late eighteenth century. Landowners in Kilfinan, for whom the middle class context was their prime contact, came to Enlightenment thought later, from the late eighteenth century at earliest. It is not that these different landowners were indoctrinated in a new process of thought or a new culture and that this then caused them to re-organize their estates. Enlightenment was linked to certain social relationships, like those undertaken by the urban middle class and outlined in brief above, and so the inspiration came as much from these new ways of engaging with others. In this case, and for example, a merchant might experience social relations amongst the middle class and between them and others in the towns in one way and this could provide inspiration for the re-formulation of relations on their country estate. The Scottish Enlightenment could provide justification both for existing asymmetrical relationships in the town and for the fundamental transformation of society in the Highlands. It was also born of these changing relationships.

ENLIGHTENMENT HISTORIOGRAPHY:
THE STAGES OF SOCIETY

According to Kidd (1993:28–29), Medieval and Early Modern Scotland had a strong ethnocentric tradition of political discourse. This was founded on a version of history that emphasized Scottish nationhood and was proud of a past of national independence closely linked to domestic constitutional freedom from tyrannical kings. However, from the late seventeenth century this view of the Scottish past was increasingly undermined as constitutional freedom came increasingly to be associated with English prosperity (Kidd 1993:Chapter 3).

Historiography in the first half of the eighteenth century was dominated by partisan Whig–Jacobite debates over the Scottish past (Kidd 1993:Chapter 5). These histories were grounded with reference to an Original Contract (in which the majority in society, where in the State of Nature each individual has the right to freedom, agree to set aside their natural right to govern themselves) or ancient constitution (giving aristocrats the right to resist the monarchy). Questions such as the nature of kingship (absolute or elected?) were debated in an arena that emphasized party, not nation. With the fading of the Jacobite threat after the mid-eighteenth century, party legitimacy ceased to be the keystone of political debate. The disappearance of this bipartisan discourse coupled with the emergence of Enlightenment historical sociology was related to historical inferiorism and the adoption of an Anglo-British institutional identity (Kidd 1993:96–99).

Scottish Enlightenment historiography was markedly different from its predecessors in theoretical terms. It rejected appeals to the Original Contract or ancient constitution, arguing that all human history was stadial and could be understood with reference to human nature, which was universal and uniform.

Perhaps the most famous of the stadial accounts of human history is Adam Smith's four-stage theory. He says:

> There are four distinct states which mankind pass thro: first, the Age of Hunters; secondly, the Age of Shepherds; thirdly, the Age of Agriculture; and fourthly, the Age of Commerce. (Adam Smith, in Broadie [ed.] 1997:479)

As we might suspect from the labels given to each of these ages, Smith defined them in economic terms. On the Age of Hunters he argues:

> If we should suppose 10 or 12 persons of different sexes settled in an uninhabited island, the first method they would fall upon for their sustenance would be to support themselves by the wild fruits and wild animalls which the country afforded. Their sole business would be hunting the wild beasts or catching the fishes. (Adam Smith, in Broadie [ed.] 1997:479)

However, these hypothetical hunters would soon feel the need to progress to the next stage of society:

> In process of time, as their numbers multiplied, they would find the chase too precarious for their support. They would be necessitated to contrive some other method whereby to support themselves.... The contrivance they would most naturally think of, would be to tame some of those wild animalls they caught, and by affording them better food than what they could get elsewhere they would induce them to continue about their land themselves and multiply their kind. Hence would arise the age of shepherds. (Adam Smith, in Broadie 1997:479)

The population growth that this economic advancement allowed would engender further change:

> ...when a society becomes numerous they would find a difficulty in sup-
> porting themselves by herds and flocks. Then they would naturally turn
> themselves to the cultivation of the land and the raising of such plants and
> trees as produced nourishment fit for them ... they would gradually advance
> into the age of agriculture. (Adam Smith, in Broadie [ed.] 1997:480)

From the Age of Agriculture, it was one more step to the end point of historical development:

> As society was farther improved, the severall arts, which at first would be
> exercised by each individual as far as was necessary for his welfare, would
> be separated; some persons would cultivate one and others, as they severally
> inclined. They would exchange with one another what they produced more
> than was necessary for their support, and get in exchange for them the
> commodities they stood in need of and did not produce themselves. This
> exchange of commodities extends in time not only betwixt the individualls
> of the same society but betwixt those of different nations ... Thus at last the
> Age of Commerce arises. (Adam Smith, in Broadie [ed.] 1997:480)

Note the inevitability of this stadial progression and the qualitative judgment implied by terms such as improved.

Others propounded this stadial view of human history in a variety of forms. John Millar's description of societal progress is similar, if more succinct (John Millar, in Broadie [ed.] 1997:491), and Adam Ferguson compares the history of mankind from "rudeness to civilization" with the development of a child from infancy to manhood (Adam Ferguson, in Broadie [ed.] 1997:499; for biographies of Millar and Ferguson see Broadie [ed.] 1997:797–798, 801), again implying an inevitability in the process and offering a qualitative judgment on the stages prior to that of the modern, civilized, Commercial Age. Hume in general, also adopts the stadial view:

> The bulk of every state may be divided into *husbandmen* and *manufactur-*
> *ers.* ... As soon as men quit their savage state, where they live chiefly by
> hunting and fishing, they must fall into these two classes; though the arts of
> agriculture employ *at first* the most numerous parts of the society. Time and
> experience improve so much these arts, that the land may easily maintain
> a much greater number of men, than those who are immediately employed
> in its culture, or who furnish the more necessary manufactures to such as
> are so employed. (David Hume, in Broadie [ed.] 1997:388–389; emphasis in
> original)

The economic basis of each stage in a society's development is referred to throughout, but the change from one age to another involved much more than the simply economic. Smith's description of the process, outlined above, comes in the context of a discussion on the origin and development of property rights. He argues that regulations concerning property rights vary according to the stage society is in at a given time (Adam Smith, in Broadie [ed.] 1997:479–487). Much of contemporary North America, he argues, was in his day in the Age of Hunters. As a result, the only injury that could be done to an individual was to deprive them of their game. This lack of personal property resulted in a lack of laws and regulations concerning it and in a lack of regard for theft. In such a stage of society, property begins and ends with physical possession. With the Age of Shepherds, flocks and herds would be considered the property of those who tamed them, with physical possession becoming less relevant in determining property rights. As a result, laws and regulations become more numerous and complex and theft is regarded more seriously, being punishable by death in Tartary, as Smith's example goes. With the Age of Agriculture, theft and open robbery is less of a threat and property laws will be less rigorous, but more complex to deal with the extension of property over areas of land. Lastly, with the Age of Commerce, property laws become proportionately increased with regard to the subjects of property. It is in this last age that private property really emerges as common land is divided once and for all. Smith's example here is the rise of a city, where an individual will farm that land adjacent to their fixed abode. The course of a society through history therefore not only involves stadial and progressive economic change, but also corresponding change in the laws and institutions of that society.

Some considered the social changes accompanying each stage to go further still and to include changes in a society's mentalité. Henry Home, Lord Kames, for example, says in his discussion on the rise and fall of patriotism:

> The members of a tribe, in their original state of hunting and fishing, being little united but by a common language, have no notion of patria; and scarce any notion of society, unless when they join in an expedition against an enemy, or against wild beasts. The shepherd-state, where flocks and herds are possessed in common, gives a clear notion of common interest; but still none of patria. The sense of patria begins to unfold itself, when a people leave off wandering, to settle upon a territory which they call their own. Agriculture connects them together; and government still more ... a man's country, and his countrymen, are to him in conjunction an object of peculiar affection, termed amor patriæ, or patriotism: an affection that rises high among a people intimately connected by regular government, by husbandry, by commerce, and by a common interest. (Henry Home, Lord Kames, in Broadie [ed.] 1997:521)

HUMAN NATURE, THE COMMERCIAL AGE,
AND HUMAN INDEPENDENCE

Enlightenment historiography posited that each stage in a society's history is quite distinct in terms of economy, social institutions and cultural values. Further, the progression from stage to stage is generally in a set order and moves gradually towards civilization (the Commercial Age). This pattern was considered to be universal and to explain the diversity of social life throughout the world, accounting for the history of contemporary western nations and the differences between the then current state of those nations and those societies increasingly encountered in areas like the American continent. Why should this progression be universal? The answer to this question was seen to lie with human nature, although other important forces for change were discussed (Chitnis 1976:104–106).

John Millar sums up the aspect of human nature of interest here:

> There is . . . in man a disposition and capacity for improving his condition, by the exertion of which, he is carried from one degree of advancement to another; and the similarity of his wants, as well as of the faculties by which those wants are supplied, has everywhere produced a remarkable uniformity in the several steps of his progression. (John Millar, in Broadie [ed.] 1997:490–491)

There is an innate drive in all people to improve their condition in life. This coupled with the stadial account of history explains the diversity in human society and history. All societies progress from the uncivilized to the civilized, it is human nature (it is *natural*) that they do so, and the diverse societies of the world are different because they have reached different stages in this development. With time all societies will reach the end point of the Commercial Age.

The Commercial Age needs further consideration as it is a value judgment on the superiority of that age that conditions much of Enlightenment thinking on society. The Age of Commerce was seen to bring prosperity and liberty, existing in a complex inter-relation with the rule of law and justice (Berry 1997:122–123). In refutation of the view that love of liberty is most perfect amongst barbarians, Millar argues:

> Where-ever men of inferior condition are enabled to live in affluence by their own industry, and, in procuring their livelihood, have little occasion to court the favour of their superiors, there may we expect that ideas of liberty will be universally diffused. This happy arrangement of things, is naturally produced by commerce and manufactures; (John Millar, in Broadie [ed.] 1997:545)

Another important association was between commercial society and England. The *literati* considered that Scotland was under a progression to the Commercial Age and were aware of England as a neighbor advanced to that position (Chitnis 1976:117). This conditioned and inspired their enquiry into human history and society. As a result, the benefits of commercial society outlined above came to be associated with English society. Although Enlightenment *literati* did conceive of social problems that the Commercial Age could bring (see, e.g., Adam Ferguson, in Broadie [ed.] 1997:497–506), it was generally held to be a superior age and such problems as there were often entered discussion not in argument against progress to the Commercial Age, but in order to define remedies to those problems and, thus, aid social progression.

The natural progress of history, then, was the stadial movement of society toward the Commercial Age, above all to be associated with English society. This line of thought linked Improvement to English and, in the case of the Highlands, Lowland Scottish rural society. However, there was one other key aspect of Enlightenment thought essential to Improvement. We might term this the introduction of a concept of human agency in relation to the material world.

Charles Camic (1983) has defined one of the major shifts in thought with the Scottish Enlightenment as that from dependency to independence. The disposition of dependency is witnessed in the cardinal documents of Scottish Calvinism, such as The Westminster Confession of Faith, The Longer Catechism and The Shorter Catechism. For Camic, it was amongst the most elemental components of early eighteenth century Scottish discourse (Camic 1983:15). It can be defined as "the orientation, or set of orientations, that renders the action, judgment, or situation of human beings primarily subservient to agents regarded as removed in essence from human control" (Camic 1983:16). This means that:

> ...in their being and in their believing, in practice and in theory, existentially and intellectually, individuals are not their own. The inescapable message of the Calvinist teachings was...that humans and their world are wholly and absolutely dependent upon the will and the grace of God. (Camic 1983:18)

One of the major facets of early eighteenth-century Scottish thought, then, was a statement that in this world a sovereign God is the source of everything from predestination for everlasting life to a summer shower (Camic 1983:20). *Everything* was governed according to God's will and human beings were perceived as passive actors on His stage, playing out a role defined for them.

With the Scottish Enlightenment, this view of dependency began to be replaced by the distinctly modern attitude of independence.
Independence is defined as "the orientation, or family of orientations,
which regards the human condition (human actions, judgments, or
situations) as essentially autonomous, rather than as primarily subordinate to agents transcending human control" (Camic 1983:46). David
Hume argued that the ideal character is "entirely master of his own
disposition" and that "every wise man will endeavor to place his happi-
ness on such objects chiefly as depend upon himself" (quoted in Camic
1983:56). Further afield, for Kant, the motto of the Enlightenment was
"have the courage to use your own reason" (Berry 1997:2). With the
ideological shift from dependency to independence the premise of the
fall of man and original sin were supplanted with the notion that people are born pure and untainted, with the result that they were no
longer deprived of moral and intellectual worth and predestined to everlasting dependency. Rather, their dignity was constantly proclaimed in
a universe inhabited by capable beings who no longer demanded per-
petual supernatural assistance (Camic 1983:57–59). Hume and Smith
admitted Providence no role in explaining human action and granted
God no direct entry into the sequence of events in this world. Indeed,
Hume considered the purpose of his work as being in order "to free
men from unexamined beliefs," to render them independent (quoted in
Camic 1983:63–65).

This new orientation of independence justified a new attitude to the
physical environment that stressed human agency and that involved an
exponential rise in the exploitation of land as a resource. It was not that
God was no longer said to be the creator of the Earth. The complexity
of and order within the world was seen as evidence of divine creation,
as James Hutton, farmer, chemist, and geologist, explains:

> When we trace the parts of which this terrestrial system is composed, and
> when we view the general connection of those several parts, the whole
> presents a machine of a peculiar construction by which it is adapted to
> a certain end. We perceive a fabric, erected in wisdom, to obtain a pur-
> pose worthy of the power that is apparent in the production of it. (James
> Hutton, in Broadie [ed.] 1997:773; see Broadie [ed.] 1997:800 for a brief
> biography)

Rather, with Enlightenment the important philosophical innova-
tion was the consideration that people could act to alter the created
material environment and their relationship with it. In doing so they
could also act outside of the constraints of tradition, as autonomous
individuals.

There are a few problems with this simplified picture of shifting cultural orientations. Whether Camic's reading of the orientation of dependency is entirely appropriate for all social contexts of the time is unclear. Further, the attitude of human agency in the material world had been developing since the Renaissance (Berry 1997:70) and, so, was not an entirely new phenomenon. However, several obvious material aspects of Improvement show a relatively greater intervention in the natural world than had previously been the case. Courtyard farmsteads in particular were abstract and geometric in from, commonly forming a rectangular courtyard, where the *bailtean* had been disposed according to the pre-existing local topography of the site. Pre-Improvement agriculture had predominantly been located on the naturally draining lower slopes of hills, but with Improvement lower and previously boggy areas could be drained and colonized. The Enlightenment disposition of independence provided ideological justification for and came from the dramatic transformation of the physical nature of the rural world with Improvement.

EXEMPLARS FOR IMPROVEMENT: LOWLAND SCOTLAND AND ENGLAND

Settlement

The general pre-Improvement, or sixteenth to eighteenth century, settlement pattern in the Lowlands was one of nucleated farming townships, known as fermtouns (Whyte and Whyte 1991:4). These fermtouns were generally clusters of between six and twelve households with buildings loosely scattered or strung out in an irregular line, with no indication of planning (Whyte and Whyte 1991:4; see Whyte 1981:12–15 on variation in Lowland settlement morphology and size).

From the 1760s, and in places the 1740s, Lowland settlement form saw comprehensive change with the fragmentation of the fermtoun (Fenton and Walker 1981:102). However, as we shall see in relation to landscape and domestic space, Improvement in the Lowlands was underway in the seventeenth century. An early example of a planned farmstead layout is West Gagie in Angus, the form of which can be reconstructed from an inventory of 1649 which includes the compass orientations of the various buildings and indicates which of these are under the same roof (Whyte 1975:65). There, the dwelling house and some of its offices formed three sides of a courtyard, with a wall and gate forming the fourth. The remaining outbuildings formed a separate cluster, possibly enclosing a second yard. Elsewhere, different but equally planned and geometrical forms were introduced in the late seventeenth century, as with the L- and Z-shaped steadings in the barony of Lasswade near Edinburgh (Whyte 1975:66).

The courtyard farm, however, is the type that became the most popular from the late eighteenth century (Whyte and Whyte 1991:139). At first, such farm steadings were arranged in a U-shape with the fourth side open or completed with a wall and gate. Subsequently, many farms in the east and south east of the country filled the fourth side of the courtyard with an additional range of buildings, often pierced by an arched entrance. Sometimes, notably in the nineteenth century, more complex plans emerged as additional courtyards were built and farmhouses were separated from the rest of the steading. In the North East and the dairying areas of the South West, where the farms were smaller, U-shaped and L-shaped farms continued in use.

Also increasingly common through the seventeenth century were farmhouses similar to the range farmstead of the southern Highlands (see Whyte 1975:63). In these Lowland ranges, the dwelling, byre, and barn, usually in that order, were commonly placed end-to-end under one roof, divided by light partitions. Entry to dwelling and byre seems to have been by a common doorway. Other spaces could be added according to the particular requirements of a given farm, and there was significant regional variation in this respect. For example, farm buildings in arable areas often included a stable for the workhorses.

Settlement morphology and pattern in England varied from region to region, and in places was more stable from the Medieval to post-medieval period (in addition to what follows, see Newman 2001:124–129). A network of nucleated villages was typical of champion landscapes of the Medieval period, concentrating in a broad strip of lowland running from the Midlands into the northeast (Johnson 1996:23). These villages were regular or irregular in form, consisting of a church, manor house, and rows of houses. Such settlements had their origins in the period from the ninth to twelfth centuries. Many of these settlements were depopulated from the late Medieval period and replaced with dispersed sheep farms (Johnson 1996:47–49).

In other parts of England, dispersed settlement patterns were common in the Middle Ages. In wood-pasture areas, concentrating in the southeast, southwest, the Welsh Marches, and parts of the northwest, large nucleated villages were rare, although small nucleations were to be found (Johnson 1996:25). Settlement was more generally clustered in small hamlets, loose ribbon (i.e., strung out) clusters, or dispersed altogether. Upland areas, in the Pennines and in the far west and southwest, also had a dispersed settlement pattern, though settlement was much less dense than in areas of wood pasture (Johnson 1996:28).

Landscape

The pre-Improvement landscape of Lowland Scotland was in many ways similar to that described for the Highland study areas in Chapter 4 (see, e.g., Fairhurst 1960:70–71; Whyte and Whyte 1991:Chapter 3). Arable farming was in openfields separated from hill pasture, where it existed, by dykes of turf and stone.

The process of enclosure did not substantially affect the rural landscape of the Lowlands until well into the eighteenth century, but it is a process that first began much earlier. Enclosure of policies in the vicinity of the seats of landowners really began to take hold in the Lowlands in the early seventeenth century, especially around Edinburgh where deer parks and formal walled gardens were constructed around the country houses of lawyers and members of the Privy Council (Slater 1980:227). It was the nobility who took the real lead in creating enclosed policies, and the formal gardens, walled park and orchard of the 1630s at the Earl of Lothian's Ancram House, Roxburghshire, form an early example (Slater 1980:227–228).

The rural Lowlands outside of these policies was, in the seventeenth century, largely unenclosed. This was to change in the eighteenth century, especially from the mid part of that century. Third (1955:91–92; see also Third 1957) has defined three main periods of enclosure in the eastern Lowlands. The first period, between 1720 and 1760, saw the enclosure of a number of moderate estates in fertile areas by people such as prosperous Glasgow merchants, Edinburgh or London professionals, and lairds who belonged to local societies of Improvers. An even spread of Improvement was not always achieved, however, and enclosure often remained confined to policies and home farms. The second period, between 1760 and 1800, saw a more comprehensive and striking transformation of the Lowland rural landscape, with vast sums of money being expended by the great landowners. Enclosure in this phase was often well organized and strictly supervised by estate officials and could cover wide areas, resulting in uniform adherence to current doctrines and theories on landscape Improvement and in grids of rectangular enclosures. Such could be the will to adhere to a predetermined plan that little regard was shown for the courses of streams or the position of previously existing farm steadings. Hundreds of laborers were employed in such projects by families like the Hamiltons, resulting in rapid and uniform changes (see Third 1955:91). The third phase of enclosure, between about 1800 and 1820, saw the Improvement of estates above 200 meters, which were hampered by poor terrain, transport difficulties, and low financial resources. There, Improvements were initially tentative and the form of enclosures was heavily influenced by the previous arrangement of arable under the open-field system and by the local topography. This three stage phasing of the enclosure process is generally true for large parts of the Lowlands, but is not universal. For instance, large-scale commercial orientated enclosure came much earlier (first, in fact) to Galloway, where it was related to the cattle trade (Whyte and Whyte 1991:130). In places, such enclosure was happening as early as the late seventeenth century (Dodgshon 1981:262).

As just discussed, in form, Lowland enclosure could assume a grid-like pattern of rectangular fields or, on higher ground, a more irregular pattern where the shape of fields was more dependent on local topography and previously existing patterns of land use (see also Lebon 1946). Sometimes the individual enclosures in a grid-like system could take other forms, being wedge-shaped or arranged in long strips (Third 1955:86–91). This diversity of enclosure is similar to the arrangement in Kintyre and Kilfinan.

Shieling as a practice had existed in the Lowlands (see, e.g., Whyte and Whyte 1991:70–71). However, it had died out there much earlier than in the Highlands. A number of place names in hill areas like the Lammermuirs contain the element shiel(s) and denote former shieling sites. Many of these shielings probably went out of use in the twelfth and thirteenth centuries, in cases being converted into permanent sheep farms by their monastic landlords (Whyte and Whyte 1991:70–71). In parts of the Borders, shieling survived as late as the fifteenth and sixteenth centuries (Whyte and Whyte 1991:71). Possible survivals of shieling into the seventeenth century, in Galloway for example, are rare in the extreme (Whyte 1979:84). Glenesslin in Dumfries and Galloway has recently been subject to intensive archaeological survey (RCAHMS 1994). A sizeable number of shielings were found, but there is no record of transhumance in the area for the eighteenth and nineteenth centuries (RCAHMS 1994:7).

Enclosure in England largely predated that in Lowland Scotland and took place within many different historical contexts (for a general overview see Newman 2001:106–112). In wood-pasture areas of England, enclosures that appear on nineteenth century or modern maps can often be seen to have survived from the Roman period or even earlier, although there are cases of later piecemeal enclosure of land within such areas (Johnson 1996:25–26, 50–53). Areas of Medieval champion landscape were characterized by open arable and pasture fields

(Johnson 1996:23–25). However, from the late Middle Ages, these areas were increasingly enclosed as the farms were turned over to sheep, with a peak period of enclosure between 1450 and 1550 (Johnson 1996: 48–49). Areas of champion land that survived unenclosed into the eighteenth century were often subject to enclosure by Act of Parliament after 1750 (Johnson 1996:55–56). Fenlands around the borders of Norfolk, Cambridgeshire, and Lincolnshire were extensively drained and enclosed in the seventeenth century (Johnson 1996:50). Enclosure accompanying the reclamation of waste, that is land not under systematic cultivation, occurred in two main periods, prior to 1300 and from the seventeenth century (Johnson 1996:55). As in Scotland, the morphology of enclosure varied and both grid-like and more irregular systems exist, the latter often preserving previous patterns of land use.

Shieling was widespread over most of northern England in the Middle Ages and, in some areas, may have been practiced from the tenth and eleventh centuries, if not earlier (RCHME 1970:1, 3). As in the Scottish Borders, the practice survived in places into the sixteenth and seventeenth centuries, but was almost completely abandoned by the latter century (RCHME 1970:1, 3–8; Whyte 1979:84).

Domestic Space

The adoption of Improved domestic space in the rural houses of the Lowlands, as the Improvement of settlement and landscape, although becoming widespread in the eighteenth century, had earlier roots. As virtually no vernacular dwellings of the seventeenth century survive, discussion has centered on the evidence of estate papers (see Whyte 1975).

Perhaps the most important structural element of the house was the timberwork, and cruck framing was widespread (Whyte 1975: 57–59). The crucks were structurally important as the house walls were not load bearing (Whyte and Whyte 1991:31). Roofing in the seventeenth century Lowlands was mostly constituted of organic materials (Whyte 1975:59–60). Straw thatch was common in most of Lowland Scotland except Aberdeenshire and the Moray Firth coast. Where straw was in short supply or too precious as fodder, turf and heather were in common use. Walling was built from those materials ready to hand and the principle materials were stone, clay, and turf (Whyte 1975: 60–62). The earliest known use of lime mortar in the context of tenant housing construction was on the Aberdour estate in Fife in 1625, although the bulk of references relate to the period 1660–1700 (Whyte 1975:62).

These building traditions continued into the eighteenth century, in places into the nineteenth (Fenton and Walker 1981:Chapters 5 and 6). However, their popularity was increasingly eroded in that period (e.g., Caird 1980:216–217). Roofing was increasingly of slate or pantiles and walls increasingly of stone and lime (Fenton and Walker 1981:69–70, 90–93).

In terms of construction techniques, then, the history of the Lowland farmhouse from the seventeenth to nineteenth centuries parallels that of the Highlands closely. Originally built predominantly from organic materials, from the mid- to late eighteenth century these were increasingly replaced by stone, lime mortar and slate. Documentary sources, however, suggest that the internal subdivision of space was increasingly common in the seventeenth century, if not widespread or universal.

Ian Whyte has drawn a general picture of domestic space in the seventeenth century Lowlands from surviving estate papers (Whyte 1975:62–67). The size of the dwelling space could vary from one couple (that is, the space between two cruck trusses) to fourteen. The smallest dwellings probably had one room, heated by a central hearth, but the more common dwelling area of two to three couples was large enough to allow some subdivision of space. There seems to have been considerable variation in internal organization of the dwelling according to the occupier's status. Tenants of larger holdings seem to have lived in houses with more complex internal layouts and made from more durable materials. For example, an eight-couple house at Bridgend of Lintrathen in Angus, described in an inventory of 1656, consisted of a hall, back chamber, inner chamber, and pantry (Whyte 1975:64). Increased spatial complexity was further facilitated by some of the constructional innovations mentioned above, especially lime mortar and its associated load bearing walls. These allowed upper floors to be constructed, as at the factor's house at Belhelvie, Aberdeenshire, described in 1705 (Whyte 1975:64). Houses such as this were probably becoming increasingly common throughout the seventeenth century with the quickening pace of agricultural commercialization (Whyte 1975:65).

Such seventeenth century houses, with complex and compartmentalized internal layouts, were the forerunners of the type of house that became common from the eighteenth century, and the spatial organization of these dwellings often derived from the homes of ministers and small lairds (Whyte and Whyte 1991:138). Typically, such houses were of two or three storeys, with symmetrical facades. There was some regional variation in the specific character of Improved houses, with the South West generally retaining the single-storey farmhouse, and the two or more storey farmhouse being more common in the east (Fenton and Walker 1981:69).

Most seventeenth century houses in the Lowlands, as in the Highlands, had a single hearth in the middle of the floor (Whyte and Whyte 1991:36). Nevertheless, from descriptions in estate papers it seems that some seventeenth century houses had gable-ends incorporating a chimney (Whyte 1979:165). Presumably the two or more storey farmhouses and highly subdivided linear ranges had several individual fireplaces servicing different rooms.

The process of the increasing subdivision of internal space and the decentralization of the hearth can be traced in England for a period earlier than that in Scotland. In a study focusing on the domestic architecture in western Suffolk, Matthew Johnson has argued for the transformation from open to closed space within the houses of middling farmers in the period from the fifteenth to the seventeenth century, though primarily in the sixteenth (Johnson 1993). His conclusions in that study can be extended to other parts of England and Wales (Johnson 1996:79). The Medieval house in question in England and Wales focused on a central hall open to the roof. Over time, the importance of this open space was reduced as a ceiling was inserted, limiting its size. Separate rooms at the ends of the house increased in number and increased in importance as centers of activity in their own right (Johnson 1996:79). Upstairs rooms were also increasingly common and more heavily used. At the same time, a chimneystack against a partition wall of the hall replaced the central hearth.

Routine Practice

From the Medieval period, then, the material environment of rural England and Lowland Scotland in terms of landscape, settlement, and domestic space began to exhibit many of the traits of Improvement that were to become common in the Highlands. In parts of England at least, what were to become key material elements of Improvement, like enclosure, had much longer histories. Just as later in the Highlands, communal and familial aspects of routine practice declined with the material environments that they structured and were structured by.

Improvement in the Scottish Lowlands was associated with changes in the way the land was worked and should be considered a gigantic strategy of social and economic engineering (Devine 1994a:70). The fact that the single-tenant farm was triumphant there by the mid-eighteenth century (Devine 1994a:27) neatly sums up the decline of community. By the seventeenth century, shieling, which was probably a similar practice in the Lowlands to the Highlands (see Whyte and Whyte 1991:70–75), had disappeared. Thus, one of the main practices where the people of one fermtoun or more congregated and worked in common disappeared. As in the Highlands, enclosure negated one of the main functions of shieling, which acted to separate the cattle from the ripening crops (see Fenton 1999:138). Enclosure was also accompanied by changes in arable farming. By the end of the eighteenth century, changing plough technology allowed the reduction in size of plough teams, eventually to one ploughman and two horses (Devine 1994a:53, 154).

Enclosure in England opened the way for a commodification of the landscape and created a farming landscape more appropriate to the accumulation of private wealth by the individual tenant (Johnson 1996:206). Enclosure allowed the farming landscape to be divested of regulation by the local community and to be placed in the hands of individuals (Newman 2001:108). Dispersed settlement in England is also to be associated with the fragmentation of the community. Even in the Medieval period, champion landscapes with their nucleated villages housed communities with tighter social bonds and more emphasis on neighborliness than wood-pasture regions, where dispersed settlement was more common (Johnson 1996:25).

Returning to Lowland Scotland, the subdivision of domestic space and the multiplication and relocation of the hearth can be associated with the fragmentation of routine familial practices. Through the seventeenth and eighteenth centuries, the house of the better-off tenant farmer increasingly had a separate kitchen, living room, and bedroom/private apartment (Whyte and Whyte 1991:36). Similarly, in England there was a growth in social distance with the increasing subdivision of domestic space (Johnson 1993:107). The change from Medieval to post-medieval housing in England and Wales involved fundamental change in the ways in which people related to each other:

> ...the insertion of a fireplace and chimney stack, the flooring over of the open hall and the subdivision of living space, these changes indicate considerable differences in the use of the house and signify changes in concepts of domestic living and spatial use within society. Extra usable space was gained and comfort increased, but patterns of flow and usage were also altered, affecting and conditioned by changing social relationships. Entrance arrangements were altered to provide increased control and to facilitate social exclusion. The lobby-entry...ensured that the hall and parlour could be entered independently. This arrangement may have been adopted when the parlour was transferred to the entry end of the house, in order to provide it with greater privacy in the later sixteenth and early seventeenth centuries—a time when the social gap between householder and domestic servants was increasing. (Newman 2001:57)

The exact nature of social distancing within the house differed in parts of England and Wales compared with the Scottish Highlands. As suggested in the above quote, in the middling English household the walls separated master and servant as much as members of the same family. On top of the division of space, the removal of the hearth to an end wall and the splitting of its functions meant that it was no longer a centralizing but a dividing feature (Johnson 1993:119).

A PARTIAL UNDERSTANDING OF IMPROVEMENT

Material and social change with Improvement in Kintyre and Kilfinan had clear antecedents in Lowland Scotland and England. Some of these antecedents, like enclosure and dispersed settlement in wood-pasture areas of England, had existed for centuries and many dated from the late Medieval period on. Enclosure and the other material changes forming Improvement in Lowland Scotland, on the other hand, were generally recent by comparison. Shieling had been abandoned in some areas as early as the twelfth century, but many of the other changes outlined were only introduced in the seventeenth and did not become widespread until well into the eighteenth. I do not wish to suggest that Improvement had universally transformed the material and social environment of the Scottish Lowlands and of England before commencing in the Highlands. The concept of Improvement should be confined to the post-Medieval period and the transformation antecedent to Improvement remained partial. Changes in the use of domestic space in England were subject to both regional and social variation (Newman 2001:58). Many of the subdivided houses mentioned above were the homes of the rural middle class, the more prosperous farmers. Landscape and settlement change varied through space and time.

However, Improvement and its predecessors were widespread and established enough to provide Enlightened Highland landowners with exemplars for change and through which they could justify that change. Indeed, the fact that material forms like the highly subdivided dwelling were to be associated above all with the middling sort may have been important in the eyes of Highland landowners wishing to commercialize and modernize their estates, as they considered themselves to be doing. It was as much the social groups and patterns of social interaction associated with the Improved environment in England and the Lowlands as any abstract philosophical thought that made such an environment desirable.

Landowners' knowledge and experience of these exemplars was probably acquired in a variety of ways. For example, the Dukes of

Argyll owned an estate in the Lowlands, in Peebleshire. This they renamed Whim when embarking on a series of experimental Improvements in 1729 (see RCAHMS 1967:326–331). They had first hand
practical knowledge of the progress and character of Improvement in
the Lowlands. The House of Argyll first held land in the Lowlands
centuries before, as early as the beginning of the fourteenth century
in the Ochil Hills near Stirling (RCAHMS 2001:16). They physically
placed themselves at the center of Scottish political circles at an early
stage, acquiring Castle Gloom (later Castle Campbell) near Stirling,
which hosted a royal castle and palace, in the second half of the fifteenth century (Cruden 1999:18). Castle Campbell was set ablaze in
1654, and afterwards, in the 1660s, the Earl of Argyll acquired the
Stirling town house now known as the Argyll Lodging (Cruden 1999:29;
Fawcett 1996:8). The Argylls retained ownership of the Lodging until
1764 (Fawcett 1996:11). The family had risen to pre-eminence in the
Highlands and beyond through service to the Crown and by the eighteenth century their political activities meant they were frequently
resident in London (Cregeen 1970:5, 10). Bearing all this in mind, it
is impossible to see the House of Argyll solely as a Highland kindred,
something explored in a little more detail in the next chapter.

Some Kilfinan landowners would have repeatedly traveled to
Lowland towns in their capacity as merchants, a role more fully explored in the next chapter. Other Improving landowners in Kilfinan
were of English or Lowland Scottish extraction and had only recently
bought their Highland estates when they began to Improve (again,
more on this in the next chapter). On top of this, literature promoting Improvement and advising on the practicalities of that process was
increasingly common from the seventeenth century in Scotland (see,
e.g., Fenton 1999:17–18).

That the Scottish Lowlands and England were the appropriate
places to look for exemplars for Improvement was outlined explicitly by
the Scottish Enlightenment. Enlightened views came to some, like the
Dukes of Argyll, through their direct involvement with Enlightenment
literati during the eighteenth century *floruit* of the movement. Others,
as many of the Improving landowners of Kilfinan, came to Enlightenment's main tenets later and through their membership of the emergent
middle class.

Enlightenment social theory not only described where exemplars
for change were to be found, but also provided legitimation for Improvement. It was an elaborate ideology. Stadial history coupled with a
particular conceptualization of human nature suggested that progress
to the Commercial Age was natural, desirable, and even inevitable. The

landowners of Kintyre and Kilfinan, according to this view, were merely hastening or aiding the unavoidable course of history. Added to this was a sense of independence whereby they were rendered free to alter the world at will.

Of course, placing Highland Improvement in its context, with reference to the Scottish Enlightenment and Lowland Scottish and English exemplars, does not fully explain why it happened. In the chapter to follow, I will argue Improvement was a definite social strategy on the part of the landowners in the case study areas, through which they sought to address certain significant social contradictions.

Improvement and the Landowner | 6

The first half of this chapter considers Improvement on the Argyll Estates in Kintyre. With Improvement, the Dukes of Argyll aimed to resolve a contradiction that had been evident in the structure of west Highland society for several centuries, that between individual claims and collective and hereditary claims to land and its resources, between the co-existence of the landlord–tenant–sub-tenant relationship and that of the clan–clan gentry. West Highland society was structured according to the landlord–tenant–sub-tenant relationship *and* that of the clan gentry-clan at one and the same time, from at least the late Medieval period. This situation is evident in the Gaelic terms *duthchas,* the collective heritage of the clan, and *oighreachd*, individual heritage. When these two relationships were aligned, as when the tenant's landlord was also their clan chief, this was not the site of conflict. However, change in legally defined landholding in Kintyre, in the wake of the forfeiture of the Lordship of the Isles in the late fifteenth century, resulted in the misalignment of *duthchas* and *oighreachd*, resulting in sometimes open conflict and in the constant potential for rebellion or resistance to the interests of the House of Argyll. They came to own land in Kintyre through their close connections with the Scottish Crown, but their control of the estate was threatened by continued counter-claims to the land, its population and resources, as *duthchas*, from Clan Donald.

Contradictory relationships and associated principles of landholding were therefore a prime area of conflict resulting in the instigation of Improvement. Improvement should be seen as part of a longer-term project of the Civilizing of the west Highlands and Islands. Previously, the Crown and their agents, the Argylls, had tried a variety of strategies in attempting to render the area more peaceful and loyal on their terms. These included the plantation of Lowland farmers and the creation of burghs like Campbeltown. Improvement was part of this political and social project aimed at resolving conflict in the area.

However, Improvement was fundamentally different from earlier Civilizing projects in aiming to undermine existing routine practice and, thus, undermine associated concepts of collective and hereditary heritage. In privileging the individual in routine practice, Improvement aimed to resolve the contradiction between *duthchas* and *oighreachd* in favor of the latter, with the House of Argyll as legally defined proprietors. Improvement also sought to undermine routine familial experience. From such routine practice a tenant's traditional, hereditary right to their holding made sense. In privileging the individual, Improvement made the ideology behind the individual lease knowable. Tenants could now be required to sign a lease pledging their loyalty to the House of Argyll, and would have no basis for a competing claim to their portion of the land. In redefining the structure of everyday life, Improvement sought to bring stability to the asymmetrical relationship between the House of Argyll and the population of their estates.

The second part of this chapter considers the case of Kilfinan. Some Improving landowners there came from long-established landowning families, others had only recently purchased their estates with the profits of trade or their profession. Many of the latter came from the Lowlands or England. There are clear differences in the biographies of all these landowners and landowning families, but, where we know enough about them, they all appear to be connected through the emergent middle class.

In Kilfinan, Improvement addressed a contradiction between the landowners' position as members of the emergent middle class and as proprietors of traditional Highland estates. In this case, landowners sought to maintain their middle class status by reorganizing their estates along capitalist lines and to conform to ideals commensurate with the tenets of Scottish Enlightenment thought. As we have seen, the Enlightenment justified Improvement by connecting it to Lowland Scotland and England where, it was thought, progressive rural society was to be found. Estates that did not Improve along those lines could, literally, have been seen as backward.

But Improvement in Kilfinan was not simply about the relationship between a landlord and their peers. As in Kintyre, Improvement changed the basis of interaction between landlord, tenant and sub-tenant. The contradiction inherent in the landlord-tenant-sub-tenant relationship became exposed in Kilfinan with the increasing involvement of landowners in commercial society. These landowners increasingly came to view their estates as resources to be exploited and they acted to undermine existing social connections with the tenantry, thus exposing the exploitative nature of their position in society. In a similar way as in Kintyre, but in a slightly different historical context, Improvement acted to naturalize the landlord's position as owner.

In both Kintyre and Kilfinan, Improvement was the result of the tensions inherent in society and the tensions between differently constituted social relationships. While it brings clarity to separate one contradictory relationship from another for the purpose of analysis, it is important to remember that each relationship did not exist in isolation. Rather, each relationship existed within a constellation of others, and the practice of each relationship impacted on the practice of others.

CLANSHIP AS A SOCIO-POLITICAL SYSTEM

The importance of the clan system, and the reason why it can be regarded as a system, lies in the multi-dimensional character of clans and their chiefs (Dodgshon 1998b:7–8). It is well known that clans were structured around kin-ties, real or assumed. However, it is important to view clans as more than just communities bonded by and stratified through such kin ties. The identity and position of a clan was also given meaning through their strategic control of land and its potential resources. These resources were exploited in the distinct ideological behavior, centered on feasting and feuding, that helped structure relationships within the clan. Control over land and resources were fundamental in maintaining social relationships in the west Highlands and Islands in this period.

Chiefs might secure control over land in a number of ways (Dodgshon 1998b:32–34). First, a chief might secure overarching control over his territories through the creation of canopy clans, where land was granted to their younger sons or to the more senior branches of the clan, the *uachdaran*. Otherwise, land could be granted out to cadet branches of the clan, with senior members of those branches serving as tacksmen, or *fir-tacsa*. These cadet branches would then proceed to fill their territories with kinsmen in a process of downward genealogical emplacement (Dodgshon 1998b:33), although it would also be necessary to grant land to non-kinsmen. This process meant that the physical topography underlying a chiefdom was overlain by a social topography. Bonds of manrent and friendship could also be used to extend ties of dependence, complementing and adding to the kin-group. Such alliances could foster more composite or aggregate clans.

The result of this process of territorial control was a close association of particular territories with specific kin or allied groups. In many cases, flux in territorial control could lead to conflict:

> The estates held by the clan elite, conveyed as their individual heritage, their *oighreachd*, were usually of lesser extent than the territories settled

by their clansmen for whose collective heritage, their *duthchas*, the *fine*
were trustees. Jeopardised or frustrated endeavours to align *oighreachd*
and *duthchas* created the grounds for feuding. (Macinnes 1996:38)

Shift in control of a territory from a landlord who also bore some
relationship under the clan system to the tenants of that territory to a
landlord who did not engendered potential conflict. The previous landlord, as clan chief or as a member of the clan gentry, the *fine*, still bore
responsibilities towards his former tenants and expected certain dues
from them. This could lead to feuding between different clans, but also
to obstruction and resistance by the tenants towards their new landlord (Macinnes 1996:38). The close relationship of territory and kinship
under the clan system was a potential source of conflict, when *duthchas*
and *oighreachd* were unaligned.

Another important aspect of the clan system was the place of the
ordinary population of the clan within the overall kinship structure, and
the degree to which they were bound into that system by genuine or
putative ties of kinship. This is of relevance in assessing where the
conflict inherent in the structuring of territorial relationships around
both *duthchas* and *oighreachd* lay. That is, was the ordinary tenant's
identity sufficiently defined by the kin-ties of their clan to cause them
to consider a change of landlord a source of conflict? Again, I refer back
to Dodgshon's discussion of the subject (Dodgshon 1998b:41–50).

From extant records showing patterns of naming, it would appear
that the ordinary Highlander could build up their identity with reference to different coordinates:

1) they could identify themselves with a patronymic, emphasizing
   their immediate genealogy, for example *John MacGillychallum
   vic Gillyffadrick* (individual then father then grandfather);
2) with reference to lateral relations, noting someone by their first
   name and then emphasizing their relationship to a brother or
   cousin, for example;
3) with reference to an epithet, with first name followed by a descriptive element e.g. *more/beg* (great/little);
4) and, with reference to a clan name, such as MacDonald.

In most cases, then, people defined themselves in relation to kin-
ties. This definition, however, was at various degrees of remove and
the coordinates referenced could vary. This variation was not random,
but was structured according to context. Patronymics were often used
in situations where it might be important to emphasize a hereditary
right to a holding and a share of the local community's resources, to

duthchas. For example, patronymics might be used in rentals where no tacksmen are listed and where townships are directly divided amongst the tenants, or where a tenant's landlord was not their chief.

The use of clan names also seems to have varied according to circumstance. Clan names could be used to draw on the support of a chief and they could also be used to challenge authority. For example, all the inhabitants of Inninmore in Morvern labeled themselves as Camerons, when it is unlikely they were, at a time when the landowner of the township was the Campbell Earl of Argyll (Cregeen 1968:163). In many cases, patronymics and clan names appear side by side.

It seems, then, that kin-ties to a wider clan were significant to the bulk of the population, but that significance was dependent on circumstance. In some instances it was seen as most important to emphasize hereditary rights to a holding and its associated resources. In such cases, it is possible that the identity of the current landlord might not be too significant as long as tenants were allowed to enjoy what they saw as their customary rights. In other instances, however, clan affiliation was seen as a significant enough aspect of identity to advertise, and this sometimes in protest at the fact that their current landlord was not the tenant's chief. It is possible that these two aspects of identity can be related, with tenants using a clan name as a form of protest against perceived threats to their traditional rights, rather than simply against a change in landlord.

Members of the farming population and the landed gentry alike in the west Highlands could mobilize their membership of a clan as a strategy in relation to their claims to certain resources or rights. The clan gentry might claim access to the resources, including people, of a given territory as the collective heritage of the clan, its *duthchas*. The name of the clan could be mobilized by those inhabiting a territory in the face of threats to their traditional rights to its resources, not least their right to hereditary occupancy of a holding.

Concepts of the community of the clan and of hereditary occupancy did not exist in isolation, however. They related to routine practice. In pre-Improvement routine, in just that period covered by Dodgshon's discussion of the structuring of the clan, we have seen that a *sense of community* and a *sense of family* were fostered (see Chapter 4). They also related to more ritualized relationships, like those of involved in feasting and feuding (see Dodgshon 1988).

In general terms, everyday experience of the world as part of a community would have made the more abstract idea of the community of the clan knowable. In other words, abstract notions of the clan would appear as common sense. Routine practice also helped to structure the clan in more tangible ways. The community of the *baile* was related to the clan in practice, through the tacksmen. While a tacksman's holding need not be confined to one *baile*, this was the prevalent pattern (Macinnes 1996:16). In some cases, the tacksman certainly lived within the *baile* (see, e.g., Stewart and Stewart 1988). Thus, the tacksmen were at once part of the community of the *baile* and members of the *fine*, the clan gentry. This link allowed the clan elite to mobilize a series of small groups who attained some coherence as such through their everyday experience of living and working together.

It was also argued in Chapter 4 that the pre-Improvement material environment and associated routine practice would have fostered experience of the world as part of a family. This form of experience above all took place in the domestic setting. Again, routine practice made certain more abstract understandings of the world knowable. In this case, concepts of hereditary occupancy were common sense as they were in agreement with general experience of everyday life as part of the family.

DUTHCHAS AND *OIGHREACHD* IN KINTYRE

Kintyre and the Lordship of the Isles

Conflict could arise, then, if *duthchas* and *oighreachd* became misaligned. This is just the situation we find in Kintyre. The Lordship of the Isles, of which Kintyre was a part, has been described as the largest and most powerful province of fifteenth century Scotland (Bannerman 1977:211; the brief historical sketch of the Lordship to follow here is derived from Steer and Bannerman 1977:201–205). The earliest known record of the title of Lord of the Isles is in an indenture of 1354 wherein the chief of Clan Donald, John, styled himself *Iohannes de Ile, Dominus Insularum*. However, the history of the institution may be extended back further if we consider his Gaelic title *Ri Innse Gall*, "King" or "Ruler" of the Hebrides, first ascribed to Somerled (d.1164). Somerled seems to have been responsible for bringing a level of political cohesion to an area including the Isles and parts of the western mainland. After Somerled's death the Clan Somairle, named after him, separated into three main branches: Clan Dugall, after Dugall son of Somerled; Clan Ruari, after Ruari grandson of Somerled; and, Clan Donald, after Donald, also a grandson of Somerled. Clan Donald was the paramount kin group in the Lordship by the fifteenth century and that most relevant to Kintyre.

Until the fourteenth century, the overlordship of Clan Somairle and, with it, the title *Ri Innse Gall* fluctuated amongst the leaders of the three main kindreds. However, the close association of the Clan Donald with the Bruces during the Wars of Independence in the early fourteenth century laid the foundations for their elevation within Clan Somairle. For example, the Clan Dugall possessions of Mull and Tiree were granted to Clan Donald in light of Clan Dugall's support for the Balliols in opposition to the Bruces. In the second quarter of the fourteenth century, Clan Donald allegiance switched to the Balliols and in 1336 they were granted extensive lands as a result, most of which were already under their authority. Their position seems to have been strong enough by this time, however, that David II, son and successor of Robert the Bruce, confirmed most of these lands. The territories of Clan Ruari were brought directly under the authority of Clan Donald through marriage in 1337. Clan Ruari disappeared as a distinct political entity thereafter. By the fifteenth century, therefore, Clan Donald had established their control both of the Lordship and of a patrimony of extensive lands within it.

The rise of Clan Donald within the Lordship is particularly relevant here as Kintyre formed one of their key territories. Kintyre came within the bounds of the later Lordship as far back as the time of Somerled, who was styled *Ri Indsi Gall & Cind Tire*, "King of the Hebrides and of Kintyre," on his death (Steer and Bannerman 1977:202). After his death, Kintyre passed to Clan Donald (Steer and Bannerman 1977:202). It was also amongst those territories granted by Balliol in 1336 (Steer and Bannerman 1977:203). Though excluded from the later grant of confirmation by David II, it could not conceivably have been alienated in any effective way from Clan Donald because of its position at the very center of their power (Steer and Bannerman 1977:203).

In the fifteenth century, Kintyre was possessed by that section of Clan Donald known variously as Clan Ian Mor (after Ian, or John, Mor (d.1427), younger brother to the Lord of the Isles), Clan Donald South, or the MacDonalds of Dunivaig and the Glens/MacDonalds of Islay and Antrim. The designations "of the Glens" and "of Antrim" refer to the fact that their territory extended into the north of Ireland. So, Kintyre not only formed part of the patrimony of Clan Donald, but of a senior lineage within that clan. The head of that lineage held a prominent position in the *Concilium Insularum*, the Council of the Isles. The heads of the kindreds who attended the council in the fifteenth century were divided into four grades, with the highest grade of "four great men of living of thair royal blude of Clan-donald lineally descendit" including MacDonald of Dunivaig (Bannerman 1977:221–222). Further, a deed of 1475 describes Donald Balloch of Dunivaig as "primus et principalis conciliarus" (Bannerman 1977:222, note 48).

The heads of Clan Ian Mor were probably primarily based on Islay, where the principle meeting place of the council is to be found on an island in Loch Finlaggan (on which see Caldwell and Ewart 1993). However, Kintyre was more than just territory to the Clan Donald, having a certain cultural significance. The Crown rentals for North and South Kintyre drawn up in 1505 and 1506, after the forfeiture of the Lordship, make interesting reading in this respect (see Bannerman 1977:219). They show the contemporary head of the MacMhuirichs, hereditary poets to the Lords of the Isles, possessing five named holdings *per po- etam*. Further, the MacIlshenaich harpists are also recorded as holding lands in the area. Hereditary bards and musicians played an important role in the feasts, in particular, that were an important aspect of the ideological behavior surrounding the control of resources and the territory from which they came (Dodgshon 1988; 1998b:8). The cultural importance of Kintyre in the fifteenth century is further underlined by the existence of a school of late Medieval monumental sculptors there, producing a corpus of carved stones that contributed to the distinctive sculptural tradition associated with the Lordship of the Isles (see Steer and Bannerman 1977 on this subject in general). The Kintyre school of sculptors, probably based at Saddell Abbey, came into being some time after 1425 and ceased operation before 1500, with the forfeiture of the Lordship (Steer and Bannerman 1977:48–50).

Forfeiture and Unrest: Kintyre and the Decline of the Lordship of the Isles

From the late fourteenth or early fifteenth century, the Lords of the Isles held a claim to the Earldom of Ross (Steer and Bannerman 1977:205). This came by virtue of the marriage of Donald, Lord of the Isles, to an heiress, in MacDonald eyes at least, to the Earldom. A campaign to make good her claim culminated in the battle of Harlaw in 1411 and the Crown's subsequent formal recognition that the right of inheritance to the Earldom belonged to Donald's son, Alexander. Despite this, the MacDonald's hold on the Earldom remained precarious and depended on their military presence and strength at any given time. Conflict with the Crown over attempts to consolidate their possession of the Earldom, together with a penchant for treating with the English, helped lead to the forfeiture of the Lordship in the late fifteenth century (Steer and Bannerman 1977:206–207). Forfeiture finally came in 1493. The weakness of the Lordship at that time and an expansionist policy of the Crown formed the context (Bannerman 1977:212–213; Nicholson 1974:541–542). Legal annexation of the Lordship's territories by the Crown, however, did not simply lead to its control of the area.

Crown annexation was followed by a series of military expeditions and the garrisoning of several key strongholds, which included the construction of a new castle at Loch Kilkerran, later the site of Campbeltown (Nicholson 1974:542–544). The Earl of Argyll played an increasingly prominent role in governing the former Lordship on behalf of the Crown. He was granted custody of Tarbert Castle in 1499; was an essential member of the commission of assessment, set up in 1500, to grant tacks of the lands of the Lordship excepting Islay and Kintyre; and, was to be the King's lieutenant-general in the lands subject to that commission (Nicholson 1974:544). Despite all this, the Crown had not introduced order, in its terms, to the region. Rather, it had created a power-vacuum that led to what the MacMhuirich seannachies recorded as "a great struggle among the Gael for power," a struggle that took three main forms (Nicholson 1974:548). First, there were several attempts to restore the Lordship up until the death of Donald Dubh in 1545. Second, the heads of cadet branches of the MacDonalds struggled to achieve some of the pre-eminence that had formerly belonged to the senior branch. And third, other clans strived to increase their territory and power at the expense of the MacDonalds.

There were at least seven major risings before the inhabitants of the Lordship finally accepted its forfeiture, risings in which Clan Ian Mor were prominent (Steer and Bannerman 1977:210). Indeed, the pronouncement of forfeiture did not become effective for more than 50 years, until the death of Donald Dubh, grandson of the forfeited Lord (Bannerman 1977:213). Despite this, Kintyre seems to have remained in Crown hands from soon after 1493. The Crown rentals of 1505 and 1506, previously mentioned, bear testament to this, as does that of 1541, which was drawn up after the Kintyre lands were inalienably annexed to the Crown in 1540 (McKerral 1948:12).

This is not to say that Clan Ian Mor had no interest in Kintyre in the sixteenth century. They survived the forfeiture and became the most powerful of the branches into which Clan Donald split (Stevenson 1980:22). In 1545, large tracts of land in Kintyre and elsewhere were granted to James MacDonald of Dunnyveg (McKerral 1948:14). He had restored the House of Dunnyveg and the Glens to its former power and prestige, being viewed by the Crown at this point as the most likely leader of the west Highlanders. However, this situation was not to last long. Following James' death in 1565, Somhairle Buidhe, his brother, seized possession of the clan's Antrim lands (Stevenson

1980:22). Clan Ian Mor thus split into the MacDonalds of Dunnyveg and the MacDonnells of Antrim, or Dunluce. The final downfall of the House of Dunnyveg came soon after. In 1607, Kintyre formed part of a Crown grant to the Campbells of Argyll following from a feud between the MacDonalds of Dunnyveg and the Macleans that came to involve most of the clans of the Western Isles, and as such led to serious Crown intervention (Stevenson 1980:23–27).

Clan Campbell and Clan Donald from the Late Sixteenth Century

The Campbells, as the MacDonalds, had supported Bruce in the Wars of Independence and profited thereby, mainly at the expense of the MacDougalls of Lorn (Steer and Bannerman 1977:210). They remained, however, within the confederacy of clans that looked to the authority of the Lords of the Isles, until the fifteenth century when they began to take a more independent line (Steer and Bannerman 1977:210). From that time, they began to distance themselves culturally from the Lordship. Within the Lordship, a distinct Gaelic identity was fostered. This can be seen archaeologically in the late Medieval carving tradition unique to the region (Steer and Bannerman 1977). The Campbells, on the other hand, increasingly fostered a Lowland identity from the fifteenth century. Again, there is surviving archaeological material that suggests this. Most notable is the collegiate church at Kilmun in Cowal erected by Sir Duncan Campbell of Lochawe in the mid fifteenth century, and where he and many other heads of the House of Argyll were subsequently buried (Cowan and Easson 1976:223; RCAHMS 1992:174–186). He was of that lineage of Clan Campbell later to become the Earls and, then, Dukes of Argyll. Significantly, this was the only collegiate church founded outside of the Lowlands (Steer and Bannerman 1977:210). The sculpture associated with Campbell burial at Kilmun is distinct from the Medieval West Highland tradition, with the effigies of Sir Duncan Campbell of Lochawe and his second wife related stylistically to Lowland Scottish examples, for instance (see RCAHMS 1992:179–181).

Campbell genealogies from the fifteenth century onward also display a marked Lowland orientation. The earliest surviving Campbell genealogy, of the first half of the fifteenth century, and another dating from about 1550 trace Campbell genealogy to a British (and thus Lowland) root (Sellar 1973:117). The earlier of the two takes the genealogy back to Arthur, and possibly Uther, and the later takes it back to the eponym of the British race, *Briotain*. These genealogies unquestionably claim a British descent for the Campbells (Sellar 1973:118), but it is also clear that a parallel Gaelic identity was maintained in this period, and in some form down to the eighteenth century (Gillies 1978:257–263). This shows that the Campbells were not simply attempting to divorce themselves from the Gaelic world. Indeed, the Campbells seem to have aspired to a prominent, even dominant, position in Gaelic society, which would have required them to place themselves culturally within that context. However, in aspiring to this position, they seem to have felt it necessary to distance themselves to some degree from the MacDonald Lords of the Isles and, so, tactically fostered a parallel British identity.

A close political relationship with the Scottish Crown was no doubt concerned in this fostering of a part Lowland identity. Certainly, this relationship was instrumental in the rise of the Campbells to a dominant position in the southwest Highlands (Cregeen 1968:153–156). The original Highland patrimony of the House of Argyll was the Barony of Loch Awe, although Colin Campbell of Loch Awe, created Earl of Argyll in 1457, moved the family seat to Inverary on Loch Fyne. For much of the fifteenth century, there is no evidence that the Campbells were in any way in conflict with the Lords of the Isles (Steer and Bannerman 1977:211). Indeed, it seems that they did not wish to destroy the Lordship itself, but to take over the position of power held by the MacDonalds as Lords of the Isles (Steer and Bannerman 1977:211). This takeover was instituted in the late fifteenth century, from the time when the Earls of Argyll became the Crown agents charged with the "daunting" of the west Highlands and Islands (Cregeen 1968:156–157). A commission to carry out the forfeiture decreed against the fourth Lord of the Isles was given to the first Earl in 1475, and with this the Campbells acquired some MacDonald territory, such as Knapdale in 1493, and extended their overlordship over many former MacDonald vassals. In some ways they did take over the position of the Lords of the Isles, receiving a commission of lieutenancy with fullest powers over the Lordship in 1500 and 1517 (Steer and Bannerman 1977:211–212). Despite the position of authority into which the Campbells then rose, there is no evidence of hostilities between them and the clans of the former Lordship between 1493 and 1529, and this in spite of major risings in the interval by MacDonald claimants to the Lordship (Steer and Bannerman 1977:212). The Crown evidently had considerable doubt about a large increase in Campbell power within the region and measures were taken to curb this (Steer and Bannerman 1977:212). It is from this point of view that we should see the MacDonalds of Dunnyveg and the Glens being received back into Crown favor for a time, as mentioned above.

The rise of the House of Argyll in this period, then, was at the expense of the former MacDonald Lords of the Isles in terms of political control of the region, with a stress on the continuity of the institution of the Lordship, in form if not name. Further, there was still scope for the Clan Ian Mor to maintain a position of some status and exercise a fair degree of territorial control in the area. The infamous feud between the MacDonalds and the Campbells does not seem to have broken out until the late sixteenth century, a period when the focus of Campbell aggrandization shifted from the takeover of the Lordship as a political institution to the acquisition of new territory (Hopkins 1998:18). The Lordship of the Isles had consisted of and exercised authority over various different clans. The Campbells, from the second half of the sixteenth century, threatened the very existence of those clans in moving to expand their territory. Control of a wide territory by assuming the authority of Lords of the Isles as heads of a confederacy of different clans had very different implications from achieving control of that territory through the expansion of personal ownership of land. In the latter situation, there was extensive scope for the *duthchas* (collective heritage) of a given clan to become severely compromised as it was increasingly unaligned with the *oighreachd* of the clan (the personal patrimony of the clan *fine*), as Campbell *oighreachd* expanded at its expense. It is perhaps no surprise, then, that when we turn to the specific case of Kintyre, acquisition of the territory by the Campbells was followed by serious unrest.

Kintyre in the Seventeenth Century: Campbell Territorial Expansion and Resulting Civil Unrest

The Campbells of Argyll began to acquire territory and influence in Kintyre in the sixteenth century. As early as 1502, the lands of Skipness were granted to Archibald, second Earl of Argyll, and in 1576 they obtained superiority to the church lands of Iona at Skierchanzie, with those of Whithorn at St. Ninians following in 1584 (McKerral 1948:13). Substantial territorial gains in the peninsula were made in the early seventeenth century when the then Earl of Argyll obtained a charter to the lands of the Lordship of Kintyre itself (McKerral 1948:13). This territorial advance into Kintyre largely came in the context of general Campbell territorial expansion, whereby the House of Argyll roughly quadrupled its estates (*oighreachd*) to not less than 500 square miles (Cregeen 1968:157). Further, the Earl of Argyll was by this time feudal superior of an area of around 3000 square miles in the Highlands and, as Sheriff of Argyll, the Earl represented the law of Scotland in the west Highlands, being charged with the administration of justice and having control of the region's official armed forces and ample powers to use them with impunity (Cregeen 1968:157).

In 1594, the lands of Angus MacDonald of Dunnyveg were forfeited as a result of actions related to a MacDonald-Maclean feud, but he was still in actual possession of a good part of them in 1605, if only as a Crown tenant (McKerral 1948:15–16). Following several Crown military expeditions, the Earl of Argyll was granted charter to the lands of Kintyre in 1607 in light of his services in subduing the MacGregors and others (McKerral 1948:15–19). This grant was on condition that all broken men of the surnames of MacDonald and Maclean were expelled from the lands granted and that none of these lands were set to anyone of the name MacDonald. The grant was made despite the Privy Council's opinion that trouble would arise from the MacDonalds as a result.

On receipt of the news of the change in possession of Kintyre, Sir James MacDonald, son of Angus MacDonald of Dunnyveg, attempted to escape his captivity in Edinburgh Castle, but was re-taken, brought to trial, and convicted of treason for earlier offences (see McKerral 1948:17–22 on this and what follows). He had been imprisoned in 1603 after actions, including an unsuccessful attempt on his father's life, aimed at settling the Crown-MacDonald dispute on his own behalf. Despite the conviction of treason, sentence was not carried out and he remained captive until 1615. In that year, he made a successful escape, finally reaching Islay and retaking Dunnyveg. From there he proceeded to Kintyre, raised his clan, and captured the castle at Kinloch or Lochhead (Campbeltown). This rebellion was ultimately unsuccessful and Sir James fled the country, returning to London on a pardon in 1620, where he died. Sir James' death, and that of his father previously in 1614, ended the male line of the MacDonalds of Dunnyveg.

Subsequent to this, the main threat to Campbell control of Kintyre came from the MacDonnells of Antrim and from the population of the peninsula itself (McKerral 1948:34–71, 114–130). In 1635 Lord Lorne (first son of the Earl of Argyll) actually granted charter of the lands and Lordship of Kintyre to Viscount Dunluce (son of the first Earl of Antrim, who was head of the family of MacDonnell of Antrim). This followed from Lorne's displeasure that control of Kintyre had been granted to his younger half-brother. However, the Privy Council stopped the grant to Antrim and Kintyre was granted to Lorne in 1636. On his insistence, Lochhead castle was garrisoned and a proclamation was issued warning the people of Kintyre not to attend any courts set up by the MacDonnells. From that time, the MacDonnells recurrently jeopardized the House of Argyll's position in Kintyre through military expedition, real or threatened.

With the first Bishops' War of 1639, the Earl of Antrim was fully expected to invade the west of Scotland, with Lochhead perceived as the most likely landing place. In response to this perceived threat, the first, and only, Marquis of Argyll constructed an entrenched camp on the north side of the Loch, Fort Askamylnemoir, now commemorated in the place names Trench Point and Fort Argyll. However, the threat of invasion waned with the victory of the Covenanters in 1640. The fort was maintained, however, and a grant of permission to keep it manned speaks of the "known inmitie" of the Earl of Antrim and of Clan Donald towards the Marquis and his friends.

Maintenance of the fort was perhaps prudent, for in 1644 surviving lineages of Clan Ian Mor again posed a threat to Argyll's position. In that year, the Marquis of Montrose took up arms on behalf of King Charles I, and against Argyll. Montrose found an ally in the Earl of Antrim, who sent a force of some 1500 to join him under the command of his cousin, Allaster, or Alexander, MacDonald of Colonsay. The Colonsay MacDonalds were, like the Antrims, a branch of the Clan Ian Mor. Allaster fought with Montrose for over a year, but after the Battle of Kilsyth in 1645 split off to wage a private war against the Campbells, aiming to win back the MacDonalds' old patrimony of Islay and Kintyre. For two years from 1645, Allaster and his father, Coll Ciotach, worked their will on the inhabitants of Campbell lands in Argyll (McKerral 1948:44). Argyll's estates were extensively raided with houses burnt, their inhabitants slain, crops destroyed, and cattle driven off. The MacDonalds actually took possession of Kintyre and, in 1647, the Marquis of Argyll reported to Parliament that he had had no rents from his Kintyre lands in three years. It is notable that in all the provisions for ameliorating the affects of the raids none was made for Kintyre, which was outside of Campbell and Crown influence at the time. In 1647, an expedition to Kintyre ended MacDonald control of the district.

For the remainder of the seventeenth century, threats to Campbell control were less overt in nature, but the peninsula was continually held under suspicion of being a nest of rebellion. This suspicion continued into the eighteenth century in the context of the Jacobite rebellions. Suspicion of rebelliousness, at times and in specific circumstances, extended beyond the indigenous population to include members of the Lowland plantations that Argyll, ironically, had fostered in an attempt to increase the security of his control of the area (see below). This climate of suspicion can be seen in the context of the Pentland Rising of

1666. Although Argyll had not been asked to take to the field against the rebels and on behalf of the Crown, he proceeded to Kintyre on his own initiative. After rounding up the entire Lowland colony there he was able to state that although he found the place in no rebellious state, the people were not principled as he wished (McKerral 1948:115). Around this time, Argyll determined to have the sub-tenants on his Kintyre lands each take out a written lease. He had some control over the activities of the tacksmen through written leases, but their sub-tenants did not hold land directly of him or by written agreement and were seen to be freer to engage in political activity opposed to his own interests. In his eyes they had formed an unwelcome clique.

That the indigenous Highland population remained a problem for Argyll can be seen in the context of his own rebellion of 1685. During this, he managed to recruit many of the Kintyre Lowlanders. However, none of the old MacDonald vassals joined him and some even joined the Marquis of Atholl, positioning themselves against Argyll.

Argyll's suspicion of the loyalty of the population of Kintyre continued into the eighteenth century. During the '45, part of a regiment was dispatched to Tarbert at the northern tip of the peninsula by Colonel Campbell (Argyll's cousin). This was with a view to controlling the southern approach to Inverary from Knapdale and Kintyre, following intelligence that a force under MacDonald of Largie and others was to advance that way to join the Jacobite army (Ferguson 1951:25–26). Having said this, sections of Kintyre society, most notably the Lowland colonists, were considered loyal. Upon the arrival of General Campbell (the Colonel's father) in Campbeltown, he "found 450 men rais'd for His Majesty's service in that corner of the country and ready to march at one day's notice" (quoted in Ferguson 1951:49).

The Legacy of Unrest: Improvement and the Civilizing of Kintyre

From the late sixteenth century, James VI sought to deal with unrest in the west Highlands through means other than the military. In a series of legislative actions, he attempted to pacify the region by *Civilizing* its inhabitants, according to his understanding of the term. Civilizing essentially involved undermining the traditional basis of clanship and re-structuring Highland and Island society in a way more akin to that of the Lowlands. For example, in 1597:

> The Kingis Majestie . . . found it meit and expedient, baith for the reductioun of the Illis to his Heines obedience, establisching of justice and quietnes, and

furthsetting of his Hienes commoditie and proffeit within the samyn, that
certane tounis should be erected and sett doun in Kintyre, Lochabir, and
the Lewis, upoun commodious pairtis maist proper for the saidis effectis.
(reproduced in Masson [ed.] 1882:455)

Burghs had long been a feature of Lowland society and are clearly
associated here with the maintenance of Crown control. As we shall
see below, the suggestion that a burgh be planted in Kintyre was soon,
though not immediately, acted upon.

Perhaps the best-known piece of legislation associated with the
process of Civilizing is the Statutes of Iona (1609). In the Statutes,
an attempt was made to systematically undermine the practices that
sustained feasting and feuding and, thus, played an important role
in the display behavior that ideologically structured the clan system
(Dodgshon 1998b:105–107). Such legislation, and other associated actions, in part suggested a strategy to the House of Argyll in securing its
control of Kintyre and other of its estates.

Following the grant of Kintyre to the Argylls, they sought to Civilize
the area. In the seventeenth century, this project largely found form
in plantation. The first phase of plantation involved the creation of
the burgh at Lochhead, later Campbeltown (McKerral 1948:23–29).
Originally, the Campbell charter to lands in Kintyre had been granted
in feu-farm, with attendant feu-duties owed. In 1609, the Exchequer
passed an Act discharging the Earl of Argyll from the payment of
these feu-duties on condition that he planted a burgh in Kintyre. Further, the conditions included that this burgh should be inhabited by
"Lowland men and trafficking burgesses" (quoted in McKerral 1948:24).
On these terms, the idea was to create not only a burgh in Kintyre,
but also a Lowland plantation. Such plantation was a common means
at the time of addressing political and other disputes, as with the
settlement of the Fife Adventurers in Lewis around 1600 and the
plantation of Ulster about 1610. The political context of the plantation of Kintyre is further underlined by the conditions of the char-
ters granted to the first of the Lowland planters. These forbade the
sub-leasing or sub-feuing of any of the lands granted to those of the
names of MacConnell or MacDonald, Maclean, MacLeod, MacAllaster,
or MacNeill.

Despite a Decreet of the Lords of Council in 1609 giving Argyll
permission to eject 53 Kintyre tenants of old stock, the creation of the
burgh seems to have been delayed until at least 1617. This is when the
Earl received an Act of Ratification with regard to his Kintyre lands.
Perhaps in part due to this delay, the planned clearance of indigenous
Kintyre tenants did not take place.

The main phase of Lowland plantation seems to have begun later, under the Marquis of Argyll, from around 1650 (McKerral 1948:80–86, 118–119). The initiative for this phase of plantation came not from the Crown, but directly from the Marquis himself and this plantation differed in its constitution. Grants of land were now given to Lowlanders higher on the social scale than the original Lochhead burgesses, including lairds and barons. These second phase planters were commonly connected to the Marquis through the Covenanting party. Grants were also made to members of the Clan Campbell from other parts of Argyllshire. These grantees then sub-let, as tacksmen, to tenants from their own estates. McKerral (1948:80) has suggested two motives for this phase of plantation. First, the intention was to secure a strong political and, if necessary, military backing for the Marquis in the area. Second, the plantation introduced tenants to recover the value of the Kintyre estate, recently wasted through war, famine, and plague. These plantations began in 1650 and continued through the next quarter century and beyond. The first planters of this phase seem to have settled principally in the old parishes of Kilkerran, Kilchousland, Kilkivan, Kilmichael, and at Saddell. However, from 1669 settlement increasingly focused in the far south of Kintyre, in Southend parish, which was by 1678 the center of gravity of the Lowland population, along with the burgh at Lochhead.

We can perhaps understand these projects of Lowland plantation better if we return to consider the cultivated orientation of the House of Argyll towards Lowland Scottish society. The cultivation of genealogies emphasizing a Lowland ancestry was connected to their course of action with regard to securing control of Kintyre. A British ancestry is particularly emphasized in Campbell genealogies of the fifteenth century. However, the active creation of Campbell genealogy continued into the seventeenth and eighteenth centuries. Indeed, in these later centuries the writing of manuscript histories of the family seems to have been a considerable growth industry (Sellar 1973:112). These accounts all tell roughly the same story and have been referred to as the later approved Campbell tradition (Sellar 1973:112). They all derive from two earlier seventeenth century manuscript histories of which that given in Duncanson's *Ane Accompt of the Genealogie of the Campbells* will serve here as illustration of the main emphases (see Sellar 1973:112–117).

In this, the earlier tradition of British ancestry remains and the line is traced back to Arthur, who is given a son, Smerevie or Merevie (Merlin), supposedly born at Dumbarton. The main difference to earlier genealogies occurs in the eleventh generation after Smerevie. There, it is related that Malcolm son of Duibne and grandson of

Diarmaid O'Duibne traveled to France where he married the heretix of Beochamps (or Campus Bellus), niece to William the Conqueror. Malcolm's second son, Gillespic, returns to Scotland where he marries his cousin, Eva, the heiress of Lochawe. This account also includes the popular etymology of the name of Campbell that derives it from *de Campo Bello* and, thus, relates it to Beauchamps by way of *Campus Bellus* and *Bellus Campus*. Campbell genealogy in the seventeenth and eighteenth centuries, then, attempted to reconcile a Gaelic past (particularly prominent with Diarmaid O'Duibne, a companion of Finn), with earlier traditions of British descent. Further, the name of Campbell and the ancestry of that family are linked to a Norman past and, even, to William the Conqueror himself.

The creation of a part Lowland identity would have accorded well with the Campbell's important role in both Highland and wider Scottish affairs in this period and their ownership of large estates in both the Highlands and Lowlands (as noted briefly in the last chapter).

Summary

So, from the late fifteenth century in Kintyre a struggle for political control of the area was bound up with changing control of the land and its resources. Eventually, this resulted in the misalignment of *duthchas* and *oighreachd* and conflicting and contradictory claims to land in the peninsula and the support of its population. By the seventeenth century, the Campbells, and the House of Argyll in particular, were the dominant legally defined landowners in Kintyre. However, various descendants of Clan Donald, or allied kindreds, maintained claims to land in Kintyre as the collective heritage of their clan. Even when this misalignment of *duthchas* and *oighreachd* did not result in overt conflict, the peninsula was considered a potential nest of rebellion against the House of Argyll and, in many instances, the Scottish Crown.

Efforts of the Crown and the Campbells to Civilize the area were intended to address opposition to their interests there. With plantation this is obvious, as tenants disposed to Argyll physically replaced the old stock. Plantation also worked on a more subtle level, being intended to introduce Lowland practices that were considered more lawful and peaceful. Most notable is the attempt to introduce commerce through the creation of the burgh at Lochhead and, thus, perhaps the attempt to draw the population of Kintyre into a more concrete relationship with the rest of the country through trade.

Thus, from the early seventeenth century, the House of Argyll sought to address opposition to their ownership of land in Kintyre by introducing Lowland people and practices. Improvement should thus be situated as part of a long-lived process. The House of Argyll had actively been cultivating their association with the Lowlands from at least the fifteenth century. This is clear from the manipulation of their genealogy. The fact that suspicion of unrest in Kintyre continued into the eighteenth century, however, shows that the Civilizing of Kintyre had not been entirely successful. While many of Kintyre's occupants may have been far from rebellious, the conditions still existed for them to question the legitimacy of Campbell *oighreachd* in the area. The possibility of thinking in terms of the clan and in terms of their own hereditary right to land and its resources still existed.

Although Improvement is connected to earlier actions, like plantation, it is also radically different. Improvement was different from earlier Civilizing projects in two main ways. First, it became a sustained enterprise where previous projects had been more sporadic. Secondly, Improvement sought to fundamentally alter routine practice and the everyday environment on a wide scale. Where previous projects involved relatively small-scale plantation or attempts to induce aspects of Lowland practice, Improvement in Kintyre sought to undermine routine practice in such a way as to make the ideology of clanship unknowable. With Improvement, experience of the daily round was increasingly from the perspective of the individual isolated from community and family. Claims by an absent clan gentry to the resources of farms of Kintyre and the loyalty of their inhabitants would become increasingly absurd in such a situation. Further, hereditary claims to occupancy of a given portion of land would equally be undermined. At the same time, claims to legitimate legal ownership by the House of Argyll, as their personal property, would make more sense, as would occupation of the land on individual lease. Improvement, for the House of Argyll, primarily sought to resolve the contradiction between *duthchas* and *oighreachd* in favor of *oighreachd* and, thus, to legitimate ownership of their vast estate to their tenantry.

IMPROVEMENT IN KILFINAN AND THE EMERGENT MIDDLE CLASS

Contradiction in the nature of the land rights of the gentry, between *duthchas* and *oighreachd*, is significant for Kilfinan. As we shall see below, many Kilfinan landowners of the Improving period were in the same position as the House of Argyll in Kintyre in that they owned their estates as private property, *oighreachd*, but were not of the clan of their tenants. Many came from a Lowland or English background and only purchased their Highland estates in the nineteenth century. This change in landownership could have exposed the exploitative nature of the relationship between landlord and tenant, as it had in Kintyre. Some Improving landowners in Kilfinan came from old stock, from kindreds who had been established there for centuries. However, the contradictory nature of their relationship with their tenantry was equally exposed. Commercialization of these established estates had been underway for some time prior to the nineteenth century and the period of Improvement, and the connections essential to the clan had been seriously undermined as a result.

Contradiction between *duthchas* and *oighreachd* is not known to have resulted in overt conflict in Kilfinan. There is no real indication that landowners' possession of their estates was threatened in the same way as in Kintyre. However, the potential for conflict was there and an influx of new landowners in the nineteenth century could only have made the nature of the landlord–tenant–sub-tenant relationship more starkly obvious. The tenantry could have mobilized their connection to a clan and their hereditary right to occupation of a holding if their perceived traditional rights were threatened. For many, these concepts would have remained viable well into the nineteenth century, considering the continuance of pre-Improvement routine practice and the pre-Improvement material environment into that century. MacDonald lands in Kintyre were granted to the Campbells and the wider Clan Donald maintained a claim to these lands, their resources and population, as *duthchas*. This is perhaps the vital difference with Kilfinan, where the land transfers in question occurred much later and in a different way. Many of the new landlords of the nineteenth century bought their estates from the previous owner, and these estates were not subject to any ensuing counter-claim. This does not mean that the population of an estate could not have continued to maintain notions of their clan membership or hereditary rights, but their capacity to resist their landlords was compromised by the lack of a wider clan context.

Other relationships are also key to our understanding of Improvement in Kilfinan. One significant issue in Kilfinan is the contradiction between the landowners' simultaneous position as members of the emergent middle class and as proprietors of traditional Highland estates, traditional as seen from a middle class perspective. In considering this below, it will first be necessary to trace the history of landholding in the parish. No comprehensive summary of landholding in Kilfinan has previously been published and that given below is a summary of a more detailed analysis that I have chosen to abbreviate here for clarity (see Dalglish 2000:289–304; some material is available in Anon. 1871; Atkinson et al. 1993; Bannatyne Club 1854; Barrow 1981; Cairns 1961; Lamont 1914; Marshall 1983; McKechnie 1938; RCAHMS 1992; Renwick [ed.] 1908; Timperley [ed.] 1976; useful unpublished nineteenth century Valuation Rolls and Road Assessments are held by the Argyll and Bute District Archive, Lochgilphead, under the references 1/13/6; 1/13/33; 1/13/47; 1/73/12; 1/73/13; DR1/12). Some Improving landlords were from long established landholding families in the parish, most notably the Lamonts. However, their landholding history is not straightforward, periodically losing their lands in the aftermath of the Civil Wars of the mid-seventeenth century, for example. This trauma in landownership is particularly significant for the ensuing and connected commercial reorientation of the estate economy.

This reorientation encouraged already existing commercial activities, particularly trade in cattle, and led to the eventual inclusion of the Lamont gentry in the middle class, emergent from the late eighteenth century. Membership of the middle class was something the Lamonts had in common with other Kilfinan landowners of the nineteenth century. As suggested in the last chapter, middle class membership was the common point of contact with the Scottish Enlightenment for most of them.

Continued membership of the middle class engendered a contradiction between their position within that middle class and within their estates. With the emergence of the middle class, its attendant social relations, and Enlightenment-based ideology, an unImproved estate would have been seen as backward. This would be in the sense that such an estate existed in a stage of society one step behind that of the urban middle class and the Commercial Age. So, from the late eighteenth century, established landowners long engaged in mercantile activity and new landowners who purchased estates with the profits of trade or their profession can both be seen to have Improved their estates as a strategy in establishing or maintaining their membership of the middle class. Estates organized in terms of certain forms of social relationship where the individual was articulated within the community and kin-group were a threat to middle class ideals in that they hampered the free exploitation of the land (and its inhabitants) by autonomous individuals. They stood in the way of commercial progress.

In Kilfinan, the landowner's relationship with their tenantry was transformed as the landowner addressed another social concern, inclusion within the middle class. It is important to remember that both changing relationships are basic to our understanding of Improvement in Kilfinan. Each is as important as the other and both are reflexively linked. Improvement, in promoting the autonomous individual, serviced the landowners concern for middle class inclusion and also acted to naturalize the landlord–tenant–sub-tenant relationship in the face of the increasing exposure of the commercial and exploitative nature of the estate. Some estates in Kilfinan sought commercial re-orientation from the mid-seventeenth century at least. In the nineteenth century, the existence of the estate as a commodity to be bought, sold and exploited was starkly underlined by an influx of many new landowners. Improvement thus addressed the social contradiction inherent in the landlord's relationship with their tenantry.

The Landholding History of Kilfinan

The parish of Kilfinan was, at the time of the first Statistical Account in the early 1790s, largely divided into two unequal parts (McFarlane 1983:204–205). At that time, the Campbells of Otter were proprietors of nearly the whole of the smaller northern division, Otter, and the Lamonts of Lamont of the most part of the southern division, Kerry. This pattern of landholding, with the parish divided into two major geographical divisions and essentially between two different kin groups, can be traced back into the late Medieval period. In the nineteenth century, the Lamonts remained dominant in landholding terms until the sale of their property there in 1893. Alongside this, the Otter estate fragmented, with an influx of new landowners there and in some of the minor holdings of the parish.

The story of the largest estate in the parish, Kerry, is largely one of continuity. However, this apparent continuity masks periodic traumas to ownership and the erosion of the Lamonts' territorial and social influence outside of Kilfinan. A recurrent theme is their loss in opposition to the Campbells.

In the late twelfth century Laumon, the eponym of the kindred, sided with Balliol and the MacDougalls against Bruce. In general, those Highland kindreds who sided with the victorious Bruce faction benefited in local and regional terms, while those who sided with Balliol suffered (see, e.g., McDonald 1997:Chapter 6). This is partly true for the Lamonts. The Campbells gained territory in Cowal at their expense. However, diplomatic initiative seems to have led to the survival of the Lamonts as a locally significant kindred and to have allowed them to retain a portion of their lands.

In the fifteenth century, we witness the consolidation of the Lamont chief's position in territorial terms and in social and political terms as head of the clan. This is to be seen in the erection of the Barony of Inveryne in 1472, the privileges of the Barony including the superiority of several Lamont cadet lairdships that had previously been largely independent. At this time, the chiefs of the Lamonts held their lands in two main blocks, the Nether Cowal estate in Inverchaolain parish and the Kerry estate in Kilfinan. Despite an apparent continuity in the records of landholding of the fifteenth century and the mid-eighteenth century, there were fluctuations and serious reversals in the interim.

In the fifteenth and into the sixteenth centuries, the Lamont chief's sphere of influence and landholding was not only consolidated, but expanded. This was also a period of friendly relations with the Campbells and the two situations are probably related. Through the sixteenth century, new lands were acquired in Kilfinan, elsewhere in Cowal, and beyond. The holdings of one significant Lamont cadet family were absorbed into the Barony of Inveryne. In the later sixteenth century, relations with the Campbells and the Crown soured, but serious conflict was avoided. The early seventeenth century saw another period of the pacification of Lamont-Campbell relations, as well as the fostering of good relations with the Crown. At that time, Lamont landholding remained fairly stable, though a few lands in Kilfinan previously sold by the kindred were re-acquired.

The period of the Civil Wars in the mid-seventeenth century is one of the most significant in this narrative for our understanding of subsequent Improvement, and I will return to it later. During the Wars, the Lamonts eventually sided with the Royalists, against the Covenanters and the Campbells. This led to the execution of many of the *fine*, the wasting of Lamont lands, and the forfeiture of the estates of the clan gentry. This forfeiture was not permanent and the bulk of the estates, along with the Barony of Inveryne, were restored by the end of the century.

By the mid-eighteenth century, the position of the chiefs, then referred to as Lamont of Lamont, was further strengthened by the consolidation of the Lamont cadetships under their personal ownership. This was a significant change in the manner in which the clan's territory was controlled. Previously, control had been achieved through a territorial umbrella of cadet kindreds. Now it took the form of personal ownership. There was some increase in Lamont of Lamont holdings in the later eighteenth century when, as mentioned above, they held the largest estate in Kilfinan. For the whole of the nineteenth, until the sale of the estate in 1893, the estate remained static overall.

So, from at least the fifteenth century to the end of the nineteenth, the Kerry estate remained a fairly stable Lamont possession, despite

serious fluctuation in their landholding elsewhere and with the notable exception of the immediately post-Civil War period. This stands
in marked to contrast to the situation in Kintyre. There, Campbell expansion in the wake of the forfeiture of the MacDonald Lordship of the
Isles resulted in a serious misalignment of *oighreachd* and *duthchas*.
Conflict between the legal right of ownership over and the traditional
kin-based relations within the territory in question was the core problem addressed by Improvement.

The Lamonts had been on the receiving end of Campbell aggran-
dizement, most notably in the fourteenth and seventeenth centuries.
The extent of their territorial and social control had been reduced as
Campbell estates expanded. Lamont *duthchas* and *oighreachd* did conceivably become seriously misaligned as a result of this process. However, in this case, as with other kindreds such as the MacDonalds, the
situation was the reverse of that experienced by the Campbells. If anything, and theoretically, any attempt to restore Lamont territorial control to its height could perhaps more properly have been based in the
structuring of social and territorial relations under clanship than those
of capitalism. However, as mentioned, in the eighteenth century if not
before, the Lamonts of Lamont themselves began to undermine the traditional structure of their clan. The emphasis became firmly placed on
personal ownership of clan territory under the person of the chief as
landlord.

Thus, Improvement in the case of the Lamonts cannot be explained
in the same way as Improvement on the Argyll Estates in Kintyre, although the problems of social and territorial control resulting from the
misalignment of *duthchas* and *oighreachd* remain relevant. Lamont
Improvements in Kilfinan have to be explained with reference to a further context. This is their increasing involvement in mercantile activity
and the society of the nearby Clyde burghs, from the early seventeenth
century. This context perhaps became even more significant after the
Civil Wars.

Throughout the rest of the parish, the history of landholding stands
in contrast to the (troubled) continuity of Kerry. The Otter estate, noted
as the second largest in Kilfinan in the 1790s, enjoyed some kind of stability from the later Middle Ages until the early nineteenth century,
but with a major change in ownership. The MacEwens controlled Otter
in the fifteenth century and probably the fourteenth, if not before.
Ownership passed to the Campbells of Otter during the fifteenth century and this most probably happened by peaceful means.

Little is known of the subsequent history of the estate up until
the eighteenth century. However, it seems that Otter expanded in the

aftermath of the Civil Wars. This seems largely to have been at the expense of the Lamonts, though certain lands passed through several hands before eventually ending up with the Campbells of Otter. Certainly from that time, and most likely before, the Otter Campbells were politically aligned with the House of Argyll. This placed them in opposition to the Lamonts during the Civil Wars. Support for Argyll continued in the 1685 uprising and during the first Jacobite rebellion.

In the second half of the eighteenth century, the size of the Otter estate remained stable overall. There was some flux in the ownership of individual holdings, however. This period represents the initial significant phase of a process whereby a new group of proprietors came to be established in the parish. In many cases, they were new to the Highlands. In the second half of the eighteenth century, several farms on the Otter estate passed into the ownership of three of these new heritors—Mungo Campbell, John MacIvor, and Thomas Harkness. Two of these, Campbell and MacIvor, were later to become prominent landowners in the district. However, the overall size of Otter was maintained by the absorption of the small estate of the McLeas of Lindsaig. The McLeas themselves had only recently acquired land in the parish, at some time in the eighteenth century, with profits from mercantile activity. They may previously have held this land, though, for service as surgeons and notaries to the Lamonts.

The first half of the nineteenth century saw the intensification of change in landholding. This part of the process can perhaps be divided into two main phases. Although there were significant changes in landholding at the end of the nineteenth and beginning of the twentieth centuries, it is the first half of the nineteenth century that is of importance here. This was the period when intensive Improvement began.

First, by 1818, the Campbells of Otter were bankrupt and their loss of the Otter estate at that time resulted in its fragmentation. Several farms eventually passed to John MacIvor in 1826. These farms and MacIvor's previous acquisitions were formed into the new estate of Ardmarnock. Two further new estates were created from the remains of Otter. First was Ballimore, owned by Mungo Nutter Campbell. Second was a smaller incarnation of the Otter estate, also under Campbell ownership. Thus, by 1844, three new estates had been created, largely at the expense of Otter. These estates were the most significant in extent in Kilfinan after Kerry.

The next significant phase belongs to the mid-nineteenth century. Then, two of these new estates changed hands. By the early 1860s, the estate of Otter had passed to Patrick Rankine. Ardmarnock passed to Dr. John Nicol of Liverpool in 1852.

Alongside the creation of these three new major estates, several small estates changed hands through the eighteenth and nineteenth centuries. The majority of the small estates existing around 1750 were subsumed within Kerry and Otter during the remainder of the eighteenth century. Others were in the hands of a Dr. Colquhoun, an Andrew MacFarlane, and of John MacIvor by the start of the nineteenth century. These were subsequently all included in the Ardmarnock estate under John MacIvor. There were two small estates that survived from around 1750 into the nineteenth century, although they did change hands. These were originally the holdings of John Murray of Blackbarony and Colin MacLachlan. By 1802, they had passed to Arthur MacArthur Stewart and John Moodie of Inins respectively. By 1844, the first estate had passed to Niell Malcolm of Poltalloch and the latter to Arthur Scoular of Inans. A new estate, if that word can be used for a holding of one farm, had been created with the transfer of Calves from MacArthur Stewart's estate to John Oldham. Calves, renamed Glencaladh, passed to George Robert Stephenson by the beginning of the 1880s. The other two holdings remained with the Malcolm and Scoular families.

The main estate in the parish, Kerry, was owned throughout the period of Improvement, and previously, by the Lamonts. A local and established family likewise owned the estate of Otter up until the early nineteenth century. It remains to establish the background of the other landowners of the eighteenth and nineteenth centuries.

As we have seen, by the early nineteenth century, the Otter estate had absorbed some smaller estates that had probably belonged to local families (Campbells and McLeas). However, during the early nineteenth century Otter fragmented. A portion passed to John MacIvor. He had also acquired several other small estates in the area. Although it is not specifically certain who John MacIvor was, there is a reasonable chance that he was either local or had local connections. The MacIvors were a sept of Clan Campbell (Anon. 1871:172–178). The main branch of the family is synonymous with the Campbells of Asknish (in Knapdale), which family preferred that surname to MacIvor from the late seventeenth century. Evidence of the interchangeability of these names is to be seen in several seventeenth century sasines relating to that family and to other branches (e.g. Campbell [ed.] 1933:100; [ed.] 1934:10, 69, 128–129, 136). If John MacIvor of Ardmarnock was not of the family of Asknish, which was commonly referred to as Campbell from around 1700, he may still have had strong local connections.

In the mid-nineteenth century, Ardmarnock passed to the Nicols. As has been said, the first Nicol of Ardmarnock was a medical doctor from Liverpool. The estate had, thus, passed to an English professional and to someone quite unlike the traditional landed proprietors of the region. Ardmarnock remained in Nicol hands into the twentieth century.

The main portion of Otter fragmented into the estates of Ballimore and (a reduced) Otter. At its inception, Ballimore was the property of Mungo Nutter Campbell and remained with his family through the nineteenth century. As with MacIvor, it is possible that Campbell had strong local connections or might have been of a local family. However, what information is available relates to his life in Glasgow. From the burgh records it seems that Campbell was a prominent Glasgow burgess, presumably a merchant of some description, in the first half of the nineteenth century. He was elected Dean of Guild in 1822 and 1823 and Provost in 1824 and 1825 (Renwick [ed.] 1940:697; [ed.] 1941:57, 122, 174, 223).

It is unclear who the Campbells who owned the reduced estate of Otter were. They may have been of the same family as the previous Campbells of Otter, or have been related. This estate passed to the Rankines in the mid-nineteenth century. Again, little is known of them. Certainly, they were not established landowners in the district. No Rankines at all appear in a Valuation Roll of 1751 for Argyll (Timperley [ed.] 1976:28–45).

Of the smaller landholders in the parish, little can be said of most. John Murray of Blackbarony owned the estate of Inniens, Calves, and Blackbarony in 1751. The Murrays of Blackbarony had held that title and barony in Peebleshire in the south east of Scotland from the late Middle Ages (Burke 1856:720). The estate passed to Arthur MacArthur Stewart by 1802. The MacArthurs held a small amount of land in Cowal in 1751, and small pockets of land elsewhere in Argyll (Timperley [ed.] 1976:31–33). By that time, Stewart holdings in Argyll were confined to Lismore and Appin, although Stewart expansion from Renfrewshire in the Medieval period had previously given them estates in Cowal (Rennie 1993:73; Timperley [ed.] 1976:40–41). So, on his name alone it is possible that Arthur MacArthur Stewart had connections to local landed family, but this of course remains pure speculation.

By the mid-nineteenth century, and from then into the twentieth century, most of this small estate belonged to the Malcolms of Poltalloch. They were a local kindred (see Macinnes 1998a:173–174). They had originally been a satellite family of the Clan Campbell. They became established as landowners in Mid-Argyll in the sixteenth century and consolidated that position during the seventeenth. However, their real rise as significant proprietors in the area came on top of the fortune they acquired as colonial adventurers in the wake of the Union of Parliaments in 1707. Principally, they were plantation owners in Jamaica, which allowed them to cut loose from political clientage to the House of Argyll and involved the re-orientation of their interests to the Imperial context. The latter process is witnessed by the Anglicization of their name from MacCallum to Malcolm.

A small portion of MacArthur Stewart's estate, Calves, passed first to John Oldham by 1844 and subsequently to George Robert Stephenson. Again, little is known of these landowners and neither came from established landholding families in Argyll (see Timperley [ed.] 1976:28–45).

The other small estate that survived from 1751 into and through the nineteenth century was Innens. In 1751 this belonged to Colin MacLachlan. It is possible that he was related to the MacLachlans of MacLachlan who were significant landowners in the neighboring parish of Strathlachlan. That family was established in the west of Cowal by the thirteenth century at least (Rennie 1993:72). Innens passed to John Moodie by 1844 and then to Arthur Scoular. Yet again, little is known of these two and they do not belong to established Argyll landowning families (see Timperley (ed.) 1976:28–45).

By 1844, the Lamont properties of Kilfinan, Drum, and Inveryne had passed to Alexander MacAlister of Loup and Torrisdale and remained with him until some time between 1861 and 1870, when they became part of the Otter estate. His kindred were well established locally, being a sept of Clan Donald (MacMillan 1960:26–29). In 1751, their landholding concentrated in Kilcalmonell parish in Kintyre and in South Knapdale (see Timperley [ed.] 1976:35, 43).

The remaining landowner to consider is Thomas Harkness of Clachaig, who had acquired the farm of Derinakerochmore from the Otter estate by 1802. This had passed to Archibald Harkness Clachaig of Derrynacharachmor by 1844, but to Campbell of Ballimore by the early 1860s. Harkness was not an established Argyll landowner (see Timperley [ed.] 1976:28–45). The title *of Clachaig* may refer to a Clachaig in Dunoon and Kilmun parish nearby. However, this property was in the possession of Archibald Campbell of Knockbuy in 1751 (Timperley [ed.] 1976:31). If Harkness derived his title from that property, this could only have come about sometime in the late eighteenth century.

So, from about 1800, there seems to have been significant flux in landownership in Kilfinan. Outside of the Lamont estate, ownership passed from traditional landholders to a wide variety of newcomers. Several of the new landowners can definitely or presumably be associated with established local kindreds, like the Malcolms of Poltalloch, MacAllisters of Loup, and MacIvors. Many, however, are likely to have been from outwith the area, from the Lowlands or England, or would at least have spent much time there. Such is the case with the Campbells of Ballimore, the Rankines of Otter, and the Nicols of Ardmarnock.

This situation fits a general pattern of changing landownership found throughout the west coast of the Highlands and the Islands in the nineteenth century (in general see Devine 1989a, 1994b; for a parish-based case study see Gaskell 1996; similar trends have also been noted for the central Highlands (Stewart 1990:Chapter 16)). The period 1800 to 1860 in particular saw the disappearance of many traditional landed families from the west Highlands. Those who did survive were often forced to sell large parts of their patrimony. By the 1850s, about 60% of the larger estates outside of Sutherland had passed to a new elite, and this does not include those estates of less than 3000 acres that many new purchasers tended to acquire (Devine 1989a:110). Further, most of these land transfers involved non-resident Highland purchases, that is the buyers were mostly of non-Highland stock, and many were English landowners, merchants, or financiers (Devine 1989a:111). These new landowners had varied backgrounds, previously having been landowners elsewhere, merchants and financiers, professionals (such as lawyers and academics), or industrialists, for example (Devine 1989a:112).

The landholding history of Kilfinan fits broadly into this pattern. The Lamonts continued as significant landowners through the nineteenth century, but with a slightly reduced patrimony. The Campbells of Otter may have continued to hold a much-reduced estate until this passed to the Rankines. There were two main phases of estate transfer, both in the early to mid nineteenth century. The background of the new landowners included an English professional (Dr. Nicol) and several prominent merchants (Campbell of Ballimore in Glasgow and the Malcolm of Poltalloch family in the colonies). Those newcomers about whose background nothing is known overwhelmingly came from families previously not established in Argyll. However, one contrast with the model is the significant number of new landowners from previously established Highland families (such as MacAllister of Loup and Malcolm of Poltalloch). The reasons behind the transfer of these estates will be returned to below.

Urban Society and the Emergent Middle Class

The Lamonts and Campbells of Otter were established Highland landowners and might readily be viewed in a context of traditional clan-based society, as *ceann-cinnidh* (chiefs, head of the kindred) or *fine.* However, it is also possible to include the Lamonts, and perhaps the Campbells of Otter, within the emergent middle class introduced in the last chapter and thus give them a part common biography with the new landowners of the nineteenth century.

From the early seventeenth century, various members of the Lamont family were admitted as Glasgow burgesses. The first of these was in 1609 and probably traded in Loch Fyne herring (McKechnie 1938:128). In 1628, we find Sir Coill Lamount of Innerin (the head of Clan Lamont), his son James Lamount, and Robert Lamount of Silvercraigs (a cadet) admitted as burgesses (Anderson (ed.) 1925:70). So, both chiefs and other members of the *fine* were becoming involved in burgh life.

Inclusion of the clan gentry as Glasgow burgesses can be traced into the eighteenth century. For example, Duncan Lamont of Auchshilag (Auchinshelloch) was admitted in 1716 (Anderson (ed.) 1925:325). In 1774, John Lamont of Lamont's brother, Hugh, left Scotland for America after serving an apprenticeship as a Glasgow merchant (McKechnie 1938:321). The Lamont Laird of Ascog features in the burgh accounts for 1737 to 1738 and 1752 to 1753 "for two braces in his shop and drawing them up in the touns corner house" (Renwick [ed.] 1909:510; [ed.] 1911:560). Other untitled Lamonts were also admitted during this period. Such is the case with Archibald Lamont, servitor to the above Duncan Lamont of Auchinshelloch (1706), and Duncan Lamont, servitor to the Earl of Bute (1720) (Anderson [ed.]1925:267, 351). Aside from those clan gentry acting as merchants, then, there were members of the kindred entering the burghs in a professional capacity.

The activities of some of the eighteenth century chiefs also testify to their continued inclusion in commercial society. Perhaps most obvious is John Lamont of Lamont's entering into partnership in a firm established to trade with British America in the 1770s, when he was already a stockholder in the Royal Bank of Scotland (McKechnie 1938:321).

Aside from their inclusion within Glasgow society, various Lamonts were also active in the surrounding local burghs. Coll Lamont of Inveryne was the first laird to do regular business in Rothesay on Bute (McKechnie 1938:135). The family's connection with that town was long established. The Ardlamont Lamonts had a property there from the early fifteenth century and the chiefs acquired property there in 1540 and 1563 (McKechnie 1938:88). Members of the *fine* are also recorded as regularly purchasing meal and other goods in Port Glasgow and Greenock in the seventeenth century (McKechnie 1938:235, 251).

Dugald Lamont, merchant in Kilfinan, is listed as a burgess of Inverary in 1724 and 1726 (Beaton and MacIntyre [eds.] 1990:24, 27). However, he and other similar merchants are of little relevance here. As Devine (1995:22–24) has pointed out, the Scottish merchant class was far from homogenous, being a complex and diverse grouping ranging from the petty shopkeeper to the merchant elite, like the Tobacco Lords of Glasgow. It is likely that Dugald Lamont, merchant in Kilfinan, was an innkeeper rather than a merchant in the sense of the John Lamont of Lamont involved in trans-Atlantic trade and mentioned above. Dugald Lamont's sphere of action was probably extremely localized.

In terms of the burghal roles of these various Lamonts, we have seen that they were largely merchants and professionals. The landowning clan gentry, however, were almost exclusively merchants. This mercantile role largely concerned the marketing of local produce within Scotland, though, as we have seen, they were occasionally involved in trans-Atlantic trade.

Reference has been made to the trade in Loch Fyne herring. The Loch was well known for the product and references to it appear in a variety of contemporary sources (e.g., Mitchell [ed.] 1907:146; McFarlane 1983:215). Certainly, Lamont of Stillaig was engaged in a speculation in Loch Fyne herring in 1689 (McKechnie 1938:251). It is probable that others among the Lamont *fine* were too.

Perhaps more important here was trade in produce of the land, which is greater in recorded extent, particularly for the Lamonts of Lamont. There is some evidence for the marketing of meal, by Lamont of Stillaig again (McKechnie 1938:235). However, the more significant trade seems to have been in cattle.

The Argyllshire cattle droving trade can be traced back into the sixteenth century, at least, and was most significant in the eighteenth and early nineteenth centuries (Haldane 1952:84–85). Cattle bred on the islands, principally the Isle of Mull in the north and Islay and Jura in the south, were ferried or swam to the mainland (Haldane 1952:86–88, 94–97). The destination of the droves was the Lowland cattle trysts, and, ultimately for many, England. There were many routes by which these droves could pass to the Lowlands. With the shifting of the main tryst from Crieff to Falkirk, from the mid-eighteenth century, the focus of the Mull area droving traffic shifted further south, towards Inverary and Loch Fyne (Haldane 1952:89, 112). At Loch Fyne, the northern droves met up with others from the west, from Islay and Jura via Kintyre and Knapdale (Haldane 1952:91, 94–94, 97). Their immediate destination was the major local tryst at Kilmichael-Glassary in the valley of the River Add (Haldane 1952:97). From there they would proceed to the Lowlands. The route to the Lowlands from Kilmichael-Glassary passed through Glen Kinglas, on the northern boundary of Cowal (MacDonald 1994:6).

From this it may seem that Cowal was largely by-passed by the droving trade. This was not the case. As early as 1613, Coll Lamont (the Glasgow burgess) is recorded as raising an action against three burgesses of Linlithgow, a noted Lowland cattle mart, for the price of 85 "ky," or cows, and three "bullis" purchased by them from his tenants (McKechnie 1938:136). Coll was probably acting as an organizing go-between, dealing cattle to the Lowlands on behalf of his tenants. The chiefs of Lamont also bought and fattened cattle on their own behalf. For instance, in the mid-eighteenth century, Archibald Lamont of Lamont took an active role in the cattle trade (McKechnie 1938:305). This was in partnership with Lamont of Auchagoyl and a MacAllister from Ardpatrick at the mouth of West Loch Tarbert. They bought cattle in Kintyre, Knapdale, and Cowal and sold locally and in the Lowlands. The cattle they bought were often collected at cattle ranches in Kilfinan, as well as in Knapdale. The principal Kilfinan depots were at Craignafeich and Auchinshelloch (McKechnie 1938:305). Ground at Ardlamont was also enclosed with dykes intended to control cattle in the 1750s (McKechnie 1938:304–305). It therefore seems likely that the first enclosures were associated with the droving trade and, certainly, there is a complex of irregular enclosures at Craignafeich. Later Improvements have obscured much at Ardlamont, however.

The cattle in question probably reached Kilfinan by ferry across Loch Fyne to Otter. Such a ferry is noted in the records of the Commissioners of Supply (MacDonald 1994:2). The Commissioners, of whom John Lamont of Lamont was one in 1771, were responsible for highways, bridges, and regulation ferries from 1686 and, therefore, had a major aspect of the droving trade as their concern (MacDonald 1994:1, 6).

Cattle dealing from Kilfinan certainly continued into the nineteenth century under Peter Lamont in Stillaig (McKechnie 1938:351). He was a gentleman farmer, Justice of the Peace, and a grandson of the Lamont cadet Stronalbanach.

The Campbells of Otter likewise had connections with Glasgow from the seventeenth century. Archibald Campbell of Otter was admitted as a burgess in 1628, as was John Campbell of Otter in 1715 (Anderson [ed.] 1925:70, 309). Information regarding this family's inclusion in burgh society is scant, however. Presumably they were engaged in similar mercantile activity to the Lamonts, principally the herring and cattle trade.

The landowners of Kilfinan were closely involved with the burghs of western Scotland, principally as merchants. This burgh context is relevant from at least the early seventeenth century, certainly for the Lamonts and perhaps for the Campbells of Otter. The majority of the new landowners of the nineteenth century can also be linked to a similar context, as merchants or professionals. Perhaps the key significance of the burgh context is the emergence of a self-professed middle class there in the late eighteenth and early nineteenth centuries. This middle class cohered through common experience of social relations and a related ideology. This ideology had its roots in the Scottish Enlightenment of the eighteenth century and exhibited those Enlightenment traits previously highlighted as providing justification for Improvement. Such justification came with faith in future progress. An intellectual and spatial framework for developing rural settlement and landscape came from the inspiration provided by the emphasis on ordered geometric space, exemplified by the new-town, of which Edinburgh is the outstanding example. This was accompanied by disdain for Scotticisms in speech, but no doubt also for traditional forms of architecture and landscape conceptualization and organization, and by the heralding of rational and scientific enquiry. Membership of the middle class also entailed other more political and social motives for Improvement.

Improvement and the Establishment and Maintenance of Middle Class Status

Improvement in Kilfinan can be understood in part as a strategy in the maintenance of middle class status. In the case of the Lamonts, consideration of this begins with the Civil Wars of the seventeenth century and the subsequent commercial reorientation of their estate economy. As Allan I Macinnes (1998a:166–169) has pointed out, the trauma of the Civil Wars was followed by the reconstruction of many estates in the Highlands along commercial lines. The clan *fine* in many areas changed in status from tacksmen to proprietors and the exercise of power within the clans was transformed as the clan elite was gradually redefined as a commercial network of landed entrepreneurs. New opportunities were increasingly sought outwith the Highlands and were facilitated by social networking within Lowland and English society. This re-orientation of *fine* interests and networks had material and social ramifications within their Highland estates. The clan gentry were increasingly physically distanced from their tenants with the construction of policies and the introduction of mansion houses. Further,

Lowland tenants were introduced to many estates to counter the depopulation of the War years (Macinnes 1996:106–107).

The Lamont's position in Kilfinan suffered catastrophic reverse during the Civil Wars. This was followed by the exile of the chief for a number of years on Arran and on the Lowland mainland, under the protection of the Semples, the Duchess of Hamilton, and the Earl of Wintoune, as well as for five years on Bute (McKechnie 1938:205–206, 211). This exile no doubt strengthened their links with Lowland society, previously initiated in their context as merchants in Glasgow. The management of their estates after their restoration included aspects of those strategies outlined in general by Macinnes. Lowland tenants were introduced (Macinnes 1996:106–107). Furthermore, following the destruction of Toward castle, Ardlamont House became the principal residence of the Lamont chiefs (RCAHMS 1992:309). The most part of the mansion house as it stands today dates from the early eighteenth and early nineteenth century phases of construction, although elements of it may have been influenced by the late seventeenth century structure (RCAHMS 1992:24, 309, 311). However, it does seem that the shift from Toward to Ardlamont represents a shift from the old style of estate center to the new. Toward consists of a fifteenth century tower house with sixteenth and seventeenth century additions (RCAHMS 1992:297). It is evident, however, that the formal policies on the Lamont of Lamont estate predate the Civil Wars and the move to Ardlamont. During the Wars, Campbell of Achavoulin and Campbell of Evanachan "did cut doune and destroy the wholl planting in and about the hous of Towart, orchzairds, parkis, and wallis thereof" (quoted in McKechnie 1938:195).

The dislocation of the Civil Wars also came at a time when Sir James Lamont was heavily in debt (McKechnie 1938:147). This, with the devastations of the Wars, threatened the survival of the Lamont estates and the social position of the chief. Commercial reorientation was a common strategy in his situation at the time. For the Lamonts, a focus on mercantile activity, and the associated partial restructuring of their estates, would have been a strategy suggested by their pre-war burgh context and no doubt further naturalized during their period of exile. Commercial reorientation towards Lowland mercantile interests was a strategy intended to reconstitute and maintain their social position. However, the nature of that position had now changed and was increasingly associated with their role as proprietors and estate managers, rather than their role as clan chiefs. This is evidenced in the changing way in which territorial control was exercised. As seen above, during the eighteenth century, the lands of the

various Lamont cadets were consolidated under the personal ownership of the Lamont chiefs. This represents the erosion of the traditional means by which territory was organized and controlled through
kin ties under the clan system. In the late seventeenth century, the
basis of the cadetships had already been placed on monetary terms,
as opposed to the previous tenure under the clan system (McKechnie
1938:230).

The commercial reorientation of the estate provides a background
context for Improvement. From the seventeenth century, the proprietors were increasingly associated with and orientated towards
Lowland commercial society. Their estates, though, were still largely
managed along previously established lines. Furthermore, the material
environment of the estate was probably largely unchanged by the personal reorientation of the chiefs. The construction of a mansion house-
and-policy estate center was a limited acceptance of new architectural
and landscape ideals. Such changes were largely confined to the personal domain of the proprietor. Enclosure of land outside of the policies
did occur. Again, however, this was limited and confined to those areas
associated with the droving enterprises of the chiefs and the remaining
fine. While the products of the estate might now be sold as merchan-
dise, where they had previously been consumed in the maintenance
of the clan, they were still produced in a fairly non-capitalist manner. Townships remained in joint-tenancy until the nineteenth century,
as the Valuation Rolls quoted above show, and fields and grazings remained organized along communal lines. However, the new landscape
around the home of the landowner points to an increasing social differentiation and distance between them and the population of their
estates. A contradiction arose between the landowners' new mercantile, Lowland orientated relations and their relations with those living
on and maintaining their estates.

This contradiction became exposed further with the emergence of
a distinct middle class from the late eighteenth century. Improvement
can in part be thought of as an attempt by the Lamonts of Lamont to
establish their position within the emergent middle class and maintain
their mercantile role. Improvement of their Highland estates would
demonstrate their understanding and acceptance of a new pattern of
social relations founded on the autonomous individual. The acceptance
was expressed in the geometric ordering of space, seen in some forms of
enclosure and in the layout of Improved farms, and the desirability of
progress, conceived in conjunction with the stadial organization of history. Improvement was not inevitable for the Lamonts, but would have
been essential for the maintenance of their connections with the new

middle class. It was in this context that the potential conflict between the organization of their estates and their wider, mercantile relations emerged and had to be addressed. The need to address this issue perhaps became more acute with the growth of tourism in the area from the early nineteenth century (see Lloyd-Jones 1991:Chapter 4 on tourism in Kilfinan; Rennie 1993:115–117, on tourism in Cowal in general), exposing estates in Kilfinan to the scrutiny of leisure seekers from Glasgow and other burghs.

A similar understanding can be drawn for Improvement on the other Kilfinan estates. The Campbells of Otter were similarly increasingly involved in burgh life. However, little is known of the Campbell of Otters' role in burgh society, and they were not noted Improvers. The fragmentation of Otter in the early nineteenth century is the key context for Improvement.

Mungo Nutter Campbell of Ballimore *was* a noted Improver (Stark 1845:367–368). He and the other new proprietors, such as the MacIvors and Nicols of Ardmarnock and the other smaller proprietors, are of most interest here. As has been said, the majority of these new landowners were associated with the emergent middle class, as merchants or professionals. This provides a context for the Improvement of their estates. However, the specific reasons why a new landowner Improved in this context would have been slightly different from those of the Lamonts.

Devine (1989a:124–126) has suggested that the purchase of Highland estates during the nineteenth century does not represent rational economic self-interest, although such estates clearly did provide an income. The key factors were the romanticization of the Highlands, the growing interest in certain forms of leisure, and conspicuous consumption (Devine 1989a:126–130).

Prior to the mid-eighteenth century, many external observers perceived the region as a barren and sterile wilderness, inhabited by a barbarous population largely disaffected to the British Crown. In the early nineteenth century, a different perception came to be adopted by many in the affluent and leisured classes of British society. From modern ideas of the sublime and picturesque it followed that the ascribed characteristics of isolation and wildness came to be viewed as a positive attraction.

Growing interest in the sports of hunting, shooting, and fishing and the growth of the Highlands as an area for leisure are connected to this change in attitude. Sport was not the only leisure. With the hunter came the scientist (like the geologist and botanist) and the artist.

That the leisure aspects of a Highland estate were important to nineteenth century landowners in Kilfinan is clear from the Valuation

Rolls. The Valuation Roll of 1860/1861 describes several properties as shootings or shootings let (ABDA 1/73/13:52–54). These lands occur on the estates of John Nicol of Ardmarnock and John Malcolm of Poltalloch. It is possible that lands unlet and in the hands of the proprietors Mungo Nutter Campbell, Archibald Lamont of Lamont, and Arthur Scoular of Ininns may have included areas set aside for sport. The Malcolm of Poltalloch estate in Kilfinan also contained fishings (ABDA 1/73/13:54). By the Roll of 1870/1871, the Lamont, Campbell of Ballimore, and Rankin of Otter estates all had shootings listed (ABDA 1/13/33:105–108). However, the sporting aspects of the Kilfinan estates do not appear significant until the mid-nineteenth century and later. For those landowners who purchased in that period, such as the Rankins and Nicols, the sporting estate may have been what they had in mind. For others this may not have been an initial reason for purchase.

On top of those leisure and scenic aspects, Devine (1989a:129) suggests that the acquisition of a Highland estate also served the psychological drives of the wealthy:

> ... [the land's] main function may have been simply to satisfy the urge for territorial possession. It became a form of conspicuous consumption, a means by which material success could be demonstrated, status and place in society assured and a family line established. In this sense, buying a Highland estate and 'improving' it gratified the same passion for possession as the collection of fine art or the acquisition of expensive and elaborate furniture. (Devine 1989a:129)

Putting such "psychological" motives aside, I would draw attention to the social aspects of the desire for land. The emergent middle class may have viewed estate acquisition as a way to secure their social position through reference to and entrance into the traditional basis of social and political power (Campbell 1988:98).

The establishment and maintenance of the newly consolidated and increasingly dominant social position of the middle class is perhaps the key to understanding why its members purchased Highland estates. The key to understanding why they Improved these estates is in part the fact that, at the time of purchase, they had a specific conceptualization of how such an estate should be constituted—along capitalist lines. The Highlands were becoming known for their isolation and wildness and appropriate for sport and leisure. However, the middle class context of the new landowners meant they would have professed and wished to be seen as adhering to ideas of progress. They would have considered that the farmed areas of an appropriate estate should resemble the farms of the Lowlands, just as the mansions built at the center of these new estates were in the Georgian style (see Figure 14). Furthermore, they

Figure 14. Ardmarnock House, Kilfinan. A residence of the new landed elite (National Monuments Record of Scotland reference D63863; crown copyright: RCAHMS).

would have considered a Highland estate organized with reference to community and kindred as an impediment to the proper progress of commercial exploitation of the land, which was dependent on the relations of capitalism.

This means that the new landowners, on buying their Kilfinan estates, would have experienced the same conflict as did the Lamonts. Their acceptance or continued inclusion within the middle class would have naturalized and required the reorganization of their estates. New and established landowners alike also faced potential conflict with their tenantry, who might expect some right to occupancy of the land in contradiction to the increasingly commercial nature of the estate as an asset for rationalization and exploitation. The situation of the landowner in Kilfinan might have seemed particularly tenuous at a time when many estates were changing hands and where many new landowners could claim no right to the land other than their ownership as private individuals. In this situation, Improvement could act to head off conflict between landlord and tenantry by naturalizing the existence of the autonomous individual and private property.

IMPROVEMENT AS A STRATEGY IN RESOLVING SOCIAL CONTRADICTION

For the House of Argyll, Improvement formed part of the longer-term project of Civilizing the Highlands and aimed to consolidate their dominant landholding position in the southwest Highlands. Their position as landholders in Kintyre was threatened by a counter-claim to their estates by Clan Donald and by the continued non-compliance of their tenantry, who refused to define themselves solely as the tenants of their landlord. Opposition to the interests of the House of Argyll was not constantly manifest as overt resistance, but continued to exist in potential all along. Improvement sought to address the contradiction inherent in the landlord–tenant–sub-tenant relationship and to address problems arising from the existence of competing claims to land as *duthchas* and as *oighreachd*.

In Kilfinan, Improving landowners sought to consolidate their position within the middle class, contingent upon the growing coherence of that class from the late eighteenth century. Here, the contradiction was between their simultaneous existence within what would have been conceived of as progressive (Enlightened, commercial) middle class society and backward Highland society. Improvement also attended to the increasingly exposed contradiction existing in the landlord-tenant-sub-tenant relationship. Improvement would have served to naturalize this contradictory relationship.

Improvement, therefore, did not simply come with exposure to Scottish Enlightenment thought. Improvement, involving the fundamental reorganization of routine practice in the Highlands, was instigated by landowners in order to address a variety of specific social problems, or contradictions, peculiar to their own situation. To understand Improvement simply as an aspect of the intellectual enterprise that was Enlightenment would be to ignore the fact that, as Devine has said of the Lowlands, it was a gigantic strategy of social and economic engineering (Devine 1994a:70). It would be equally wrong, however, to assume without consideration that Improvement was a simple and homogenous process of social transformation. The following chapter explores how the rural population of Kintyre and Kilfinan actively engaged with Improvement and sought to manipulate their changing routine environment in accordance with their own agendas. As will be seen, we should not simply oppose two social groups, the landlord and the people, in a dialogue of domination and resistance. Most recent histories of Improvement in the Highlands have done just this. Rather, we should see social change as composed of a series of actions that were structured by previous experience, contingent on changing circumstance, and constrained by relations of power. The rural population of Kintyre and Kilfinan did not address Improvement as a body. Rather, their individual response was contingent on what Improvement meant for them, above all in relation to their continued occupancy of the land. The acceptance of Improved routine practice and its associated material environment revolved around the question of land rights. The degree to which members of the rural population could determine their own lives according to their own interests depended on their position within an asymmetrical network of relationships.

Improvement and the Farming Population | 7

The last two chapters have weighted discussion towards the landowners of Kintyre and Kilfinan and have framed Improvement in a somewhat abstract way. But Improvement was not a one-way process whereby landlords imposed fully formed capitalist social relations, and the material environment that helped maintain those relations, on the rural population. The landlords were never fully free to act without reference to others. It remains and is essential to consider how the farming population engaged with Improvement. Was it promoted, accepted, or rejected, and by whom? In fact, response to Improvement was subtler than this, with different individuals and groups manipulating their material environment and related routine practices in complex, but variously constrained ways. Here I have chosen to examine the progress of Improvement in relation to changing understandings of land tenure and in relation to different social groups as defined by tenurial status, such as tenant or (landless) laborer. How different groups engaged with Improvement was contingent on where Improvement sought to position them in relation to others and to the land. It was also contingent on their position in these respects as it existed at a given time—that is, their position within an asymmetrical network of social relations.

Continued occupancy of the land was a key concern for many. It had been a concern prior to Improvement, evidenced in concepts of hereditary tenure. The concern for occupancy converged with people's varied circumstances with Improvement as large or middling tenants, smallholders, or laborers to produce a material world that was complex. All groups were concerned with continued occupancy and use of the land and the maintenance of social relations structured to facilitate this. For some, their position on the land was fairly secure with Improvement, as they occupied their farms on long leases and were financially comfortable. Others were dispossessed or lived in insecurity. Those who were favored under a lease system that dealt with the individual, might readily accept Improved domestic space. For others, the maintenance of unImproved forms of domestic space was connected to the maintenance of hereditary claims to occupancy, which provided a form of resistance to their dispossession or insecurity. Their maintenance of routines not founded in relationships between autonomous individuals potentially represented a frustration of their landlord's attempts to construct his relationship with them in these terms.

This resistance was limited in scope, however. Aside from significant variation in the changing form of domestic space, Improvement at the levels of landscape and settlement seems to have been much more uniform and was connected to the abandonment of pre-Improvement routine practice in these environments. This suggests that the routine structuring of community was undermined effectively.

The chapter begins with a discussion of the recent historiography of Improvement. Despite the fact that there have been conflicting interpretations of the process, there are several common themes running through most narratives. The engagement of the farming population with Improvement is often considered largely in terms of overt, often violent resistance. This concern has come with a concentration on land clearance and, thus, with the northwest Highlands and Islands. In such narratives, the Highland population is often characterized as two diametrically opposed and individually homogenous social groups, the landlords and the people.

Later, these two propensities (the concentration on overt resistance and the bipolar division of the population) are questioned on theoretical grounds and on the basis that they ignore the potential complexity of Improvement as a process that was at the same time promoted, accepted, rejected, and manipulated by the population at large. The remainder of the chapter considers varied responses to Improvement from an archaeological perspective. That is to say, from a perspective that aims to understand past society from the starting point of its material environment. The data available for Kintyre are more useful here. There are, for example, a greater number of explicit documentary sources defining the use of domestic space. It is for this reason that I have concentrated on that region. However, a comparison of the situation described for Kintyre with what can be said for Kilfinan does allow some significant contrasts and similarities to be drawn.

A contrast between widespread Improvement in the landscape, but more varied adoption of Improved domestic space, will be argued for Kilfinan as well as for Kintyre. However, nucleated settlement continued on some farms in Kilfinan, where it did not in Kintyre. Considering the importance of the *baile* in structuring a sense of community, this continuity in settlement is potentially significant. There are problems, though, in defining the routine practices associated with these post-Improvement townships. The other significant contrast between

Kilfinan and Kintyre with Improvement is between the different horizontal social divisions that emerge in these two areas. In Kintyre, the farming population came to be divided between large, middling and small tenants, and farm laborers. In Kilfinan, the group of middling tenants was largely absent. Significantly, the range farmstead, argued below to be associated above all with the middling tenant, is common in Kintyre but rare in Kilfinan. It will be argued that distinct uses of domestic space and the maintenance of materially distinct houses by different tenurially defined groups were both a cause and result of the emergence of these groups. A comparative archaeology of Improvement can explore the different social consequences of Improvement in different areas and underline the fact that Improvement was not a homogenous process. This is equally clear in the fact that, just as the path of Improvement varied from region to region, it varied from house to house.

NARRATIVES OF RESPONSE TO IMPROVEMENT

Literature on the eighteenth and nineteenth centuries in the Highlands has grown significantly since the 1960s and has been characterized into two main schools (Carter 1981; Macinnes 1998b:180–184). Sharon MacDonald (1997:69–75) has labeled these two groups *people's historians* and *economic historians*, while admitting the simplification inherent in these categories. Here I will focus on their work relevant to the themes of Improvement and related social change.

The first group, the people's historians, includes writers such as John Prebble (e.g., 1963), James Hunter (e.g., 1992; 2000), and Ian Grimble (1962), who might in a longer term perspective be placed together with authors of the period in question itself (e.g., MacKenzie 1986 [1883]). Their writings focus on the common people through themes such as:

> ...the projection back of the notion of a 'people' and the materialisation of this through descriptions of the people's 'way of life'; oppression of 'the people' by those in power—a conflict which may also be mapped onto an ethnic divide (e.g., Scotland versus England); and the resilience or rebellion of 'the people'. (MacDonald 1997:69–70)

People's histories have primarily focused on the period of the clearances and issues surrounding the history of crofting. They are, above all, concerned with the removal of people from the land, a process most associated with the north and west Highlands, and their resettlement in individual crofts.

The view presented of Improvement, primarily clearance in this case, is one of bipolar opposition. The people are oppressed by their landlords, who have betrayed their paternal charge. In this view both people and landlord are homogeneous categories. Prebble says in his preface to *The Highland Clearances*:

> This book . . . is the story of how the Highlanders were deserted and betrayed. It concerns itself with people, how sheep were preferred to them, and how bayonet, truncheon and fire were used to drive them from their homes . . . The chiefs remain, in Edinburgh and London, but the people are gone. (Prebble 1963:11)

The impression of the process of Improvement given is one of (selfish, profit-oriented) landlord action and (laudable, justified) popular reaction. In a simple cause and effect relationship, clearance of the people for sheep is followed by overt resistance on the part of the people, which is followed by suppression by the landlords, often with the aid of state-sanctioned legal and military force (e.g., Prebble 1963:15–18 and *passim*.). The landlords *act* and thus initiate conflict, while the people *react* to oppression and are, thus, further oppressed. People's histories effectively deny the people agency. Their actions are, rather, reactions to an infringement on traditional rights, relationships, and a traditional way of life. I am not suggesting that there were no acts of oppression or that, in cases, people were sometimes forced into a position where they had little room to define their own way of life. Rather, I am suggesting that such accounts as Prebble's emphasize such narratives at the expense of all others.

Some historians who could be assigned to this group, like James Hunter, have produced more subtle work. Hunter's *The Making of the Crofting Community* (2000 [1976], see especially the preface to this new edition, which discusses the book's place in the historiography of the recent Highlands) describes how crofters, not just their landlords, actively shaped modern Highland and Island society. It also recognizes different groups within the populations of the various estates it discusses (large tenants, crofters, sub-tenants). However, Hunter's study focuses predominantly on the landlord–crofter relationship and in doing so acts to reinforce the people–landlord dichotomy.

Sharon MacDonald's economic historians differ in approach from the people's historians and mutual criticism has been marked (MacDonald 1997:73–75; see, by way of example, the complementary articles of Hunter (1975) and Richards (1975) on the Sutherland Clearances).

Perhaps best known amongst the economic historians are Thomas M. Devine (e.g., 1989b; 1994b:Chapter 14; 1995:Chapter 12), Philip Gaskell (1996), Malcolm Gray (1957), and Eric Richards (1973, 1982, 1985). Their approach has focused less on themes of exploitation and oppression and more on the broader, inevitable consequences of agricultural and economic developments. Indeed, in cases, the statement that agrarian capitalism in the Highlands was inevitable is explicit (Gray 1957:89).

People's historians have criticized the economic historians for being too sympathetic to the Highland landlords and for ignoring questions of the people affected by Improvement, while the economic historians have suggested that the popular historians romanticize the pre-clearance period and exaggerate the extent of the brutality involved in clearance. The class-conflict model of Prebble and others is criticized as too simplistic, ignoring as it does the wider forces affecting the landowners.

There has been some heated and often polarized debate surrounding the historiography of Improvement, and particularly clearance. On the face of it we are being asked to choose between a model that emphasizes the oppression of a betrayed people at the mercy of profit-mongering landlords and one that underlines the fact that landlords were subject to impersonal economic forces beyond their control, inevitably leading to the rationalization of the estate economy. The difference between the two models in these terms is stark, and both are rooted in contemporary political and social circumstance (MacDonald 1997:74–75). The choice between these histories is largely a political one. MacDonald (1997:74–75) consciously avoids adjudicating between the two, taking a more anthropological approach and concentrating on the role they play in "contemporary social imaginings" within Highland localities. However, such an attitude is rare. Even philosophers have been enjoined to discuss the thorny issue of assessing the value and ethics of passionate and economic realist histories of Highland clearance (e.g., Sutherland 1975).

Despite their entrenched differences, I would argue that if the question of the social dynamics of Improvement is assessed with reference to both schools, we find several significant assumptions common to both. As seen above, Prebble and others have tended to write the history of Improvement with reference to two homogenous and competing social groups, the landlords and the people. This is also the case in economic histories of the process. In considering popular resistance in the Highlands, Devine discusses the development of certain cultural stereotypes of the Highlander in the nineteenth century (1994b:211–212). However, throughout the rest of the chapter in question, the existence of the High-lander/the Highland people in reality is not questioned. With state-ments like "[t]he Highland people were mainly devoid of power during the clearances" (Devine 1994b:212) it is clear that people is not to be taken in a general sense of those that inhabited the Highlands. The Highland people were a homogeneous and coherent ethnic group. *Their* language and *their* culture had long been under attack (Devine 1994b:212).

As with the people's histories, this definition of the Highland people as an homogenous ethnic group in opposition to an equally homogenous landowning group seems to logically demand overt reactionary protest to Improvement from the people. Rather than simply relate cases of protest to the introduction of sheep, as Prebble does for example, the economic historians approach the subject in a more sober and seemingly objective manner. They ask two key questions: how much overt resis-tance was there; and, why was there not more? (see e.g., Devine 1989b; 1994b:Chapter 14; 1995:Chapter 12; Fraser 1988:269–272). To ask why there was not more resistance implies that overt reaction to Improve-ment is a logical expectation. This leads Devine to follow the argument of Eric Wolf that "[p]easants cannot rebel in a situation of complete impotence" (quoted in Devine 1994b:212) and state that the Highland people appeared docile in the nineteenth century because they did not have the power to act otherwise. He says:

> The Highland people were mainly devoid of power during the clearances. They did not own the land and only had access to it through short-term leases at the landlords' will.... The power of the authorities was overwhelming and the landowners had full legal control over their properties. The army was engaged ... and on the appearance of troops from Inverness, Aberdeen, Fort William or Glasgow, resistance tended to disintegrate rapidly. (Devine 1994b:212)

The Highland people were thus weakened in economic, legal and political terms. This was apparently compounded by a cultural weak-ness whereby the concept of *duthchas* brought with it a reverence for the landlord/chief (Devine 1994b:214–215).

From this perspective overt and often-violent protest was the log-ical reaction of the people to the impositions of their landlords. The seeming lack of protest is to be explained not with reference to a lack of will on the part of the people, but to the efficiency of the oppres-sive functions of the State. Reverence on the part of the people for their landlord also meant that any overt protest that did occur was directed away from the landlord and towards others, such as the estate factor, the sheep farmer, and even the sheep themselves (Devine 1994b: 215).

There are some interesting and useful points made in such discussions of resistance, or the lack thereof. However, the characterization of the Highland population as a homogeneous people in opposition to a homogenous landowning group and the related concern with overt resistance to Improvement restrict our ability to produce nuanced and dynamic histories of the process. Those living on Highland estates probably did not have access to a conception of themselves as members of a definable Highland people prior to the late nineteenth century (MacDonald 1997:81). We need to consider that the power of the tenantry and sub-tenantry to define their relationships with their landlord and with each other was not homogenous and that the changing relationships between different groups were diverse. The dialogue between the various individuals and groups concerned in Improvement need not be seen as confined to one of imposition and simple acceptance or overt resistance. Our consideration needs to expand beyond the protests associated with clearance. We should consider more varied manipulations of the social material aspects of Improvement, which may or may not be conceived in terms of resistance.

ARCHAEOLOGY AND THE DYNAMICS
OF IMPROVEMENT

A general model of Improvement, in terms of the changing material environment of dwelling, settlement, and landscape, has been developed in previous chapters. This model has been tied to a consideration of changing routine practice. As argued in chapter three, different practical understandings of the world are developed in routine practice. Explicit ideological statements that claim to describe the true nature of the world and to justify asymmetrical social relationships will be evaluated by individuals and groups in relation to their practical understanding of the world. Some ideological statements will appear as common sense because they conform to that practical understanding, others will appear as false because they do not. Similarly, practical experience of everyday relations with others conditions the way in which other relationships are approached, and vice versa. So, asymmetrical relationships between landlord and tenantry will not only be assessed in terms of the explicit ideology justifying or refuting them, but in terms of how the practice of those relationships accords with the practice of others, such as within the family. This inter-connection between different relationships works at a variety of levels and I do not want to suggest that we should simply oppose landlord–tenant–sub-tenant and intra-familial relations. There would have been many more connections, between a tenant farmer, their landlord, farm workers, family, and so on. While we cannot explore all possible relationships at once, it is worth recognizing their existence and connection to each other.

Pre-Improvement routine was seen to play a role in structuring the community and family ties that made the community of the clan and hereditary conceptions of land occupancy and ownership knowable. Improvement, progressing in slightly different ways in the two case study areas, sought to reorder this routine and thus reorder the nature of social relationships. Improvement created a routine world in which it made sense that the individual was more significant than kin and community and in which occupancy of land was to be by legal agreement and not related to traditional rights. Capitalism as a network of social relations was introduced to the Highlands in no small part through the manipulation of material culture and lived space. Routine practice with Improvement made the individual knowable and, thus, allowed the pre-eminence of relations of absence over those of presence. However, if we reconsider the archaeology of Improvement in Kilfinan and Kintyre in more detail and in light of what has been said in the first part of this chapter, this general model can be seen to mask a world of diverse experience.

Dual Material Response to Improvement

The first edition OS maps of Kintyre make it clear that enclosure, on a grid pattern where possible, was advanced by the mid-nineteenth century. Other aspects of Improvement associated with the reordering of the wider landscape and environment and the processes of daily work in that landscape were also adopted. In Southend parish, the tenants were industrious in draining at that time (Kelly 1845:433). Earlier, it had been reported that the tenants were readily using lime in improving the fertility of the ground (Smith 1798:199).

Externally, houses appeared Improved too:

> One or two white farm-houses, with slated roofs, are seen in the valley, and by their neat and cared-for appearance show that . . . [the landowner] is improving the property in the spirit of the age. We also see on the opposite hill-side, some scattered cottages, with their whitewashed walls and dark thatch . . . (Bede 1861, volume 2:41–42)

To the traveler passing through Kintyre, the impression might well be that the population had come to live and work in a fully Improved manner within wholly reordered space, from the landscape to the domestic scale.

However, as seen in Chapter 4, Improved space was not universal to or homogenous within all houses of the mid-nineteenth century. To quote Lord Teignmouth's 1836 description of houses in Kintyre again:

> The farm-houses are generally, throughout Cantyre, old and poor habitations, *far behind the general improvement visible in this part of the country.* The entrance is usually through the byre, which is a continuation of the house in the same line: the fire is placed in the middle of the floor, contained in a grate, either square or shaped like a bowl, and raised a little above the ground, a custom peculiar to Cantyre.... There are some few farm-houses in the modern style, indicating the slow growth of Improvement. (Teignmouth 1836:388; my emphasis)

In several cases, in Kintyre and beyond, Improvement seems to have meant different patterns of change in different material and social domains. In some cases, we can see a distinction between external Improvement and change (in landscape organization, settlement morphology, external appearance of the house) and internal (domestic) continuity in the use of space. Considering this material pattern with reference to the role played by the form of the dwelling, settlement, and landscape in structuring the social relationships of the clan and the social changes attendant on the adoption of Improved space we can begin to understand some of the complexities of the process.

The adoption of enclosure and the dispersal of settlement that was widespread by the mid-nineteenth century would have facilitated the deconstruction of community ties that had previously been maintained by the congregation of people in the nucleated township. Everyday tasks had also previously reinforced the sense of community. To take a few examples, ploughing of the openfields was a communal exercise and the shieling of cattle and other animals in summer was the task of a large part of the township community, or of several townships. Enclosure was associated with the destruction of this interdependency and activities like ploughing were carried out by fewer people.

Enclosure and dispersed settlement need not necessarily imply the complete destruction of a sense of community. The club farms of Morvern, in northern Argyll, for example, involved the operation of individual smallholdings together with communally owned and managed sheep flocks or cattle herds (Gaskell 1996:51). However, the routine structuring of community would at least partly be undermined in such a situation. Certainly in Kintyre, communal practice decreased with Improvement in some key areas of farming. Improved farm machinery was becoming increasingly popular there in the first half of the nineteenth century (Bede 1861, Vol. 2:101–104). This machinery included labor-saving devices such as new types of plough, requiring fewer people to operate them, and the wheeled cart. Adoption of this new machinery no doubt reflects a changing attitude to the everyday tasks in which they were used. Fewer people were needed, or available, with Improvement.

Alongside this seeming acceptance of the decline of pre-Improvement social structure at the level of the township community we can see the continued use of unImproved space within the house, suggesting that traditional concepts of tenancy could have continued to operate. The continued use of the central hearth and largely unpartitioned space would have continued to foster strong family ties through proximity in everyday activities like cooking, eating, sleeping, and much more.

This varied response was related to a concern with occupancy, or continued access to land and its resources. Tacks to farms were first offered in open auction to the highest bidders in Kintyre around the early date of 1710 (Cregeen 1970:11). This occurred on the Duke of Argyll's lands, and similar reforms followed in other parts of his vast estates in the 1730s. However, such tenurial reform had its perils for the House of Argyll:

> Ironically the clan Campbell had never been more vitally important to their chief than in the years following 1737. Jacobitism was rife and a rising was preparing to overthrow the Hanoverians. Some of the native gentry had regained their old lands by outbidding the Campbells in the newly-established auction of leases.... The new landlordism of the ducal house was placing in peril the police and security of the estate, perhaps even the stability and safety of the government. Without the backing of his clan the Duke's traditional role as guarantor of peace and order in the west highlands could not be sustained. (Cregeen 1970:15)

Cregeen is writing here with reference to the Isle of Mull in particular. However, the consequences of this situation affected the whole of the Argyll estate, including Kintyre. In 1744 the third Duke, in full appreciation of the threat of Jacobite insurrection, issued instructions to his various chamberlains making political loyalty a pre-condition of tenancy on his lands (Cregeen 1970:15). He instructed that:

> You are to treat with the tenants of that part of my estate under your management for tacks of the farms where the possessors are under bad character or are not affected to the Government or my interest, and in farms that are not now under tacks you are to use your endeavours to introduce tenants that are well-affected to the Government and my family, and as I am

informed that my lands are rather too high-rented in these countrys, so that
there may be a necessity of some abatement of rent, I do approve that those
abatements be chiefly given in those farms where you can bring in people
well disposed to my interest. (quoted in Cregeen 1970:15)

So, from the mid-eighteenth century political loyalty to the House
of Argyll and the Hanoverian succession was an explicit condition of
tenancy on the Argyll estates. Considering the political and social implications of Enlightenment thought for the nature of settlement and
landscape, we need not consider the expression of this loyalty as simply
being conceived in terms of agreement to a clause in a lease. The cultivation and acceptance of an Improved farm, as part of a landscape of
dispersed settlement and enclosed fields, would be as much an expression of disposal to Argyll's interest as would a signature on a lease. The
settlement and landscape changes associated with Improvement were
intended to foster social change that would undermine the structuring
of social relations under clanship and remove the basis for rebellion
against that interest.

In this context, continued occupancy of a farm required Improvement. This occupancy seems, in the end, to have been an overriding
concern for many tenants. The continuity of community seems to have
been less significant, if we consider the prevalence of Improved landscapes and settlement patterns in this area. Under clanship, tenants
might hold land by lease, but people more generally considered themselves to have a heritable right to a portion of land. With the acceptance of both internal and external Improvement, some tenants were
accepting a change to the nature of their holding and the structuring
of their everyday life. However, they were also servicing the traditional
expectancy of the occupancy of a particular holding, despite the fact that
the nature of that occupancy had changed radically. Tenant response
to Improvement was in no small part with reference to certain past
concepts of landholding that had been maintained through everyday
practice.

In contrast to the concern with occupancy, the community ties that
had been constantly reaffirmed through the everyday experience of the
nucleated township and the practices of communal farming seem to
have been more readily altered. A more detailed consideration of the
pre-Improvement nature of the community in the Highlands than has
been attempted here is required in order to understand this situation.
It may be that more detailed analysis of the pre-Improvement environment will reveal longer-term changes in the everyday structuring of
community that prefigured Improvement. However, it can be said that
the widespread nature of Improvement in landscape and settlement

terms is testament to the fact that the landlord occupied a privileged position of power, and I will return to this issue in the concluding chapter. However, even if we accept this, it does seem that this power was far from absolute. Improvement had such an impact in no small part because many accepted or sought after tenancies on dispersed and Improved farms or undertook to carry Improvement through. Others were less enthusiastic and many people did not live entirely Improved lives.

The given response of groups within the farming population need not necessarily be expressed as reactionary protest. Improvement might be actively accepted by a new tenant wishing to establish themselves on the estate or, for a previous tenant, in the maintenance of previously structured relationships, in this case that of the tenant and their immediate family to the land. This would of course entail change within those relationships. As seen in chapter six, traditional rights to land were justified with reference to kin-ties of the individual to previous occupiers. This relationship was constructed and its validity continually strengthened in everyday practice. Unpartitioned space as the locus of a wide variety of daily activities, with its focus on the central hearth, would have encouraged the individual to conceive of themselves as an integral part of the familial unit. Their experience in almost every facet of life was experience as part of that unit; it was shared experience.

Viewed from this perspective, the discrepancy between the external acceptance of Improvement, in terms of landscape and settlement, and internal rejection of it in some houses becomes informative. Improvement could be rejected in one sphere and accepted in another in relation to the same general issue, occupancy. The situation here is clearly not simply one of landlord (Improving and oppressive) versus tenantry (traditional and reactionary). A member of the latter group could accept Improvement in the external sphere to ensure continued occupancy, but reject it in the traditional locus of the structuring of the relationships that justify heritable occupancy.

This response to Improvement might be viewed as contradictory. Indeed, a report by the Duke of Argyll's chamberlain, dated 1810, shows that some contemporaries perceived such contradiction, commenting on some of the settlements discussed here as an evil standing in the way of further Improvement (Gailey 1960:104). It would be easy to dismiss this apparent contradiction in practice within and outwith the house as a lack of understanding of Improvement, which would be to cast the latter as a bounded and monolithic set of practices and concepts, a culture.

However, there is, I think, a more useful way to conceive of the situation. Those who Improved in landscape and settlement terms, but maintained the traditional structuring of space within the house were not displaying some kind of pathological, fractionated cultural identity that was neither traditional nor modern. Neither were they misunderstanding Improvement. Rather, we should see engagement with Improvement as contingent. Improvement in one material sphere and not another should be seen as part of the creation of a pattern of social relations where both the Improved and unImproved are mobilized in different contexts in relation to the same question of continued occupancy.

Improvement might be rejected or adopted as contextually appropriate within a strategy where continued occupancy of the land was key. One result of this would be the continued existence of seemingly contradictory principles of occupancy, maintained through daily practice, and it is interesting in this respect that one of the main aspects of conflict between crofters and their landlords in the north west Highland and Islands, from the later nineteenth century, revolved around the issue of hereditary and communal as opposed to legal rights to land (see Cameron 1998:54; Hunter 2000). It would be worth considering the role of material culture and lived space in maintaining these attitudes and relationships amongst various individuals and groups in those areas.

Improvement and the Horizontal Division of the Farming Community

Working in an Improved landscape and living in dispersed settlements could be seen as tacit or enforced acceptance of Improvement, where it was being rejected in some houses. In other cases, Improvement was more completely accepted as it entered the house. A more detailed look at domestic space in the period of Improvement shows that response to Improvement within the house varied amongst the farming population in a meaningful way, related to occupancy and contingent upon what Improvement meant for that concern.

In some houses in the period of Improvement, routine practice was restructured in such a way as to make hereditary concepts of tenure increasingly unknowable and the individualized landlord–tenant–subtenant relationship more natural. In other houses, the opposite was the case. This complicated situation in the adoption of Improved practice seems to relate to the significance of continued occupancy of the land, something that will now be explored in more detail. Furthermore, the variable character of Improvement played a part in the structuring and restructuring of social relationships amongst the farming population itself, as well as between its various elements and the landlord. Improvement played a role in creating and maintaining specific social divisions and dependencies within the rural community, those of class.

Improvement in Kintyre was associated with the growth of a three-fold division of tenant farmers into the small tenant, the middling tenant, and the gentleman or large tenant farmer (Cregeen 1970:14). This was accompanied by the creation of a rural proletariat engaged in wage-labor (Cregeen 1970:9). The detailed historical and archaeological work required in order to consider the daily material environments of these groups simply has not been done. However, there are at least some indications that material culture, and the use of space in particular, did play a role in constructing these divisions.

The Rev. D. MacDonald, minister for Killean and Kilchenzie parish in the mid nineteenth century, has left us with a description of the situations of two different social groups as he saw them. The farmers were "upon the whole, comfortably enough lodged" (MacDonald 1845:386). It is, of course, impossible to say quite what MacDonald means by comfort. However, considering the context of his writing for a text of the Improving movement, it is likely that comfortable and Improved go together.

Of the other group, the cottagers or day-laborers he says they "live in wretched hovels, rudely constructed without any mortar, one division of which is occupied by the family, and the other converted into a kind of byre" (MacDonald 1845:387). Lord Teignmouth suggested that a distinction between the houses of cottagers and of farmers was a new phenomenon, arising in the fifty years or so prior to his writing in the 1830s (Teignmouth 1836:388–389).

Edward Bradley (*alias* Cuthbert Bede) is more informative on the differing nature of the houses of the farmers. He describes a visit in Kintyre to the house of "Mr and Mrs Mac" and compares their dwelling with those of neighboring farmers (Bede 1861, Vol. 2:110–124). The Macs' house may be fictional, and certainly their name is, but Bradley intends it as an example of a type of dwelling in Kintyre that he encountered on his travels and, as such, the picture he draws was at least representative to him.

The Macs' house is a "low range of building one story high," a "long, low hovel" (Bede 1861, Vol. 2:110). Bradley entered one of its several doors into an earthen-floored passage, allowing access to a byre on the left and dwelling on the right (Bede 1861, Vol. 2:113–114). The living quarters contained box beds against one wall, with a gable fireplace opposite:

> A suffocating smoke pervades the room, and makes your breath catch, and your eyes smart. It proceeds from the peat-turf, heaped on the fire...[that] is laid upon a low brick hearth; over it hangs a gigantic cauldron.... The smoke, after making a complete tour of the room, finds its way out through a hole in the thatch that does duty for a chimney.... The side walls of the room are not so high as a grenadier, and the timbers of the pitched roof

rest upon them, and are all laid open to view, together with the heather
that forms the thatch. A pitched roof it may well be called; for the peat
smoke has blackened it.... Two small windows in the low walls face each
other.... On the third side of the room is the hearth before mentioned; and,
on the opposite side, the whole extent of the wall, save a small space for a
doorway, is taken up by a rudely-enclosed cupboard, divided into four parts,
two above the other two. These four divisions... proclaim themselves to be
the sleeping berths of the family... (Bede 1861, Vol. 2:114–115)

To this description we might add other furniture like the spinning
wheel, kist (chest), and aumbry (dresser, adorned with platters and
jugs) (Bede 1861, Vol. 2:116–117).

The traveler is next led by Mrs Mac into "an inner room, of which
she is visibly proud,—a room reserved for visitors, and high days and
holidays, the *spence* or parlor" (Bede 1861, Vol. 2:118):

The spence is a step higher than the other room; it has a boarded floor, a
plastered ceiling, a good sized window... and a fireplace after the new and
improved fashion, with a mantelpiece.... There is a shiny mahogany table,
ditto chairs, *ditto* chest of drawers, on the top of which is a writing desk [on
which lie several, mostly theological, books]... by far the chief object in the
room is an enormous four-post bed, reaching to the ceiling.... It is covered
with snowy linen, and a smart patchwork counterpane, and looks as though
it had never been slept in, and was not intended to be occupied—as, indeed,
I found that it was not, except by extraordinary visitors on extraordinary
occasions. (Bede 1861, Vol. 2:119)

Mrs Mac goes on to entertain Bradley in the spence, with sherry and
cake (Bede 1861, Vol. 2:120).

This general description of a Kintyre farmhouse in the mid-
nineteenth century accords well with several surviving archaeological
examples of the range farmstead (see Chapter 4). What is of interest
here about this type of structure is the fact that it is associated with
the upper ranks of farmers. On the spence, Bradley informs us that Mr
and Mrs Mac are "bettermost people" and that some of the neighboring
farmers had no such room (Bede 1861, Vol. 2:118–119). These neighbors
not only had no such spence, but did not have the cake and sherry of
the Macs with which to entertain the traveler (Bede 1861, Vol. 2:122).

In the New Statistical Account for Southend, a distinction was likewise drawn between the houses of the "inferior" tenant, which were
"low," "narrow," and "cold," and those of the "better class" of tenant,
which were "excellent and substantial" (Kelly 1845:433). A distinction between the dwellings of a lower and substantial class of tenants
had been put forward some fifty years previously for Argyll in general
(Smith 1798:15).

The picture is still vague in many respects, but we can begin to see
the role that Improvement might have played in defining and redefining

the social position of various individuals *within* the rural population as well as negotiating their occupancy. Although we cannot define a type of dwelling for each of Cregeen's tenurially-defined social groups, and there is no reason to necessarily correlate social group and house type on a strict one-to-one basis, we can see variation in the use of domestic space that equates roughly with tenurial status.

The houses of those tenants with large holdings, the bettermost or substantial tenant, seem to display a greater division of space. This greater subdivision of space was associated with the separation of daily routines and social distancing within the family and between the family and other members of the farm, such as the laborers. In the Macs' house a separate room exists for entertaining and accommodating special guests. In known archaeological examples of this type of house, we can see the separation of other functional areas, such as the dairy.

Quite what a substantial tenant might be is unclear. However, houses such as the Macs' might be associated with the middling class of tenant rather than the gentleman farmer.

There is also some suggestion that amongst the upper classes of the tenantry, the gentlemen farmers, houses had a greater division of space again. The New Statistical Account of Southend certainly seems to equate a better class of tenant with large, two storey courtyard farmsteads like Machribeg, near the village of Southend itself (Kelly 1845:433). These large farmhouses had a greater internal division of space. The sleeping, cooking, eating, and working activities evidenced in the box beds, hearth and cauldron, and spinning wheel in the main room of the Macs' house were separated in a house like Machribeg. There you would find bedrooms, a kitchen, a dining room, and much else.

The smaller tenant in Kintyre generally may not have had a house with a separate spence. Although it is unclear how space may otherwise have been arranged there, it is likely that some of these tenants lived in the unpartitioned houses with central hearth, seen in chapter four above.

Cregeen is clear that the existence of the middling farmer in Kintyre had much to do with the fact that the presence of Campbeltown produced an economic situation there differing from elsewhere on the Argyll estates (Cregeen 1970:14). Elsewhere, the farming population was divided into the small tenant, gentleman farmer, and laborer (Cregeen 1970:9, 14). If such a situation operated at the excavated settlement of Lix in Perthshire, then we might equate the inhabitants of the longhouses with central hearths there with the small tenant. Certainly, the size of their holdings seems to have been small (Fairhurst 1969). Above, we also saw the suggestion that the agricultural laborer inhabited an unpartitioned house also, perhaps with a central hearth.

Despite many uncertainties, there does appear to be a general pattern of the increasing division of space within the house with increasing size of holding. I would also suggest that this increasing division of space is related to the nature of occupancy of the land. Those with houses with the most internal division were the gentlemen and middling farmers who enjoyed the securest tenure, holding long leases by this point in time, perhaps of as long as nineteen years (Martin 1987: 7–8). The smaller tenantry may also have held long leases, but their situation was rendered less secure by the smaller size of their holdings. On the Argyll estates in Mull, Morvern, and Tiree, eighteenth century small tenants reverted from long leases to holding year by year due to insolvency and other factors, and the small tenantry of Kintyre have in general been seen as impoverished by the competitive system of leasing (Cregeen 1970:14). Those with the least security of tenure and the minimum amount of land were the day-laborers:

> They hold their dwelling-houses from year to year, and the tenants, who are their landlords, can dispossess them at pleasure. A rent of L.4 or L.5 Sterling is exacted for a house kept in bad repair, a small kail garden, the scanty pasture of a cow, and some ground for planting potatoes, in the outskirts of the farm. (MacDonald 1845:387)

In general then, with decreasing security of tenure under the new conditions of occupancy in the era of Improvement we can see increasing concern for the maintenance of the environment in which established concepts of hereditary tenure made sense. Here we can see a level of resistance to Improved housing forms when Improvement was accompanied by a fall in tenurial security. However, as shown above, we should expect the situation to be more complex than a simple case of resistance to *or* acceptance of Improvement. These small tenants and laborers still worked in Improved fields, often lived in dispersed settlements, accepted positions as paid laborers, or signed Improving leases.

For the larger tenant, continued occupancy was more secure under the lease system and, as such, they had less cause to mobilize concepts of hereditary right. The maintenance of a sense of family in everyday practice including the experience of space was less important than for the smaller tenantry and the dispossessed. Thus, we find a decreasing emphasis on near constant familial interaction as we move from the house of the laborer through that of the small and middling tenant to the large tenant. For the larger tenantry, continuity of tenure and Improvement in the house were commensurate. Theirs were also the houses where provision was made to welcome and impress the extraordinary visitor. For them the concern with impressing the outside world with their efforts to Improve may, therefore, have extended from the landscape into the home. Part of this concern may well have been with showing solidarity with the interest of the estate and the landlord and retaining their position, both in terms of retaining their lease and in separating themselves from the lower classes.

Material culture played a role in some individuals' strategies in coping with their varied situations as occupants of the land. They attempted to negotiate their relationship with their landlord through structuring and restructuring the routine conditions that made different conceptions of tenancy knowable.

However, the varied responses to Improvement discussed above also affected other social relationships. In creating differing material environments the various members of the rural community were playing a part in the creation of new social divisions within that community, consciously or not. The horizontal social divisions noted by nineteenth century writers were vague. However, they appear more marked than those of the pre-Improvement period. It is not that horizontal division at this level had been absent before, rather that it was now to be emphasized over the vertical divisions of clanship. Class was now predominant, not status. The prosperous tenant farmer, in living in a large and highly subdivided farmhouse, was not simply defining their relationship with their landlord in terms of their interaction as autonomous individuals, they were defining their relationship with their laborers and, to no small extent, their family in the same terms.

A concern with occupancy also structured the response of those who in part rejected the spatial restructuring of Improvement. Their use of material culture as part of a strategy in regulating this occupancy was different from that of the larger tenants, but they approached Improvement with the same basic concern. The impact of such an act of resistance was conditioned by their situation with regard to their landlord or their employer, the farmer (again, I shall return to this point in the concluding chapter). In responding as they did to Improvement, they, somewhat ironically, would have played a role in widening horizontal social division by placing themselves within a distinct material environment.

Regional Variation in the Construction of Modern Highland Society

With the above arguments in mind, differences in the archaeology of Improvement in Kilfinan, as opposed to Kintyre, suggest that

Improvement in the two different areas meant slightly differing changes in social structure.

It was argued in Chapter 4 that the range farmstead is largely absent from Kilfinan. Alongside the courtyard farmsteads of Kilfinan we find cottage ranges, also found in Kintyre. These latter structures are often located on the periphery of large single-tenancy farms. The structure at Low Stillaig lies on the lands of Stillaig. Both the cottage range and the large modern farmhouse at Stillaig itself appear as roofed on the first OS map of the area (1863).

The suggestion, then, is that these agglomerated ranges are to be associated with large single tenancy farms. It is likely that the ranges represent the habitations of farm laborers. Certainly, Stillaig was a single or double tenancy from at least the time of the 1850 Assessment for Roads (ABDA DR1/12). There we find one tenant and twelve cottars listed under the farm.

Alongside the isolated farmhouses and agglomerated ranges of laborers' cottages we find a third contemporary element within this Improved landscape in Kilfinan, and absent from Kintyre. There are a series of nucleated settlements that are shown as roofed on the first OS maps. In places, such as at Ascog, all the buildings are shown as roofed. At others, such as Ardgaddan and Craignafeoch, only some of the buildings are shown as roofed. These settlements may represent survivals from the pre-Improvement period, reduced in size in some cases.

At Craignafeoch and Ascog we are almost certainly dealing with settlements of farm laborers, or smallholders in the sense of cottars. Ascog is listed as a single tenancy in the 1860/1861 Valuation Roll (ABDA 1/73/13:52). However, by 1870/1871 it had become joined with Stillaig in a large single tenancy (ABDA 1/13/33:107). So, certainly by the latter time, the settlement at Ascog had become one element in a large single-tenancy, where the tenant presumably lived in the farmhouse at Stillaig. Previously, a tenant may have lived at Ascog with the cottars. Certainly, the 1850 Assessment for Roads lists nine inhabitants of whom only eight are cottars (ABDA DR1/12). Craignafeoch was a single tenancy from at least 1844 (ABDA DR1/12). This single tenancy farm, at the time of the first OS map, had both the isolated farmhouse that presumably housed the tenant and his family and a small nucleated settlement to the north.

The situation at Ardgaddan is different (see Figures 15 and 16). This was a double tenancy from at least 1844 (ABDA DR1/12). Presumably this explains the existence of a northern and a southern settlement cluster there. The first OS map shows only five structures roofed at the northern cluster and two at the southern. One of the structures at North Ardgaddan is definitely a mill. Of the remaining structures, only one

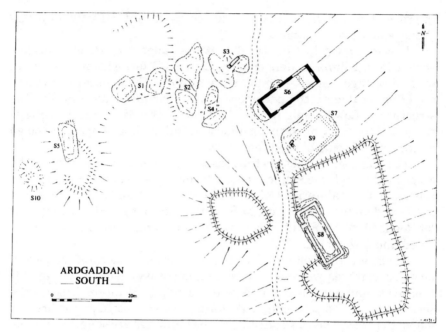

Figure 15. Plan of South Ardgaddan, Kilfinan. The well-preserved S6 is surrounded by an amorphous nucleation of less distinct buildings (copyright University of Glasgow).

at South Ardgaddan and one certain and two possible others at North Ardgaddan are likely to be houses, on the basis of size and internal features. It seems then that the amorphous nuclear clusters consist of the dwellings and outbuildings of the two tenants, possibly, though not certainly, with accommodation for laborers at North Ardgaddan. This accounts for the absence of a large, two-storied farmhouse at the site.

The post-Improvement social structure of Kilfinan, as seen from the archaeological settlement pattern in conjunction with the documentary sources, appears slightly different to that in Kintyre. In Kilfinan we find a general twofold division of the rural population. There is the tenant, generally housed in a large, isolated farmhouse and the laborer/cottar housed on the periphery of these large tenancies either in a division of a cottage range or in an amorphous, nucleated settlement.

The middling farmer of Kintyre with their linear domestic range, with its spence and byre, is largely absent. This situation accords well with Cregeen's characterization of the social structure of Kintyre as exceptional to the area, with the twofold division between large tenant and laborer/smallholder found in other areas. Ardgaddan may be an

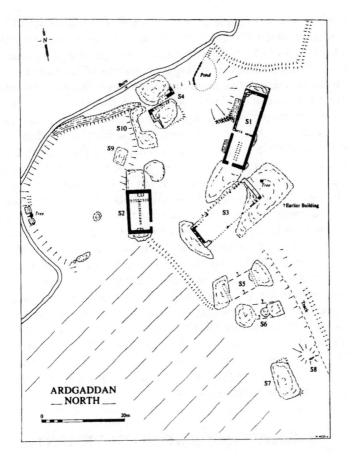

Figure 16. Plan of North Ardgaddan, Kilfinan. S1 is probably a dwelling with appended byre. S4 is a mill. The functions of the other structures are less clear (copyright University of Glasgow).

exception. The small population of perhaps just the two tenants, maybe with one or two laborers, might suggest that the situation of those tenants might compare with the middling farmer of Kintyre. They would fall somewhere in between the large tenant and the cottar. However, the two tenants here might themselves just have been smallholders, working at times for others.

In common with Kintyre, the large tenants seem to have adopted highly Improved, that is much subdivided, domestic space. The response of the smallholders/laborers to Improvement, though, is at present even less clear than it was for Kintyre. For Kilfinan we do not even have the documentary sources used above. The continued occupation of a few nucleated settlements is suggestive of at least a partial rejection of the reorganization of settlement. Continuity of nucleated settlement might suggest some form of continuity of the pre-Improvement spatial structuring of community. The response of some of Kilfinan's smallholders/laborers to Improvement might have been to resist by maintaining different patterns of routine interaction than their counterparts in Kintyre. Their response may have been to maintain a township-like community under the conditions of encroaching individual rights to land. Perhaps they had more room to determine their everyday lives.

However, a fuller analysis of the everyday activities within these post-Improvement nucleated settlements and the single-tenancy farms of which they formed a part is required. Nucleated settlement does not in itself necessarily induce a sense of community. In the pre-Improvement township and landscape, this community was created through communal practices. Nucleated settlement in itself is only a part of the process of constructing and maintaining a sense of common interest. Furthermore, many of these nucleated settlements of the period of Improvement are small and did not necessarily house a much greater population than the cottage ranges found elsewhere. Also, excavation of some of Kilfinan's deserted settlement sites is needed if we are to consider the ways in which the structuring of domestic space played a role in maintaining different concepts of occupancy. At the moment we do not even have the fragmentary and ambiguous sources that at least proved suggestive for Kintyre.

THE DYNAMICS OF IMPROVEMENT

A simple bipolar opposition of people and landlord engenders concentration on overt resistance to Improvement as the proper response of the "people," whether this resistance occurred in actuality or not. Looking at how people lived their day-to-day lives provides another way into the problem of understanding how they engaged with Improvement and what it might have meant for them.

Changes in material culture during the period of Improvement, in landscape organization, settlement pattern and morphology, and the use of domestic space, vary from region to region. In comparing the archaeology of Improvement in Kintyre with that in Kilfinan we can see that the course of Improvement varied significantly between these two geographically adjacent areas. In Kintyre, we find a middling class of tenant that seems absent from Kilfinan. This social class may be detectable archaeologically, as having a distinct approach to the construction of domestic space. The reasons behind these different regional trajectories remain to be explored.

However, the above discussion does suggest that any explanation of regional variation in the material and social process of Improvement must consider the farming population as playing an active, though not freely determined role. The tenants of varying sizes and the laborers did not passively step into a new, pre-fabricated, and homogenous social world handed down from a landlord, who might variously be conceived as beneficent or oppressive. The rural population engaged Improvement from a past. They evaluated Improvement with reference to continued occupancy, with reference to land rights. They were concerned with continued access to the land and its resources. They also evaluated the impact of Improvement on their complex relationships with others, with their landlord, their employer, their laborers, their family.

The concern with occupancy did not produce a homogenous acceptance or rejection of Improvement. Rather, occupancy was negotiated in contingent circumstances. The individual or group worked and lived within an Improved external environment, with its enclosed and often grid-like fields, dispersed settlement pattern, and rectilinear settlement morphology. At the same time, they might have inhabited unImproved domestic space, where in daily routine the family was in constant physical proximity in the single undivided space of the house, with its central hearth for a focus.

This seeming material contradiction is understandable if we consider both patterns as contingent manifestations of the same concern for occupancy. Material responses to Improvement varied with individual security of tenure. Those with access to the most secure forms of tenure inhabited more subdivided domestic space. They were less concerned to maintain the routine conditions in which traditional concepts of hereditary tenure would continue to make sense. The provision of the spence in the house of the middling farmer, and the drawing room in the large, two-storied farmhouse, neatly evidence a concern on the part of these tenants to appear to the outside world as promoting the new order. These are the spaces, separated from the rest of the house, where visitors were received.

Many who were least secure in their occupancy, the smallholders and laborers, continued to organize domestic space on more traditional lines. They thus allowed the survival of the concept of a hereditary right to land and continued to maintain a strong familial environment. Their response to Improvement was conditioned by the fact that it did not satisfy their concern for continued occupancy, and so they looked elsewhere. However, this was not resistance in simple oppositional terms.

Laborers and smallholders still worked and lived within an Improved landscape, and so at least gave that landscape and the social relations it helped to construct tacit consent or consent under duress. This was perhaps as their response in the external domain was publicly obvious and, therefore, their continued occupancy required expression of solidarity with the landlord's interest or the interests of their employer, the large farmer.

Engagement with Improvement related to continued occupancy, but also to relations within the rural population itself. Rural society became increasingly structured along horizontal lines as the divisions between its various tenurially defined groups were emphasized. This was in no small part a result of the fact that these different groups increasingly inhabited contrasting material worlds. Nineteenth century travelers and ministers could define several classes within the rural population and did so with reference to their houses.

Of course, there are many other interactions with Improvement that might prove significant. We might consider the restructuring of domestic space as accompanying the restructuring of gender relations, for example. Differing responses within the various groups discussed above might also become evident. Discussing such variation requires more detailed reconstruction of the changing material worlds of the people in question. Despite the fact that modern domestic space, settlement pattern and landscape organization, stemming from Improvement, seem familiar and self-explanatory, their social characteristics depend on use. Highly subdivided space only constructs marked social divisions within the family and community if associated with the separation of daily routines.

Conclusion

IMPROVEMENT, THE MATERIAL ENVIRONMENT, AND ROUTINE PRACTICE

Improvement was a transformation of the ways in which people related to each other. The restructuring of the physical environment was a central part of this process. Prior to Improvement, the physical environment and routine practice were structured in such a way that people related to each other as part of the community of the *baile* or several *bailtean* or as part of the family, and these relationships produced and were structured by a related sense of the community and of the family. With Improvement, changes in routine practices and their environment meant that people increasingly experienced their relationships with each other as autonomous individuals, and held a related sense of the individual. Daily structuring of the community and the family were undermined.

From at least the sixteenth to the eighteenth centuries the majority of the population lived in nucleated farming townships, or *bailtean*. Buildings within the *baile* were disposed according to the natural topography of the site, often resulting in an amorphous plan layout. These buildings were the dwellings, barns, byres, and other elements of the farm. Occasionally there were others, a church for example. These various structures were frequently accompanied by small enclosures, by kail, stock, and stackyards.

The origins of the *baile* as a settlement form probably lie somewhere in the late Medieval period. It may have come to replace small, dispersed farms as the predominant settlement form. There seems to have been some variation in the physical structuring of the eighteenth century township, some being tightly clustered and others more dispersed. There were probably many different variations on the *baile*, and settlement form was probably ordinarily in flux. There was a constant process of aggregation and disaggregation. Despite this, a general pattern of communal organization, where the individual was articulated within the community, can still be seen.

The landscape immediate to the *bailtean* was composed of unenclosed rig and furrow fields. These fields, as with the buildings of the *bailtean*, were disposed according to the natural topography, avoiding boggy areas and concentrating on the naturally draining lower slopes of the high ground. This intensively cultivated zone was defined ups-lope by the head dyke. The landscape was thus physically divided into the two broad zones of cultivated land and hill ground. One main use of the hill ground was as pasture, and shieling settlements are some-times found up to several kilometers from the parent settlement. Such shieling groups can be as large as forty or more structures and were associated with areas of communally held open pasture.

A pattern of late-Medieval enclosed fields may have existed prior to the predominance of the openfields. There is some ambiguous evidence that the agricultural lands of some immediately pre-Improvement townships were divided by low stone dykes, not entirely stock-proof and created through the consumption of stones cleared from ploughed land. Such enclosures would have been quite different from those of the period of Improvement.

Houses within the *bailtean* of Kintyre and Kilfinan were typically round-ended, and thus hip-roofed, and constructed from any of a num-ber of different materials, principally turf, turf and stone, unmortared stone, or lime-mortared stone. The roof was thatched and supported on cruck trusses. The size of these dwellings ranged from 6 to 12m by 4 to 8m. Many had two opposed entrances in the long walls, but this was not universally the case. Inside, the house consisted of a single, uni-tary space focusing on a central hearth. It is debatable whether these dwellings were generally longhouses, with cattle and humans inhabit-ing a common space.

With Improvement, the *bailtean* were almost universally replaced by dispersed and isolated settlements, principally consisting of court-yard farmsteads and linear range farmsteads, with the former accom-panied by ranges of laborers' dwellings. These new settlement forms came into widespread use from the late eighteenth century in Kintyre and by the mid-nineteenth century in Kilfinan. Where the *bailtean* had been amorphous in plan and disposed according to the local topography, these new settlements were markedly geometric and, thus, disposed ac-cording to abstract ideals without regard to the nature of the site. The courtyard and range farmsteads brought previously separate elements of the farm, like the dwelling, barn, byre, and sometimes the mill, to-gether in one structure. The linear range of laborers' dwellings were likewise composed of several units, although in this case they were mostly houses. They differed from the courtyard and linear farmsteads in that the farmstead was ordinarily the dwelling and associated out-buildings of a single family. In the cottage ranges, several families or individuals might be housed side by side. The courtyard farmsteads and rows of laborers' dwellings represent distinct elements of the large Improved farm, with the former housing the farmer and family and the latter their workers. These workers were frequently housed on the outskirts of the farm and distant from the farmstead. The Improved settlement pattern of Kilfinan is dominated by courtyard farmsteads and associated ranges of laborers' dwellings. In Kintyre, range farmsteads are also to be found. In both areas, the spread of this pattern of dispersed farming settlement is accompanied by the growth of a few nucleated villages and towns, re-housing those removed from the land with Improvement and providing services for the surrounding countryside.

Associated with the dispersal of settlement were the enclosure of the landscape and the decline of the shieling system. Enclosure had begun in Kintyre by the first half of the eighteenth century at least. It became widespread there from the later eighteenth century and in Kilfinan by the mid-nineteenth century. Enclosed fields are concentrated on the lower slopes of the high ground and on the valley floor. On the lower slopes they are often irregular in form and probably represent the enclosure of existing patches of arable, re-using the head dyke in cases. On the low ground, enclosure often went hand in hand with drainage, and the level topography together with the lack of previous intensive use allowed the creation of extensive geometric systems. Although the irregular and geometric forms of enclosure were largely contemporary, the former dropped out of use to leave a landscape divided between a zone of geometric enclosure and one of open hill ground. The shielings that had inhabited the hills prior to Improvement went out of use and were replaced with extensive sheep pastures and, eventually in places, with ground set aside for sport.

Improved houses were (and are) characterized by the subdivision of space and the associated multiplication of the hearth, which declined in importance as a focus for activity. Dwellings within courtyard farmsteads were commonly of two storeys and consisted of a variety of separate spaces including bedrooms, kitchens, and dining rooms. Many of the rooms within such houses had their own hearth, which no longer sat centrally in the floor, but was incorporated within a wall. Linear range farmsteads also exhibited an increased subdivision of space, but to a lesser extent than the courtyard farmstead. Commonly the dwelling area of the linear farmstead consisted of a kitchen, a room or spence, and perhaps a loft space. The spence and kitchen often had their own separate hearths, again frequently incorporated within or abutting a wall. In contrast to the farmsteads, laborers' dwellings were often a single space, perhaps still with a central hearth.

Change in the material environment with Improvement can be related to changing routine practice. Pre-Improvement routine practice was communal and familial, where everyday activities and interaction were conducted by the individual as a member of the community of the *baile* or of several *bailtean*, or as a member of a family.

Cultivation was communally organized, which made sense where tenants' individual cultivation rigs were intermixed. Communal ploughing was facilitated by the lack of enclosure. Livestock were maintained by herds whose employment was the responsibility of the whole township or at shieling grounds where the livestock of one or more *bailtean* were seasonally gathered. Communal and coordinated herding were sensible considering the lack of enclosure and the damage free-roaming livestock might do to the crop. The concentration of the farm population in the nucleated *baile* meant that people were already gathered for communal work.

The pre-Improvement house was a single unpartitioned space with central hearth. Thus, all activity within the house potentially took place in the presence of other members of the family. Activities associated with the hearth, such as cooking, eating, and some household industries like ceramic production, took center stage. Other activities, like sleeping, and crafts like spinning or weaving likewise occurred in the presence of others. The hearth and unpartitioned space of the house also provided an appropriate arena for story telling, music, discussion, and other activities that could combine in the *ceilidh*.

Improvement undermined the routine structuring of community. The *bailtean* were fragmented and houses became isolated from each other. People thus had less opportunity to socialize, and visits were now separated from the routine domain of the family, taking place in specialized spaces like the spence, parlor, or dining room. Enclosure dispensed with the need for herds or for shieling, as livestock were thus separated from the crop and from each other. Enclosure also required the consolidation of the tenant's land into discrete units separate from the land of their neighbors.

Internal subdivision of the house, most apparent in the courtyard farmstead, was associated with the segregation of routine tasks. With Improvement there was a kitchen for cooking, bedrooms for sleeping, a dining room for eating, and much else. The family experienced much more of their daily routine apart from each other. The provision of several hearths detracted from its role as a focus of activity, as did its removal from the center of the room to an end wall.

In general, then, pre-Improvement settlement, landscape, and domestic space played a role in the reflexive structuring of routine practice, which was conducted in such a way that people interacted as individuals within a community or family and held a related sense of the community and of the family. These senses of community and of family were not strictly defined or codified ways of comprehending the world. Rather, they were specific forms of practical consciousness that were vague and unspoken. However, they made certain specific, more consciously and rigorously defined ideologies knowable or unknowable. Explicit ideological statements would have been assessed by the general population in comparison with their experience of the world. In other words, some statements would appear as common sense, where others would not.

The pre-Improvement communal structuring of routine social interaction made the community of the clan possible. One relationship mirrored the other. Claims by the clan gentry to the resources of a given territory and to the support of its population, their clan, made sense in a world where daily routine was experienced as part of a community beyond the individual or the family. In reverse, the coherence of the community of the *baile* could be maintained and justified with reference to explicit notions of clanship and to relationships beyond the townships immediate bounds. Different social relations and their associated ideologies impacted on each other.

The sense of family and the familial structuring of everyday interaction made hereditary claims to land and its resources conceivable. A tenant's claim to a portion of land farmed by their family for generations was obvious and natural where routine experience of the world told them that the family was a fundamental unit of society and the focus of much daily activity.

The sense of the individual and individualized relations structured in conjunction with the Improved routine environment undermined the community of the clan. Claims by the clan gentry to a real and justifiable relationship with the farming population, and claims for access to resources based solely on their position within the clan, would have made no sense where the routine structuring of community had been destroyed. The ideology of the clan and the clan gentry-clan relationship would no longer accord with practical experience of the world in terms of routine practice, interaction, and practical consciousness. Rather, the claims of a landlord to resources, as their individual right, might seem more natural. The individualized character of the landlord-tenant-sub-tenant relationship would become universalized.

The sense of the individual was also cultivated in and through Improved domestic space, making hereditary claims to the land increasingly strange as the relationship between different members of the family became individualized. Routine experience apart from the family made individual rights to the land as a leaseholder knowable. Relationships in the home, in the fields, and beyond all interacted with each other.

However, some lived in houses lacking partitions and with a central hearth, and thus acted to maintain the familial structuring of daily interaction in the home. Improvement was not a simple and linear process of diffusion or evolution. Non-Improved domestic space and familial interaction could have continued to make hereditary claims to a portion of land knowable and would have contradicted individualized landlord-tenant-sub-tenant relations.

IMPROVEMENT AND THE NEGOTIATION OF SOCIETY

Improvement consisted of the actions of diverse people attempting to negotiate their position with regard to others by transforming the very basis of social interaction. It was composed of (unequal) social negotiation and has to be understood as a specific historical process.

Kintyre had been a part of the MacDonald Lordship of the Isles until the end of the fifteenth century. Under the Lordship it had largely been the patrimony of a prominent MacDonald kindred called, amongst other things, the MacDonalds of Dunnyveg and the Glens. After the forfeiture of the Lordship in 1493, the MacDonalds of Dunnyveg and the Glens were prominent in rebellions concerned with its restoration. These rebellions often drew on the continued support of Kintyre's population for the rights of their clan and the peninsula was held under suspicion as a nest of rebellion into the eighteenth century. The Campbell House of Argyll, the most prominent agents of the Crown in the southern Highlands, played a key role in the suppression of rebellion in the region and benefited with the legal acquisition of a large estate in Kintyre and land elsewhere. Their ownership of the Kintyre estate was actually or potentially threatened on many occasions by the continued loyalty of the population of the estate to an absent MacDonald clan gentry. The House of Argyll's claim to the land and resources of Kintyre as their private property (their *oighreachd*) made less sense to the farming population than did the claims of the MacDonald clan gentry to the same resources as the heritage of the community of the clan (their *duthchas*). Further, potentially rebellious tenants had a hereditary claim to the land, and did not rely on the consent of their landlords to justify occupancy of their holding.

The Campbells of Argyll, as agents of the Crown and on their own behalf, strove to resolve the contradiction between their personal claims to the land and its resources and competing claims to it as MacDonald clan heritage or the heritage of the tenantry on traditional right. They strove to resolve the contradiction between *oighreachd* and *duthchas*, which were in conflict when unaligned. The contradiction between *duthchas* and *oighreachd* relates to a contradiction between the relationships of the landlord–tenant–sub-tenant and the clan gentry-clan. The creation of a burgh at Campbeltown and the plantation of a Lowland farming population were intended to Civilize the peninsula, to render it more like the Lowlands. However, these and other schemes met with little success and Improvement should be seen as part of the ongoing project of Civilization.

Improvement was different from earlier Civilizing projects because it fundamentally altered routine practice and the everyday environment on a wide scale. In undermining the nature of routine social interaction, Improvement undermined the clan gentry-clan relationship and the ideology of the community of the clan associated with this. With Improvement, experience of the daily round was increasingly from the perspective of the individual disassociated from the community and the family. Claims by an absent clan gentry to the resources of the farms of Kintyre and the loyalty of its inhabitants would have become increasingly absurd in this situation. Hereditary claims to occupancy of a given portion of land would equally be undermined. At the same time, claims to legitimate legal ownership by the House of Argyll, as their personal property, would make more sense, as would occupation of the land by individual lease. With Improvement, the House of Argyll primarily sought to resolve the contradiction between *duthchas* and *oighreachd* in favor of *oighreachd*. They sought to legitimate ownership of their vast estate to its inhabitants and to naturalize their relationship with those inhabitants as a relationship between individuals.

For the Improving landlord, Enlightenment thought was a sophisticated and explicit ideology. The Scottish Enlightenment favored a stadial account of history where all societies inevitably progressed through stages to the peak of civilization, the Commercial Age. Enlightenment social theorists associated the Commercial Age with England in particular, and the Scottish Lowlands were considered to be in transition to that Age. Commercial society and private property were justified as the inevitable outcome of history. Further, the economy, institutions, and even mentalité of a given society were held to be intimately connected.

Thus, Enlightenment thought held that private property could be privileged with economic change and implied that Lowland and English ideals and institutions would come to the Highlands with Lowland and English forms of economy and material culture. Added to all this was the Enlightened notion of independence, which stressed that people were free to alter the conditions of their existence and not entirely dependent on divine will. Enlightenment, after all, was defined as the courage to use one's own reason.

It is not that an Enlightenment-based culture directed landlords to Improve their estates. An Enlightened view of the world would have been strategically deployed by them, as ideology, in justifying their actions, if only to themselves and to each other. Furthermore, just as Enlightenment naturalized certain forms of social interaction, it was also in turn naturalized by these forms of social interaction.

Improvement in Kilfinan has to be explained in somewhat different terms than in Kintyre. In Kilfinan, the contradiction between *duthchas* and *oighreachd* remains relevant to our understanding of Improvement, though it does not seem to have been a source of overt conflict. Another key social contradiction in Kilfinan was that between the position of many landowners there as both proprietors of Highland estates and members of the emergent middle class. In the period of Improvement, two groups dominated landholding in Kilfinan. There were established families like the Lamonts who had held land in the parish for centuries and there was a group of new proprietors who purchased estates with mercantile profits or the rewards of their profession. The Lamonts can also be linked to this emergent middle class, having been active as merchants in the nearby burghs from at least the early seventeenth century.

From the late eighteenth century a self-aware middle class emerged in Scotland. The Improving landowners of Kilfinan experienced a contradiction in the nature of their social interaction as part of that emergent class and as Highland landowners. Social interaction as part of the middle class was that of one autonomous individual, assessed on their own individual merits, and another. This form of interaction and its extension to the rural Highlands was expressed ideologically through a series of Enlightenment-based concepts like progress. Establishment and maintenance of middle class status would have required the Improvement of estates that would literally have been considered backward. Thus, Improvement, as the transformation of one set of relationships, impacted on the establishment or maintenance of middle class relationships. Likewise, the nature of middle class interaction impacted on relationships in the Highland estate. New and

established landowners alike faced potential conflict with their tenantry, who might expect some right to occupancy of the land in contradiction to the increasingly commercial nature of the estate as an
asset for rationalization and exploitation. Here we see *duthchas* and
oighreachd in contradiction again.

All this said, Improvement was not a straightforward process and
landowners did not simply and freely re-order the material environment
and routine practice. They may have instigated Improvement, but they
did so with reference to others and with reference to the past. As just
summarized, Improvement, for them, was a strategy in maintaining
or transforming certain relationships and, as such, Improvement was
in part "caused" by others. This is not to justify the landlord's actions,
but to suggest that they did not act in a social vacuum. Also, Improvement was not freely and uniformly carried through. The populations of
Kintyre and Kilfinan did not simply and uniformly accept it or promote
it. This does not mean they were free to reject it.

Enclosure and the dispersal of settlement were advanced in
Kintyre by the mid-nineteenth century, as were other Improved practices within the landscape, like draining, the use of Improved farm
machinery, and the use of lime to enhance the fertility of the fields.
External to the home, Improved practices and their concomitant environment were widely adopted. Within the home, the story is much
more complicated. Some people lived in highly subdivided courtyard
farmsteads, while others lived in barely partitioned cottages with central hearths. In Kintyre, there was also the range farmstead.

Improvement was neither simply rejected nor accepted. Improvement affected everyone, but it did so in different ways. The lives of
different people were affected in different ways, but different aspects of
a single person's life were also differentially affected. One person might
experience one form of relationship in the home, with their family, and
quite another form in the fields as a farmhand, or with the landlord as
a tenant.

The dispersal of settlement and advancement of enclosure would
have gone a long way towards the deconstruction of the ties of community, where community refers to face-to-face social engagement and the
demarcation of individuals by status rather than class. This process
would have been furthered, for example, by the adoption of Improved
farm machinery, which required fewer people and draught livestock
to operate. In this situation, routine experience of the landscape would
have cultivated a sense of the autonomous individual more than a sense
of community. Within the house, by contrast, routine practice was more
diverse and while some families became more and more differentiated

within themselves, others continued to interact in a singular space around the central hearth.

Variation in the transformation of people's routines with Improvement was not random, but related to a common underlying concern for continued occupancy. Occupancy is defined here as continued residence upon a portion of land and use of its resources. A hereditary right to occupancy was commonly asserted in the pre-Improvement period.

From the mid-eighteenth century at least, political loyalty to the House of Argyll and the Hanoverian succession was an explicit condition of occupancy on the Argyll Estates. Continued occupancy in Kintyre, under these conditions, would require the tenant or sub-tenant to express their disposal to Argyll's interest. Considering the links drawn in Scottish Enlightenment thought between economy, social institutions like the law, the Commercial Age, and progress, the acceptance and promotion of an Improved landscape would be an overt expression of solidarity with the landlord's interest. At the scale of landscape, occupancy seems to have taken priority over the maintenance of community for most. Here, Improvement acted to undermine one previously structured relationship, that of community, while maintaining another, that of the farmer and farmhand and their families to the land.

Variation in the acceptance of sub-divided domestic space becomes meaningful when we consider the tenurial position of the occupants of different houses. Improvement in Kintyre was accompanied by the threefold division of the tenantry into the small tenantry, the middling farmer, and the gentleman (substantial/large) farmer, and by the growth of a rural proletariat employed in wage labor. Contemporary observers equated the differential organization of domestic space with tenurial rank. Some drew a distinction between the house of the farmer, which was described as comfortable (read Improved), and that of the wage laborer or cottager (smallholder), which was unpartitioned or unImproved. The range farmstead was associated at the time of its currency with a "better class" of tenant.

It seems that the courtyard farmstead is to be associated with the large tenant/gentleman farmer, the linear farmstead with the middling tenant, and the one-room cottage with the lower tenants and the landless, although it may not always be possible to maintain such rigid distinctions. In this case, the transformation of domestic space can be related to the implications of Improvement for occupancy. Sub-divided domestic space was marked in the house of the large tenant, whose occupancy was most secure in that they held their land by a long lease and were better off financially and, thus, less prone to insolvency. The middling farmer also lived in a sub-divided house, though the separation

of activity spaces here was less distinct. The small tenant was prone
to insolvency in this period and thus insecure in their occupancy. The
laborer, employed year by year by the tenant, held little or no land with
Improvement and only insecure employment. Both these groups were
probably associated above all with a type of house still centered on the
hearth and largely unpartitioned.

Improvement, as the sub-division of activity and space within the
house, was commensurate with continued occupancy for the large tenant and, in many cases, the middling tenant. The occupants of the
house benefited in terms of occupancy under the lease system and
adopted and promoted the routine conditions that cultivated a sense
of the individual, made the lease and private property knowable, and,
restructured their relationship with the landlord as one of absence, as
one between autonomous individuals. Those dispossessed by Improvement, or whose holdings were insecure, continued to live routine lives
that positioned them as individuals within a family or kindred, made
hereditary claims to the land knowable, and, to some extent, frustrated
the penetration and effectiveness of the relations of capitalism. They
resisted Improvement of the home in order to resist the erosion of their
right to occupancy. The maintenance of unImproved space allowed the
maintenance of an alternative claim to the land, based in concepts of
hereditary tenure rather than in the individualized lease system. The
effectiveness of their resistance is another question, to which I will return.

Improvement affected different people and groups in quite different
ways. Because of this, it is not enough to discuss Improvement solely
with reference to two opposed groups, the landlords and the people.
There is a second reason that this bipolar opposition is inadequate,
and that is the fact that many would have experienced Improvement
as a series of changes in the ways in which they engaged with others
within the farming population. Likewise, and as summarized above,
Improvement for the landlord was about their relationships with other
landlords and with the emergent middle class at the same time that it
was about their relationship with those on their estates.

In living in a courtyard farmstead and farming in an enclosed landscape, the substantial tenant was not simply restructuring their relationship with their landlord, but also with their neighbors and those
who worked the fields for them. They were acting with reference to
a multitude of groups and individuals. Likewise, the laborer was acting
as much, if not more, with reference to the farmer as to the landlord.
Their primary relationship as occupants of the land was with the former,
their employer.

In many ways, the growing distinction between different tenurially defined groups with Improvement was an unintended consequence
of the actions of various groups wishing to maintain their occupancy.
The growth of class cannot wholly be defined in such a way though.
People may have acted with a strong regard for occupancy, but they
would have been aware of what was happening around them. The chron-
ically insecure position of the laborer and smallholder could have been
justified by the substantial farmer with reference to an ideology that
made the separation of the laborer from land and its produce natural.
On top of such explicit justification, this employer-worker relationship
would have seemed perfectly normal to someone who experienced other
relationships, with their family, with their landlord, from the position of
the capitalist individual. Landlord-tenant, employer-worker, husband-
wife, parent-child, and whatever else—these were relationships that
were distinct, but inextricably bound together.

RESISTANCE AND THE ASYMMETRY OF SOCIETY

To talk of various groups within Kintyre and Kilfinan as actively
and differentially engaging with Improvement does not mean that all
were equally free to determine the pattern of their own lives and to re-
negotiate their relationships with others. Everyone would have come
to Improvement from a history of past social interaction that would
have conditioned and limited, as much as enabled, their possibilities
for action. Improvement also addressed social contradictions that had
roots centuries old. How people engaged with new social conditions
under Improvement was partly with reference to how things used to be.
People acting with reference to the past also acted with reference
to their present position within an asymmetrical society. Even the substantial tenant farmer, actively engaged in commercial farming, enclosing the fields, and living in a large, standardized, highly sub-divided
house, did not act freely. To no small extent, they promoted Improvement because their tenancy depended on it.
Everyone acted with reference to others, but some had very little
freedom to act at all. I would continue to argue that those living in
single-space dwellings and gathered around the central hearth were
engaged in an act of resistance to Improvement and to what Improvement meant for them in terms of increased insecurity and separation
from the land and from others. But this resistance was limited. The inhabitants of these houses still worked in Improved fields and received
wages for doing so. They may have maintained a hereditary claim to

the land, and did so in no small part through their routine domestic
lives, but was this of much use to them when their employer decided to
make them redundant or their landlord, with the force of law, decided
to evict them?

Well, it could have been effective in another place and at another
time. In summarizing the character of agricultural organization in
Kintyre in the 1920s, James McClement said:

> The crofting system is unknown in Kintyre, and nowadays, except for per-
> haps a score of post-war small-holdings, all the farms in Kintyre are large
> and dependent on easy communications to dispose of their surplus products.
> (McClement 1927:25)

This is a generalization, of course. McClement may not have been
aware of, or wished to highlight, significant social variation. However,
the large commercial farm was certainly pre-eminent. Improvement
in this case seems to have overwhelmingly transformed rural society
and it seems that, throughout the process, acts of resistance remained
confined to the domestic environment, if they continued at all.

It is no accident that the commercial farms of Kintyre were compared to the crofting system, largely associated with the northwest
Highlands and the Isles from Mull north. In many ways, crofting
was the antithesis of the large commercial farm. The croft, both at
McClement's time of writing and today, is a specific type of holding (see
Hunter 2000:33–34 and *passim*). The crofter is the tenant of an individual holding, paying rent to a landlord not a superior tenant. The typical
croft is sufficient to supply only a part of the tenant's needs and, so, the
crofter must have an ancillary occupation.

The crofting system was instigated with Improvement, and has
its origins in the period around 1800. Originally, certain landlords created crofts at the same time they were clearing large parts of their
estates to make way for commercial sheep farms. The crofts, often
laid out in groups along the coast, re-housed the displaced population.
They also provided a concentrated work force for the increased commercial exploitation of the estate. Many crofters were initially engaged in
the collection and burning of kelp, producing an alkaline residue that
could then be shipped to glass and soap works in the Lowlands and in
England. Landlords explicitly designed the crofts so that their inhabitants could not subsist on the produce of their holding alone and, thus,
had to engage in kelping and other industries.

Crofting is a product of Improvement and is inextricably bound up
with the commercialization of the Highland and Island estate. However,
through crofting, a large population below the level of the substantial

tenant farmer maintained a stake in the land, no matter how circumscribed. This is in contrast to the southern Highlands, where crofting
was limited and where many were dispossessed with Improvement,
working the land as wage laborers, if at all.

The continued connection of the crofting community with the land,
their spatial distinction from the commercial farmers, and much else,
lies behind McClement's comparison between crofting and the farms of
Kintyre, but the distinction goes deeper than this. By the 1920s, crofting
represented the successful assertion of the subjugated and dispossessed
of their right to occupancy of the land. Crofting demonstrates what
could have happened in the southern Highlands, had the balance of
power and contingent circumstance been different. A Royal Commission
in the 1950s described the crofter's attachment to their holdings, as
their hereditary right and as the land worked and transformed by them,
thus:

> Above all they [the crofters] have the feeling that the croft, its land, its
> houses, are their own. They have gathered its stones and reared its buildings
> and occupied it as their own all their days. They have received it from their
> ancestors who won it from the wilderness and they cherish the hope that
> they will transmit it to the generations to come. Whatever be the legal theory,
> they feel it to be their own—and in this respect the provisions of the Crofters
> Acts do no more than set the parliamentary seal of approval on their own
> deepest convictions. (quoted in Hunter 2000:281)

"Parliamentary seal of approval" refers to a series of legislative
measures from 1886, the year of the Crofters' Act, through to the 1920s
intended to enshrine and extend crofters' security of tenure and to give
them more land (see Hunter 2000). In an extensive land settlement program, the sheep farms created with Improvement were taken over and
used to provide as many crofters and landless cottars as possible with
a new croft or extended holding. The key point here is that the crofters
and cottars played a significant role in bringing about this process of
land reform. From the late nineteenth century, these groups engaged in
open conflict with their landlords, occupying and squatting on land they
argued should be given over to them, resisting eviction, openly and at
times violently confronting the agents of the estate, the police, and the
military. Such actions created an explicit "land problem" which had to
be addressed. The context for the legislative and land settlement pro-
grams that followed is of course more complex, but the key point is that
crofters and cottars played a fundamental role in securing change and
in stabilizing and extending their claim to the land. These groups propounded an elaborate ideology concerning their right to the land (see,
e.g., Withers 1990) and engaged in overt action to restructure their
relationship with their landlord. In future, a consideration of routine

practice through the nineteenth century and into the twentieth will be essential to the further understanding of this process, its origins, and variability. Here I will simply mention as a point of interest that some crofters' houses in the Western Isles maintained their central hearths and limited internal subdivision well into the twentieth century (see, e.g., Fenton 1995).

The history of crofting tells in part of the triumph of resistance. However, it needs to be restated that people are not entirely free to act and do so with reference to others and within the limits of relations of power. It is ironic that the success of the crofter/cottar in asserting their hereditary rights depended on the fact that the landlord chose to keep them on the land in the first place, and on the way he dictated they should live. It is also ironic that the landlord's eventual circumscription, as occurred in some areas, was in part due to their own successful assertion of their right to determine the organization of their estates as private property. They chose to create the crofts and, so, played a part in the creation of the community who would eventually rise against them. Equally, while Improvement, clearance, and the initial creation of crofting in the north and west are often seen as a triumph of landlordism, we should not forget that the landlords achieved Improvement through others, like the commercial farmer, and relied on the crofter and cottar, the labor force, for the effective commercialization of their estates. The landlords, in pursuing their own interests, created the social contradictions that undermined their own position. The crofters may eventually have won significant rights, but in part they owed their coherence and their ability to act to capitalism and to their landlords' past actions.

Returning to Kintyre and Kilfinan, the comparison with Improvement in crofting areas to the north and west shows the importance of considering the asymmetry of social relations. That the re-orientation of the estate in accordance with the interests of the landlord was more successful in the south in the long-term is due in part to the fact that those landlords severely circumscribed the possibilities for resistance. Non-capitalist routine relations within the home and related concepts of hereditary right to the land were maintained by some during the period of Improvement. This can be conceived as resistance to Improvement, in that some people refused to allow all of their social relationships to be restructured in a certain way, but the possibilities for further action were limited. Kintyre and Kilfinan did not have a concentration of crofters and cottars in distinct settlements, as elsewhere. It is clear that farm laborers and the few smallholders there were in Kintyre and Kilfinan did form a distinct class with Improvement. Each member of this class had much in common with their peers. However, they were dispersed throughout a landscape of large farms. Routine life for a wage laborer working on a large commercial farm would have been very different from life within a crofting community where life, however hard, was conducted as part of that community. An alternative claim to the land was significant, but its impact was limited when expressed singularly.

For sure, there were other options open to those in the southern Highlands who were impoverished with Improvement. Many from Kintyre emigrated. Some went to North Carolina, for example, settling in the Argyll Colony. Occasionally, their descendants return to visit the very spot from where their ancestors set off several centuries ago, and the experience can be an emotional one (MacVicar 1977). When they arrive, they are sometimes told stories of individual emigration events, the people involved, and the ships they sailed on (MacVicar 1977).

Those emigrating to North Carolina in the late eighteenth century gave various reasons for doing so, some of which were recorded on their arrival in America (MacVicar 1977:9, 12). Many of them quoted low wages or poverty occasioned by want of work, high rents, the conversion of arable lands into sheep pastures, and their oppression by exacting landlords. Many small tenants in Kintyre were turned off the land when the Poor Law Act of 1834 made paupers chargeable to the rates paid by the landlord (McClement 1927:24).

It has long been a subject for discussion whether emigration of the sort discussed here should be seen as a defeat imposed on people who should, in a better ordered world, have remained where they were or whether it should be seen as a radical protest against Improvement (see, e.g., Hunter 2000:25–26). Emigration represents, for some, a passive reaction and, for others, active resistance. Whatever the case, it is clear that emigrants from places like Kintyre were exercising a limited power of choice. Whether forced into emigration in defeat or actively seeking it in protest, those leaving were acting with reference to others, to their landlords and to the substantial commercial farmers.

There are many issues that remain to be explored in linking archaeology, routine practice, Improvement, capitalism, and the constitution of social relations in the Scottish Highlands. The point to remember is that it is relationships between people that we are studying. These changing relationships can usefully be defined in relation to the more abstract concept of capitalism, but the distinction between capitalism and capitalist society reminds us that the relationships between people are diverse, complex, and dynamic. These relationships exist in a multitude and people not only act with reference to others, but to many others at one and the same time. Because people act with reference to others, are situated within relations of power, and have a personal and collective past, they do not act freely. They do, however, act.

References

ABDA—Argyll and Bute District Archives, Lochgilphead.

Abercrombie, N., Hill, S., and Turner, B.S., 1980, *The Dominant Ideology Thesis*. Allen and Unwin, London.

Adams, I.H., 1980, The Agents of Agricultural Change. In *The Making of the Scottish Countryside*, edited by M.L. Parry and T.R. Slater, pp. 155–175. Croom Helm, London.

Anderson, J.R. (editor), 1925, *The Burgesses and Guild Brethren of Glasgow, 1573–1750*. Scottish Record Society, Edinburgh.

Anon., 1845, Parish of Campbelton. In *The New Statistical Account of Scotland, Vol. 7*, pp. 453–468. Blackwood, Edinburgh.

Anon., 1871, *The House of Argyll and the Collateral Branches of the Clan Campbell*. Tweed, Glasgow.

Atkinson, J.A., 1995, *Medieval or Later Rural Settlement (MOLRS) Study: Recommendations Towards a Policy Statement*. Unpublished report for Historic Scotland, Edinburgh.

——, 2000, Rural Settlement on North Lochtayside: Understanding the Landscapes of Change. In *Townships to Farmsteads: Rural Settlement in Scotland, England and Wales*, edited by J.A. Atkinson, I. Banks, and G. MacGregor, pp. 150–160. British Archaeological Reports, Oxford.

Atkinson, J.A., Banks, I., and MacGregor, G. (editors), 2000, *Townships to Farmsteads: Rural Settlement in Scotland, England and Wales*. British Archaeological Reports, Oxford.

Atkinson, J.A., Driscoll, S.T., and Watson, F., 1993, *Kilfinan Parish Survey. Preliminary Report 1992*. Unpublished report, Glasgow University Archaeological Research Division, Glasgow.

Bangor-Jones, M., 1993, The Incorporation of Documentary Evidence and Other Historical Sources into Preservational and Management Strategies. In *Medieval or Later Rural Settlement in Scotland: Management and Preservation*, edited by R. Hingley, pp. 36–42. Historic Scotland, Edinburgh.

Banks, I.B.J., 1996, *Rural Society and Settlement: Isolated Monuments and Farming Communities in Northern and Western Scotland in the Late Atlantic Iron Age*. Unpublished Ph.D. thesis, University of Glasgow, Glasgow.

Banks, I., and Atkinson, J.A., 2000, Bragar Townships Project: Developing a Methodology for Locating Hidden Settlement Patterns. In *Townships to Farmsteads: Rural Settlement in Scotland, England and Wales*, edited by J.A. Atkinson, I. Banks, and G. MacGregor, pp. 69–77. British Archaeological Reports, Oxford.

Bannatyne Club, 1854, *Origines Parochiales Scotiae*, volume II part 1. Lizars, Edinburgh.

Bannerman, J., 1977, The Lordship of the Isles. In *Scottish Society in the Fifteenth Century*, edited by J.M. Brown, pp. 209–240. Arnold, London.

Barrett, J.C., 1988, Fields of Discourse. *Critique of Anthropology* 7:5–16.

——, 1994, *Fragments from Antiquity*. Blackwell, Oxford.

——, 2001, Agency, the Duality of Structure, and the Problem of the Archaeological Record. In *Archaeological Theory Today*, edited by I. Hodder, pp. 141–164. Polity Press, Cambridge.

Barrett, J.C., and Downes, J.M., 1993, North Pitcarmick (Kirkmichael Parish). In *Discovery and Excavation in Scotland*, edited by C.E. Batey, pp. 102–103. Council for Scottish Archaeology, Edinburgh.

——, 1994, North Pitcarmick (Kirkmichael Parish). In *Discovery and Excavation in Scotland*, edited by C.E. Batey and M. King, pp. 87–88. Council for Scottish Archaeology, Edinburgh.

——, 1996, *North Pitcarmick: A Radiocarbon Dated Chronology*. Unpublished report, University of Sheffield.

Barrow, G.W.S., 1981, *Kingship and Unity*. Edinburgh University Press, Edinburgh.

Basker, J.G., 1991, Scotticisms and the Problem of Cultural Identity in Eighteenth-Century Britain. *Eighteenth Century Life* 15:81–95.

Beaton, E.A., and MacIntyre, S.W. (editors), 1990, *The Burgesses of Inverary, 1665–1963*. Scottish Record Society, Edinburgh.

Beaudry, M.C., Cook, L.J., and Mrozowski, S.A., 1991, Artifacts and Active Voices: Material Culture as Social Discourse. In *The Archaeology of Inequality*, edited by R.H. McGuire and R. Paynter, pp. 150–191. Blackwell, Oxford.

Bede, C., 1861, *Glencreggan. Or, a Highland Home in Cantire*, 2 volumes. Longman, Green, Longman and Roberts, London.

Berry, C.J., 1997, *Social Theory of the Scottish Enlightenment*. Edinburgh University Press, Edinburgh.

Bil, A., 1990, *The Shieling, 1600–1840: the Case of the Central Scottish Highlands*. John Donald, Edinburgh.

Blackburn, R., 1998, *The Making of New World Slavery: From the Baroque to the Modern, 1492–1800* (paperback ed.). Verso, London/New York.

Bloch, M., 1989, *Ritual, History and Power: Selected Papers in Anthropology*. Athlone, London.

Bourdieu, P., 1977, *Outline of a Theory of Practice*. Cambridge University Press, Cambridge.

Branigan, K., 1997, Mankind on the Margin: the SEARCH Project. *Current Archaeology* 13(8):284–307.

Branigan, K., and Foster, P., 1995, *Barra: Archaeological Research on Ben Tangaval*. Sheffield Academic Press, Sheffield.

Branigan, K., and Merrony, C., 2000, The Hebridean Blackhouse on the Isle of Barra. *Scottish Archaeological Journal* 22.1:1–16.

Broadie, A. (editor), 1997, *The Scottish Enlightenment: An Anthology*. Canongate, Edinburgh.

Burke, B., 1856, *A Genealogical and Heraldic Dictionary of the Peerage and Baronetage of the British Empire*. Hurst and Blackett, London.

Caird, J.B., 1980, The Reshaped Agricultural Landscape. In *The Making of the Scottish Countryside*, edited by M.L. Parry and T.R. Slater, pp. 203–222. Croom Helm, London.

Cairns, G., 1961, The Parish of Kilfinan. In *The Third Statistical Account of Scotland*, volume 9, edited by C.M. MacDonald, pp. 316–323. Collins, Glasgow.

Caldwell, D.H., and Ewart, G., 1993, Finlaggan and the Lordship of the Isles: An Archaeological Approach. *Scottish Historical Review* 72:146–166.

Caldwell, D.H., McWee, R., and Ruckley, N.A., 2000, Post-Medieval Settlement on Islay—Some Recent Research. In *Townships to Farmsteads: Rural Settlement in Scotland,*

England and Wales, edited by J.A. Atkinson, I. Banks and G. MacGregor, pp. 58–68. British Archaeological Reports, Oxford.

Cameron, E.A., 1998, The Highlands since 1850. In *Modern Scottish History 1707 to the Present, Volume 2: The Modernisation of Scotland, 1850 to the Present*, edited by A. Cooke, I. Donnachie, A. MacSween, and C.A. Whatley, pp. 47–72. Tuckwell Press, East Linton.

Camic, C., 1983, *Experience and Enlightenment*. Chicago University Press, Chicago.

Campbell, G.D., 1887, *Scotland As It Was and As It Is*, 2 volumes. Douglas, Edinburgh.

——, 1906, *George Douglas, Eighth Duke of Argyll 1823–1900: Autobiography and Memoirs*. Murray, London.

Campbell, H. (editor), 1933, *Abstracts of the Particular Register of Sasines for Argyll, Bute and Dunbarton*. Brown, Edinburgh.

——, (editor), 1934, *Abstracts of the Particular Register of Sasines for Argyll, Bute and Dunbarton*, volume II. Brown, Edinburgh.

Campbell, R., 1988, The Landed Classes. In *People and Society in Scotland, Volume 1, 1760–1830*, edited by T.M. Devine and R. Mitchison, pp. 91–108. John Donald, Edinburgh.

Canuto, M.A., and Yaeger, J. (editors), 2000, *The Archaeology of Communities: A New World Perspective*. Routledge, London.

Carrithers, M., 1992, *Why Humans Have Cultures: Explaining Anthropology and Social Diversity*. Oxford University Press, Oxford.

Carter, I., 1981, The Changing Image of the Scottish Peasantry, 1745–1980. In *People's History and Socialist Theory*, edited by R. Samuel, pp. 9–15. Routledge and Kegan Paul, London.

Chitnis, A., 1976, *The Scottish Enlightenment: A Social History*. Croom Helm, London.

Cowan, I.B., and Easson, D.E., 1976, *Medieval Religious Houses: Scotland* (2nd ed.). Longman, London.

Crawford, I.A., 1983, The Present State of Settlement History in the West Highlands and Islands. In *From the Stone Age to the 'Forty-Five*, edited by A. O'Connor and D.V. Clarke, pp. 350–367. John Donald, Edinburgh.

Creed, G.W., and Ching, B., 1997, Recognizing Rusticity: Identity and the Power of Place. In *Knowing Your Place: Rural Identity and Cultural Hierarchy*, edited by B. Ching and G.W. Creed, pp. 1–38. Routledge, London.

Cregeen, E., 1963, *Inhabitants of the Argyll Estate, 1779*. Scottish Record Society, Edinburgh.

——, 1965, Flailing in Argyll. *Folk Life* 3:90.

——, 1968, The Changing Role of the House of Argyll in the Scottish Highlands. In *History and Social Anthropology*, edited by I.M. Lewis, pp. 153–192. Tavistock, London.

——, 1970, The Changing Role of the House of Argyll in the Scottish Highlands. In *Scotland in the Age of Improvement*, edited by N.T. Phillipson and R. Mitchison, pp. 5–23. Edinburgh University Press, Edinburgh.

Cressey, M., 1996, Loch Arnicle (Killean and Kilchenzie Parish). In, *Discovery and Excavation in Scotland*, edited by R. Turner, p. 22. Council for Scottish Archaeology, Edinburgh.

Cruden, S., 1999, *Castle Campbell* (revised ed.). Historic Scotland, Edinburgh.

Curwen, E.C., 1938, The Hebrides: A Cultural Backwater. *Antiquity* 12:261–289.

Dalglish, C., 2000, *Rural Settlement in the Age of Reason: An Archaeology of the Southern Scottish Highlands from the Sixteenth to Nineteenth Centuries A.D.*. Unpublished Ph.D. thesis, University of Glasgow, Glasgow.

Deetz, J., 1996, *In Small Things Forgotten* (2nd ed.). Doubleday, New York.

Devine, T.M., 1989a, The Emergence of the New Elite in the Western Highlands and Islands, 1800–60. In *Improvement and Enlightenment*, edited by T.M. Devine, pp. 108–142. John Donald, Edinburgh.

——, 1989b, Social Responses to Agrarian 'Improvement': The Highland and Lowland Clearances in Scotland. In *Scottish Society 1500–1800*, edited by R.A. Houston and I.D. Whyte, pp. 148–168. Cambridge University Press, Cambridge.

——, 1994a, *The Transformation of Rural Scotland*. Edinburgh University Press, Edinburgh.

——, 1994b, *Clanship to Crofters' War*. Manchester University Press, Manchester.

——, 1995, *Exploring the Scottish Past*. Tuckwell, East Linton.

——, 1999, A conservative people? Scottish Gaeldom in the Age of Improvement. In *Eighteenth century Scotland: New perspectives*, edited by T.M. Devine and J.R. Young, pp. 225–236. Tuckwell Press, East Linton.

Dixon, P., 1993, A Review of the Archaeology of Rural Medieval and Post-Medieval Settlement in Highland Scotland. In *Medieval or Later Rural Settlement in Scotland: Management and Preservation*, edited by R. Hingley, pp. 24–35. Historic Scotland, Edinburgh.

——, 1994, Field-Systems, Rig and Other Cultivation Remains in Scotland: The Field Evidence. In *The History of Soils and Field Systems*, edited by S. Foster and T.C Smout, pp. 27–52. Scottish Cultural Press, Aberdeen.

Dodgshon, R.A., 1977, Changes in Scottish Township Organization During the Medieval and Early Modern Periods. *Geografiska Annaler* 59:51–65.

——, 1981, *Land and Society in Early Scotland*. Clarendon, Oxford.

——, 1988, West Highland Chiefdoms, 1500–1745: A Study in Redistributive Exchange. In *Economy and Society in Scotland and Ireland, 1500–1939*, edited by R. Mitchison and P. Roebuck, pp. 27–37. John Donald, Edinburgh.

——, 1993a, West Highland and Hebridean Settlement Prior to Crofting and the Clearances: A Study in Stability or Change?. *Proceedings of the Society of Antiquaries of Scotland* 123:419–438

——, 1993b, Strategies of Farming in the Western Highlands and Islands of Scotland Prior to Crofting and the Clearances. *Economic History Review* 4:679–701.

——, 1994, Rethinking Highland Field Systems. In *The History of Soils and Field Systems*, edited by S. Foster and T.C. Smout, pp. 53–65. Scottish Cultural Press, Aberdeen.

——, 1998a, The Evolution of Highland Townships During the Medieval and Early Modern Periods. *Landscape History* 20:51–63.

——, 1998b, *From Chiefs to Landlords*. Edinburgh University Press, Edinburgh.

Driscoll, S.T., 1984, The New Medieval Archaeology: Theory vs. History. *Scottish Archaeological Review* 3:104–109.

Dunbar, J.G., 1965, Auchindrain: A mid-Argyll Township. *Folk Life* 3:61–67.

——, 1971, The Study of Deserted Medieval Settlements in Scotland. II The Peasant House. In *Deserted Medieval Villages*, edited by M. Beresford and J.G. Hurst, pp. 236–246. Lutterworth Press, Woking.

Evans, E.E., 1961, Review of "Highland Folk Ways". *Antiquity* 35:247–248.

Fairhurst, H., 1960, Scottish Clachans. *Scottish Geographical Magazine* 76:67–76.

——, 1967, The Archaeology of Rural Settlement in Scotland. *Transactions of the Glasgow Archaeological Society* 15:139–158.

——, 1968, Rosal: a Deserted Township in Strath Naver, Sutherland. *Proceedings of the Society of Antiquaries of Scotland* 100:135–169.

——, 1969, The Deserted Settlement at Lix, West Perthshire. *Proceedings of the Society of Antiquaries of Scotland* 101:160–199.

——, 1971, The Study of Deserted Medieval Settlements in Scotland. I.Rural Settlement. In *Deserted Medieval Villages*, edited by M. Beresford and J.G. Hurst, pp. 229–235. Lutterworth Press, Woking.

Fairhurst, H., and Petrie, G., 1964, Scottish Clachans II. Lix and Rosal. *Scottish Geographical Magazine* 80:150–163.

Fawcett, R., 1996, *Argyll's Lodging*. Historic Scotland, Edinburgh.

Fenton, A., 1968, Alternating Stone and Turf—An Obsolete Building Practice. *Folk Life* 6:94–103.

——, 1974, "Sowens" in Scotland. *Folk Life* 12:41–47.

——, 1995, *The Island Blackhouse* (new ed.). Historic Scotland, Edinburgh.

——, 1999, *Scottish Country Life* (revised ed.). Tuckwell, East Linton.

Fenton, A., and Walker, B., 1981, *The Rural Architecture of Scotland*. John Donald, Edinburgh.

Ferguson, J., 1951, *Argyll in the Forty-Five*. Faber and Faber, London.

Findlay, A.M., 1978, "Cuninghamia": Timothy Pont's Contribution to Scottish Cartography Re-Examined. *Scottish Geographical Magazine* 94(1):36–47.

Fraser, W.H., 1988, Patterns of Protest. In *People and Society in Scotland, volume 1, 1760–1830*, edited by T.M. Devine and R. Mitchison, pp. 268–291. John Donald, Edinburgh.

Gailey, R.A., 1960, Settlement and Population in Kintyre, 1750–1800. *Scottish Geographical Magazine* 76:99–107.

——, 1961, *Settlement Changes in the Southwest Highlands of Scotland, 1750–1960*. Unpublished Ph.D. thesis, University of Glasgow, Glasgow.

——, 1962a, The Evolution of Highland Rural Settlement. *Scottish Studies* 6: 155–177.

——, 1962b, The Peasant Houses of the South-West Highlands of Scotland: Distribution, Parallels and Evolution. *Gwerin* 3:227–242.

——, 1963, Agrarian Improvement and the Development of Enclosure in the South-west Highlands of Scotland. *Scottish Historical Review* 42:105–125.

Gaskell, P., 1996, *Morvern Transformed*. Cambridge University Press, Cambridge.

Gazin-Schwartz, A., 2001 Archaeology and Folklore of Material Culture, Ritual, and Everyday Life. *International Journal of Historical Archaeology* 5(4):263–280.

Giddens, A., 1979 *Central Problems in Social Theory*. MacMillan, London.

——, 1984, *The Constitution of Society*. Polity Press, Cambridge.

——, 1995, *A Contemporary Critique of Historical Materialism* (2nd ed.). MacMillan, London.

Gilbertson D., Kent, M. and Gratton, J. (editors), 1996 *The Outer Hebrides: The Last 14,000 Years*. Sheffield Academic Press, Sheffield.

Gillies, W., 1978, Some Aspects of Campbell History. *Transactions of the Gaelic Society of Inverness* 50:256–295.

Glassie, H., 1975, *Folk Housing in Middle Virginia*, University of Tennessee Press, Knoxville.

——, 1995, *Passing the Time in Ballymenone* (1st Indiana University Press ed.). Indiana University Press, Bloomington/Indianapolis.

Gomme, G.L., 1890, Archaic Types of Society in Scotland. *Transactions of the Glasgow Archaeological Society* New Series 1:144–164.

Goudie, G., 1888, The Crusie, or Ancient Oil Lamp of Scotland. *Proceedings of the Society of Antiquaries of Scotland* 22:70–78.

Graham, A., 1919, A Survey of the Ancient Monuments of Skipness. *Proceedings of the Society of Antiquaries of Scotland* 53:76–118.

——, 1920, Further Antiquities at Skipness, Argyll. *Proceedings of the Society of Antiquaries of Scotland* 54:194–204.

Grant, I.F., 1924, *Every-Day Life on an Old Highland Farm*. Longmans, Green and Co., London.

——, 1995, *Highland Folk Ways*. Birlinn, Edinburgh.

Gray, M., 1957, *The Highland Economy 1750–1850*. Oliver and Boyd, Edinburgh.

Greig, J.Y.T. (editor), 1932a, *The Letters of David Hume*, volume 1. Clarendon, Oxford.

——, (editor), 1932b, *The Letters of David Hume*, Volume 2. Clarendon, Oxford.

Grimble, I., 1962, *The Trial of Patrick Sellar: The Tragedy of the Highland Evictions*. Routledge and Kegan Paul, London.

Haldane, A.R.B., 1952, *The Drove Roads of Scotland*. Edinburgh University Press, Edinburgh.

Hall, D.W., 2000, Scottish Medieval Pottery Industries. In *Townships to Farmsteads: Rural Settlement in Scotland, England and Wales*, edited by J.A. Atkinson, I. Banks, and G. MacGregor, pp. 173–177. British Archaeological Reports, Oxford.

Harvey, K.J., 1990, The Modernization of Scotland, 1750–1914. *Scotia* 14:47–58.

Hingley, R., 1993, Past, Current and Future Preservation and Management Options. In *Medieval or Later Rural Settlement in Scotland: Management and Preservation*, edited by R. Hingley, pp. 52–61. Historic Scotland, Edinburgh.

——, (editor), 1993, *Medieval or Later Rural Settlement in Scotland: Management and Preservation*. Historic Scotland, Edinburgh.

——, 2000, Medieval or Later Rural Settlement in Scotland: the Value of the Resource. In *Townships to Farmsteads: Rural Settlement in Scotland, England and Wales*, edited by J.A. Atkinson, I. Banks, and G. MacGregor, pp. 11–19. British Archaeological Reports, Oxford.

Hodder, I., 1991, *Reading the Past* (2nd ed.). Cambridge University Press, Cambridge.

——, 1999, *The Archaeological Process: An Introduction*. Blackwell, Oxford.

Hood, F., 1996, Balmavicar, Mull of Kintyre (Southend Parish). In *Discovery and Excavation in Scotland*, edited by R. Turner, p. 26. Council for Scottish Archaeology, Edinburgh.

Hopkins, P., 1998, *Glencoe and the End of the Highland War*. John Donald, Edinburgh.

Hunter, J., 1975, The Sutherland Clearances II: Sutherland in the Industrial Revolution. *Northern Scotland* 2.1:75–76.

——, 1992, *Scottish Highlanders: A People and Their Place*. Mainstream Publishing, Edinburgh.

——, 2000, *The Making of the Crofting Community* (new ed.). John Donald, Edinburgh.

Isaac, R., 1982, *The Transformation of Virginia, 1740–1790*. University of North Carolina Press, Chapel Hill.

James, H.F., 1998, *Gunna Excavations 1998*. Unpublished report, Glasgow University Archaeological Research Division, Glasgow.

Johnson, M.H., 1989, Conceptions of Agency in Archaeological Interpretation. *Journal of Anthropological Archaeology* 8:189–211.

——, 1993a, Notes Towards an Archaeology of Capitalism. In *Interpretative Archaeology*, edited by C. Tilley, pp. 327–356. Berg, Oxford.

——, 1993b, *Housing Culture. Traditional Architecture in an English Landscape*. University College London Press, London.

——, 1996, *An Archaeology of Capitalism*. Blackwell, Oxford.

——, 1999, Historical, Archaeology, Capitalism. In *Historical Archaeologies of Capitalism*, edited by M.P. Leone and P.B. Potter, pp. 219–232. Kluwer Academic/Plenum Publishers, New York.

Johnstone, A., and Scott Wood, J. (editors), 1996, *An Archaeological Field Survey of Deserted Townships at Tirai, Glen Lochay, Killin*. Department of Adult and Continuing Education, University of Glasgow, Glasgow.

Kelly, D., 1845, Parish of Southend. In *The New Statistical Account of Scotland*, volume 7, pp. 413–436. Blackwood, Edinburgh.

Kidd, C., 1993, *Subverting Scotland's Past*. Cambridge University Press, Cambridge.

Knapp, A.B., and Ashmore, W. (editors), 1999, *Archaeologies of Landscape: Contemporary Perspectives*. Blackwell, Oxford.

Kus, S., 1984 The Spirit and its Burden: Archaeology and Symbolic Activity. In *Marxist Perspectives in Archaeology*, edited by M. Spriggs, pp. 101–107. Cambridge University Press, Cambridge.

Laing, L.R., 1969, Medieval Settlement Archaeology in Scotland. *Scottish Archaeological Forum* 1:69–79.

Lamont, N., 1914, *An Inventory of Lamont Papers, 1231–1897*. Scottish Record Society, Edinburgh.

Lebon, J.H.G., 1946, The Face of the Countryside in Central Ayrshire During the Eighteenth and Nineteenth Centuries. *Scottish Geographical Magazine* 62:7–15.

Lelong, O., 2000, The Prospect of the Sea: Responses to Forced Coastal Resettlement in Nineteenth Century Sutherland. In *Townships to Farmsteads: Rural Settlement in Scotland, England and Wales*, edited by J.A. Atkinson, I. Banks and G. MacGregor, pp. 216–223. British Archaeological Reports, Oxford.

Lelong, O., and MacGregor, G., forthcoming, *Loch Borralie, Kyle of Durness*. Unpublished report, Glasgow University Archaeological Research Division, Glasgow.

Lelong, O., and Wood, J. 2000, A Township Through Time: Excavation and Survey at the Deserted Settlement of Easter Raitts, Badenoch, 1995–1999. In *Townships to Farmsteads: Rural Settlement in Scotland, England and Wales*, edited by J.A. Atkinson, I. Banks and G. MacGregor, pp. 40–49. British Archaeological Reports, Oxford.

Leone, M.P., 1982, Some Opinions About Recovering Mind. *American Antiquity* 47:742–760.

——, 1988, The Georgian Order as the Order of Merchant Capitalism in Annapolis, Maryland. In *The Recovery of Meaning*, edited by M.P. Leone and P.B. Potter, pp. 235–261. Smithsonian Institution Press, Washington.

——, 1996, Interpreting Ideology in Historical Archaeology. In *Images of the Recent Past*, edited by C.E. Orser, pp. 371–391. Altamira, California.

——, 1999, Setting Some Terms for Historical Archaeologies of Capitalism. In *Historical Archaeologies of Capitalism*, edited by M.P. Leone and P.B. Potter, pp. 3–20. Kluwer Academic/Plenum Publishers, New York.

Leone, M.P., and Potter, P.B., 1988, Introduction. In *The Recovery of Meaning*, edited by M.P. Leone and P.B. Potter, pp. 1–22. Smithsonian Institution Press, Washington.

Leone, M.P., and Potter, P.B. (editors), 1999, *Historical Archaeologies of Capitalism*. Kluwer Academic/Plenum Publishers, New York.

Levi, P. (editor), 1990, *Journals of the Western Isles*. The Folio Society, London.

Lindsay, I.G., and Cosh, M., 1973, *Inverary and the Dukes of Argyll*. Edinburgh University Press, Edinburgh.

Lloyd-Jones, J.S., 1991, *Against the Stream: Kerry of Kilfinan 1790–1870, an Economic History*. Unpublished manuscript courtesy of Mike Davis, Argyll and Bute Library Headquarters, Dunoon.

Lockhart, D., 1996, The Planned Villages of Argyllshire, 1750–1850. *Historic Argyll* 1:31–38.

——, 1997, The Founding of Southend. *Historic Argyll* 2:16–19.

MacAdam, I., 1881, On the use of the Spindle and Whorl by the Fishermen of the Present Day. *Proceedings of the Society of Antiquaries of Scotland* 15:148–151.

MacDonald, A. (editor), 1999, *An Archaeological Survey of Loch Restil and Glen Croe*. Department of Adult and Continuing Education, University of Glasgow, Glasgow.

MacDonald, D., 1845, United Parish of Killean and Kilchenzie. In *The New Statistical Account of Scotland*, Volume 7, pp. 376–394. Blackwood, Edinburgh.

MacDonald, J. (editor), 1992, *An Archaeological Field Survey at Meall Darroch*. Department of Adult and Continuing Education, University of Glasgow, Glasgow.

MacDonald, J., and Scott Wood, J. (editors), 1995, *An Archaeological Survey of Two Settlements at Oskaig and Holoman on Raasay*. Department of Adult and Continuing Education, University of Glasgow, Glasgow.

——, (editors), 1996, *An Archaeological Survey of Four Townships at Balachuirn, Balmeanach, Inbhire and Brae on Raasay*. Department of Adult and Continuing Education, University of Glasgow, Glasgow.

——, (editors), 1998, *An Archaeological Survey of the Townships of North and South Screapadal with a Survey of the Surrounding Area on Raasay*. Department of Adult and Continuing Education, University of Glasgow, Glasgow.

——, (editors), 1999, *An Archaeological Survey of the Township of Manish Beg, with a Survey of the Surrounding Area on Raasay*. Department of Adult and Continuing Education, University of Glasgow, Glasgow.

MacDonald, M., 1994, The Droving Trade in the Records of the Commissioners of Supply of Argyllshire. *Transactions of the Gaelic Society of Inverness* 58:1–7.

MacDonald, S., 1997, *Reimagining Culture: Histories, Identities and the Gaelic Renaissance*. Berg, Oxford.

MacGregor, G., 2000, *Rannoch Archaeological Project: 1999 Pilot Season, Archaeological Survey at Bunrannoch and Walk Over Survey*. Unpublished report, Glasgow University Archaeological Research Division, Glasgow.

MacGregor, G., Lelong, O., and Johnston-Smith, D.J., 1999, *Tigh Vectican, Arrochar*. Unpublished report, Glasgow University Archaeological Research Division, Glasgow.

Macinnes, A.I., 1996, *Clanship, Commerce and the House of Stuart, 1603–1788*. Tuckwell Press, East Linton.

——, 1998a, Scottish Gaeldom from Clanship to Commercial Landlordism, c.1600–c.1850. In *Scottish Power Centres*, edited by S. Foster, A. Macinnes, and R. Macinnes, pp. 162–190. Cruithne Press, Glasgow.

——, 1998b, Highland Society in the Era of 'Improvement'. In *Modern Scottish History 1707 to the Present, Volume 1: The Transformation of Scotland, 1707–1850*, edited by A. Cooke, I. Donnachie, A. MacSween, and C.A. Whatley, pp. 177–202. Tuckwell Press, East Linton.

MacKay, D.A., 1988, The Western Highlands and Islands: A Cultural Backwater? *Scottish Archaeological Review* 5:110–114.

——, 1993, Scottish Rural Highland Settlement: Preserving a People's Past. In *Medieval or Later Rural Settlement in Scotland: Management and Preservation*, edited by R. Hingley, pp. 43–51. Historic Scotland, Edinburgh.

MacKenzie, A., 1986, *History of the Highland Clearances*. Melven Press, Perth.

MacKenzie, W.M., 1904, Notes on Certain Structures of Archaic Type in the Island of Lewis—Beehive Houses, Duns, and Stone Circles. *Proceedings of the Society of Antiquaries of Scotland* 38:173–204.

MacMillan, S., 1960, *Families of Knapdale*. Privately printed, Massachusetts.

MacNeilage, A., 1912, Farming Methods in the West of Scotland. *Transactions of the Highland and Agricultural Society of Scotland* 24:276–292.

MacVicar, A., 1977, The North Carolina Connection. *The Kintyre Antiquarian and Natural History Society Magazine* 1:9–12.

Markus, T.A. (editor), 1982, *Order in Space and Society: Architectural Form and its Context in the Scottish Enlightenment*. Mainstream, Edinburgh.

——, 1989, Class and Classification in the Buildings of the late Scottish Enlightenment. In *Improvement and Enlightenment*, edited by T.M. Devine, pp. 78–107. John Donald, Edinburgh.

Marshall, D.N., 1978, Excavations at Auchategan, Glendaruel, Argyll. *Proceedings of the Society of Antiquaries of Scotland* 109:36–74.

——, 1983, Excavations at Macewen's Castle, Argyll, in 1968–69. *Glasgow Archaeological Journal* 10:131–142.

Martin, A., 1987, *Kintyre Country Life*. John Donald, Edinburgh.

Martin, M., 1994, *A description of the Western Islands of Scotland circa 1695; by Martin Martin; including A Voyage to St. Kilda by the same author, and, A Description of the Western Isles of Scotland by Sir Donald Monro; edited with Introduction by Donald J. Macleod*. Birlinn, Edinburgh.

Masson, D. (editor), 1882, *The Register of the Privy Council of Scotland, volume V, 1592–1599*. H.M. Register House, Edinburgh.

McArthur, J., 1845, United Parish of Kilcalmonell and Kilberry. In *The New Statistical Account of Scotland*, Volume 7, pp. 408–412. Blackwood, Edinburgh.

McClement, J., 1927, The Distribution of Agriculture in Kintyre. *Scottish Geographical Magazine* 43(1):20–31.

McCullagh, R.P.J, and Tipping, R. (editors), 1998, *The Lairg Project 1988–1996: The Evolution of an Archaeological Landscape in Northern Scotland*. Scottish Trust for Archaeological Research, Edinburgh.

McDonald, R.A., 1997, *The Kingdom of the Isles*. Tuckwell, East Linton.

McFarlane, A., 1983, Parish of Kilfinan. In *The Statistical Account of Scotland, 1791–1799*, volume VIII, edited by J. Sinclair, pp. 204–237. EP Publishing, Wakefield.

McGregor, A., 1880, Notes on Some Old Customs in the Island of Skye. *Proceedings of the Society of Antiquaries of Scotland*. 14:143–147.

McGuire, R.H., 1992, *A Marxist Archaeology*. Academic Press, London.

McKechnie, H., 1938, *The Lamont Clan, 1235–1935*. Clan Lamont Society, Edinburgh.

McKerral, A., 1948, *Kintyre in the Seventeenth Century*. Oliver and Boyd, Edinburgh.

Miller, D., 1989, The Limits of Dominance. In *Domination and Resistance*, edited by D. Miller, M. Rowlands, and C. Tilley, pp. 63–79. Unwin Hyman, London.

Miller, D., and Tilley, C., 1984, Ideology, Power and Prehistory: An Introduction. In *Ideology, Power and Prehistory*, edited by D. Miller and C. Tilley, pp. 1–15. Cambridge University Press, Cambridge.

Mitchell, A., 1862, On Various Superstitions in the North-West Highlands and Islands of Scotland, Especially in Relation to Lunacy. *Proceedings of the Society of Antiquaries of Scotland* 4:251–288.

——, 1880, *The Past in the Present: What is Civilization?* Douglas, Edinburgh.

Mitchell, A. (editor), 1907, *Geographical Collections Relating to Scotland Made by Walter MacFarlane*, Volume II. Scottish History Society, Edinburgh.

Mitchison, R., 1962, *Agricultural Sir John: The Life of Sir John Sinclair of Ulbster 1754–1835*. Bles, London.

Moir, D.G., and Skelton, R.A., 1968, New Light on the First Atlas of Scotland. *Scottish Geographical Magazine* 84(3):149–159.

Morris, G.E., 1986, The Profile of Ben Loyal from Pont's Map Entitled "Kyntail". *Scottish Geographical Magazine* 102(2):74–79.

Morrison, A., 1977, The Question of Celtic Survival or Continuity in Some Elements of Rural Settlement in the Scottish Highlands. In *Studies in Celtic Survival*, edited by L. Laing, pp. 67–76. British Archaeological. Reports, Oxford.

——, (editor), 1980, *Rural Settlement Studies: Some Recent Work*. Department of Archaeology, University of Glasgow, Glasgow.

——, 1996, *Dunbeath: A Cultural Landscape*. Dunbeath Preservation Trust, Glasgow.

——, 2000, Scottish Rural Settlement Studies: Retrospect and Prospect. In *Townships to Farmsteads: Rural Settlement in Scotland, England and Wales*, edited by J.A. Atkinson, I. Banks and G. MacGregor, pp. 2–10. British Archaeological Reports, Oxford.

Muir, T.S., 1860, Notice of a Beehive House in the Island of St. Kilda. *Proceedings of the Society of Antiquaries of Scotland* 3:225–232.

Nenadic, S., 1988, The Rise of the Urban Middle Class. In *People and Society in Scotland, Vol. 1, 1760–1830*, edited by T.M. Devine and R. Mitchison, pp. 109–168. John Donald, Edinburgh.

Newman, R., with Cranstone, D., and Howard-Davis, C., 2001, *The Historical Archaeology of Britain, c.1540–1900*. Sutton Publishing, Stroud.

Nicholson, R., 1974, *Scotland: The Later Middle Ages*. Oliver and Boyd, Edinburgh.

O'Dell, A.C., 1953, A View of Scotland in the Middle of the Eighteenth Century. *Scottish Geographical Magazine* 69:58–63.

Orser, C.E., 1996, *A Historical Archaeology of the Modern World*. Plenum Press, New York.

——, 1998, Epilogue: From Georgian Order to Social Relations at Annapolis and Beyond. In *Annapolis Pasts: Historical Archaeology in Annapolis, Maryland*, edited by P.A. Shackel, P.R. Mullins, and M.S. Warner, pp. 307–324. University of Tennessee Press, Knoxville.

Paynter, R., and McGuire, R.H., 1991, The Archaeology of Inequality: Material Culture, Domination and Resistance. In *The Archaeology of Inequality*, edited by R.H. McGuire and R. Paynter, pp. 1–27. Blackwell, Oxford.

Peate, I.C., 1938, Folk Culture. *Antiquity* 12:318–322.

——, 1963, The Society for Folk Life Studies. *Folk Life* 1:3–4.

Prebble, J., 1963, *The Highland Clearances*. Secker and Warburg, London.

Pred, A., 1986, *Place, Practice, and Structure. Social and Spacial Transformation in Southern Sweden, 1750–1850*. Polity Press, Cambridge.

Rathje, W., and Murphy, C., 1992, *Rubbish! The Archaeology of Garbage*. Harper Collins, New York.

RCAHMS, 1967, *Peebleshire: an Inventory of the Ancient Monuments*, Vol. II. Royal Commission on the Ancient and Historical Monuments of Scotland, Edinburgh.

——, 1971, *Argyll: an Inventory of the Ancient Monuments, Vol.1, Kintyre*. Royal Commission on the Ancient and Historical Monuments of Scotland, Edinburgh.

——, 1975, *Argyll: an Inventory of the Ancient Monuments, Vol.2, Lorn*. Royal Commission on the Ancient and Historical Monuments of Scotland, London.

——, 1980, *Argyll: an Inventory of the Ancient Monuments, Vol.3, Mull, Tiree, Coll and Northern Argyll*. Royal Commission on the Ancient and Historical Monuments of Scotland, Edinburgh.

——, 1982, *Argyll: an Inventory of the Ancient Monuments, Vol.4, Iona*. Royal Commission on the Ancient and Historical Monuments of Scotland, Edinburgh.

——, 1984, *Argyll: an inventory of the ancient monuments, Vol.5, Islay, Jura, Colonsay*. Royal Commission on the Ancient and Historical Monuments of Scotland, London.

——, 1990, *North-East Perth: An Archaeological Landscape*. Royal Commission on the Ancient and Historical Monuments of Scotland, Edinburgh.

——, 1992, *Argyll: an inventory of the ancient monuments, Vol.7, Mid Argyll and Cowal, Medieval and Later Monuments*. Royal Commission on the Ancient and Historical Monuments of Scotland, Edinburgh.

——, 1993, *Waternish, Skye and Lochalsh District, Highland Region: An Archaeological Survey*. Royal Commission on the Ancient and Historical Monuments of Scotland, Edinburgh.

——, 1994, *Glenesslin, Nithsdale: An Archaeological Survey*. Royal Commission on the Ancient and Historical Monuments of Scotland, Edinburgh.

——, 2001, *"Well Sheltered and Watered": Menstrie Glen, a Farming Landscape Near Stirling*, Royal Commission on the Ancient and Historical Monuments of Scotland, Edinburgh.

RCHME, 1970, *Shielings and Bastles*. H.M.S.O., London.

Rennie, E.B., 1993, *Cowal: A Historical Guide*. Birlinn, Edinburgh.

——, 1984, Excavations at Ardnadam, Cowal, Argyll, 1964–1982. *Glasgow Archaeological Journal* 11:13–39.

Renwick, R. (editor), 1908, *Extracts from the Records of the Burgh of Glasgow, Vol. IV, AD1691–1717*. The Corporation of Glasgow, Glasgow.

——, (editor), 1909, *Extracts from the Records of the Burgh of Glasgow, Vol. V, AD1708–1738*. The Corporation of Glasgow, Glasgow.

——, (editor), 1911, *Extracts from the Records of the Burgh of Glasgow, Vol. VI, AD1739–1759*. The Corporation of Glasgow, Glasgow.

——, (editor), 1940, *Extracts from the Records of the Burgh of Glasgow, Vol. X, AD1809–1822*. The Corporation of Glasgow, Glasgow.

——, (editor), 1941, *Extracts from the Records of the Burgh of Glasgow, Vol. XI, AD1823–1833*. The Corporation of Glasgow, Glasgow.

Richards, E., 1973, How tame were the Highlanders during the Clearances? *Scottish Studies* 17:35–50.

——, 1975, The Sutherland Clearances I: New Evidence from Dunrobin. *Northern Scotland* 2.1:57–74.

——, 1982, *A History of the Highland Clearances. Agrarian Transformations and the Evictions, 1746–1886*. Croom Helm, London.

——, 1985, *A History of the Highland Clearances, Vol. 2: Emigration, Protest, Reasons*. Croom Helm, London.

Sellar, W.D.H., 1973, The Earliest Campbells—Norman, Briton or Gael. *Scottish Studies* 17:109–125.

Shanks, M., and Tilley, C., 1987, *Reconstructing Archaeology*. Cambridge University Press, Cambridge.

Sharples, N., and Parker Pearson, M., 1999, Norse Settlement in the Outer Hebrides. *Norwegian Archaeological Review* 32:41–62.

Shepherd, I.A.G., and Ralston, S.M., 1981, Rural Settlement in Grampian Region: approaches and sources. *Proceedings of the Society of Antiquaries of Scotland* 111:493–509.

Simmons, A. (editor), 1998a, *Burt's letters from the north of Scotland, as related by Edmund Burt*. Birlinn, Edinburgh.

——, (editor), 1998b, *A tour in Scotland and voyage to the Hebrides, 1772, by Thomas Pennant*. Birlinn, Edinburgh.

Simpson, J.Y., 1862a, Address on Archaeology. *Proceedings of the Society of Antiquaries of Scotland* 4:5–51.

——, 1862b, Notes on some Scottish Magical Charm-Stones, or Curing-Stones. *Proceedings of the Society of Antiquaries of Scotland* 4:211–224.

Skelton, R.A., 1967a, *The Military Survey of Scotland, 1747–1755*. Royal Scottish Geographical Society, Edinburgh.

——, 1967b, The Military Survey of Scotland 1747–1755. *Scottish Geographical Magazine* 83(1):5–16.

Skene, W.F., 1880, *Celtic Scotland: A History of Ancient Alban, Vol. III*. Douglas, Edinburgh.

Slater, T.R., 1980, The Mansion and Policy. In *The Making of the Scottish Countryside*, edited by M.L. Parry and T.R. Slater, pp. 223–248. Croom Helm, London.

Smith, J., 1798, *General View of the Agriculture of the County of Argyll*. Mundell and Son, Edinburgh.

Smout, T.C., 1996a, Pre-improvement Fields in Upland Scotland: the Case of Loch Tayside. *Landscape History* 18:47–55.

——, 1996b, The Landowner and the Planned Village in Scotland, 1730–1830. In *Scotland in the Age of Improvement*, edited by N.T. Phillipson and R. Mitchison, pp. 73–106. Edinburgh University Press, Edinburgh.

SRC SMR, 1993, Strathclyde Sites and Monuments Record. In *Discovery and Excavation in* Scotland, edited by C.E. Batey, pp. 70–72. Council for Scottish Archaeology, Edinburgh.

Stark, J., 1845, Parish of Kilfinan. In *The New Statistical Account of Scotland, Vol. 7*, pp. 359–372. Blackwood, Edinburgh.

Steer, K.A., and Bannerman, J.W.M., 1977, *Late Medieval Monumental Sculpture in the West Highlands*. Royal Commission on the Ancient and Historical Monuments of Scotland, Edinburgh.

Stevenson, D., 1980, *Alasdair MacColla and the Highland Problem in the Seventeenth Century*. John Donald, Edinburgh.

Stewart, A., 1888, Examples of the Survival in Scotland of Superstitions Relating to Fire. *Proceedings of the Society of Antiquaries of Scotland* 22:391–395.

Stewart, A.I.B., 1992, Regulation of Agriculture in Seventeenth Century Kintyre. In *The Stair Society Miscellany III*, edited by W.M. Gordon, pp. 212–223. Stair Society, Edinburgh.

Stewart, J.H., 1990, *Settlements of Western Perthshire: Land and Society North of the Highland Line, 1480–1851*. Pentland, Edinburgh.

Stewart, J.H., and Stewart, M.B., 1988, A Highland Longhouse—Lianach, Balquhidder, Perthshire, *Proceedings of the Society of Antiquaries of Scotland* 118:301–317.

Stone, J.C., 1968, An Evaluation of the "Nidisdaile" Manuscript Map by Timothy Pont. *Scottish Geographical Magazine* 84(3):160–171.

——, 1991, *Illustrated Maps of Scotland from Blaeu's Atlas Novus of the 17th Century*. Studio Editions, London.

Storrie, M.C., 1967, Balliekine, Arran—Survivor of Two Revolutions. *Folk Life* 5:92–99.

Sutherland, S.R., 1975, The Sutherland Clearances III: Ethics and Economics in the Sutherland Clearances. *Northern Scotland* 2.1:77–83.

Swanson, C., 1993, The Need for a Management and Preservation Strategy. In *Medieval or Later Rural Settlement in Scotland: Management and Preservation*, edited by R. Hingley, pp. 1–3. Historic Scotland, Edinburgh.

Symonds, J., 2000, The Dark Island Revisited: An Approach to the Historical Archaeology of Milton, South Uist. In *Townships to Farmsteads: Rural Settlement in Scotland, England and Wales*, edited by J.A. Atkinson, I. Banks and G. MacGregor, pp. 196–209. British Archaeological Reports, Oxford.

Teignmouth, Lord, 1836, *Sketches of the coasts and islands of Scotland and the Isle of Man, Vol. 2*. Parker, London.

Thin, J. (editor), 1981, *Recollections of a Tour Made in Scotland, A.D. 1803, by Dorothy Wordsworth*. The Mercat Press, Edinburgh.

Third, B.M.W., 1955, Changing Landscape and Social Structure in the Scottish Lowlands as Revealed by Eighteenth-Century Estate Plans. *Scottish Geographical Magazine* 71:83–93.

——, 1957, The Significance of Scottish Estate Plans and Associated Documents. *Scottish Studies* 1:39–64.

Thomas, F.L.W., 1860, Notice of Beehive Houses in Harris and Lewis; with Traditions of the 'Each-Uisge', or Water-Horse, Connected Therewith. *Proceedings of the Society of Antiquaries of Scotland* 3:127–144.

——, 1868, On the Primitive Dwellings and Hypogea of the Outer Hebrides. *Proceedings of the Society of Antiquaries of Scotland* 7:153–195.

Timperley, L.R. (editor), 1976, *A Directory of Landownership in Scotland c.1770*. Scottish Record Society, Edinburgh.

Trigger, B.G., 1989, *A History of Archaeological Thought*. Cambridge University Press, Cambridge.

Turner, R., 2000, Managing MoLRS in the NTS. In *Townships to Farmsteads: Rural Settlement in Scotland, England and Wales*, edited by J.A. Atkinson, I. Banks and G. MacGregor, pp. 34–39. British Archaeological Reports, Oxford.

Whittington, G., 1986a, *The Military Survey of Scotland: A Critique*. Geo Books, Norwich.

——, 1986b, The Roy Map: The Protracted and Fair Copies—Part One. *Scottish Geographical Magazine* 102(1):18–28.

——, 1986c, The Roy Map: The Protracted and Fair Copies—Part Two: *Scottish Geographical Magazine* 102(2):66–73.

Whyte, I.D., 1975, Rural Housing in Lowland Scotland in the Seventeenth Century: The Evidence of Estate Papers. *Scottish Studies* 19:55–68.

——, 1979, *Agriculture and Society in Seventeenth Century Scotland*. John Donald, Edinburgh.

——, 1981, The Evolution of Rural Settlement in Lowland Scotland in Medieval and Early-Modern Times: An Exploration. *Scottish Geographical Magazine* 97(1):4–15.

Whyte, I., and Whyte, K., 1991, *The Changing Scottish Landscape, 1500–1800*. Routledge, London.

Williams, B.B., 1988, A Late Medieval Rural Settlement at Craigs, County Antrim. *Ulster Journal of Archaeology* 51:91–102.

Withers, C., 1990, "Give Us Land and Plenty of It": The Ideological Basis to Land and the Landscape in the Scottish Highlands. *Landscape History* 12:45–54.

Yeoman, P., 1991, Medieval Rural Settlement: The Invisible Centuries. In *Scottish Archaeology: New Perceptions*, edited by W.S. Hanson and E.A. Slater, pp. 112–128. Aberdeen University Press, Aberdeen.

——, 1995, *Medieval Scotland*. Batsford, London.

Index

Abercrombie, N., 67
Aberdour estate (Fife), 145
Account book analysis, 24–25
Act of Bailyierie of 1672, 91
Act of Neighborhood of 1653, 93
Afforestable Land Survey, 29
Agency/structure relations, 62–63, 75
Agricultural Improvement.
 See Improvement
Alcohol bottles, 50
American archaeology. *See* Georgian
 Order
Ancram House, 143
Anderson, J.R., 182
Antrim, Earl of, 166
Archaeology of Capitalism, An (Johnson),
 53
"Archaic Types of Society in Scotland"
 (Gomme), 22
Architecture. *See* House architecture
Ardgaddan (Kilfinan), 87, 113, 211–213
Ardlamont House, 186
Ardmarnock estate (Kilfinan), 177,
 178–179
Ardnadam (Cowal), 100, 103
Argyll and Bute District Archive, 173
Argyll Colony, 232
Argyll estate (Kintyre), 4, 11, 29, 82, 85,
 92, 93, 110, 113, 119, 121
Argyll, House of
 Campbell genealogy, 162–163, 169–170
 in Civil Wars, 177
 conflict with McDonalds, 153, 165–166,
  222
 control of Kintyre, 166–167, 168,
  170–171, 223
 Enlightenment and, 129, 131–132, 134
 Lowland estates of, 150, 169, 170
 Lowland identity of, 162–163
 Lowland plantation by, 168–169,
  170–171, 223

relationship with tenants, 154, 167,
 191, 202–203, 209, 222, 223, 226
 territorial expansion of, 164–165
Argyll Lodging, 150
Ascog (Kilfinan), 87, 113, 211
Atkinson, J.A., 28, 30, 32, 89, 95, 173
Auchategan (Cowal), 103
Authority, capitalist imposition of, 52

Baile/bailtean settlements, 82–90,
 217–218, 220
Ballimore estate (Kilfinin), 177, 179
Ballygroggan (Kintyre), 91
Balmavicar (Kintyre), 83–85, 86, 88, 91,
 97–98, 103, 105, 107
Bangor-Jones, M., 28, 29
Banks, I., 28, 89
Banks, I.B.J., 28
Banks, earth and stone, 97
Bannatyne Club, 173
Bannerman, J.W.M., 158, 159, 160, 161,
 162, 163
Barns
 blackhouses, 101–102
 range farmsteads, 106, 142
Barra blackhouses, 101–102
Barrett, John C., 28, 29, 31, 62, 70,
 72
Barrow, G.W.S., 173
Basker, J.G., 133
Battle of Harlaw, 160
Battle of Kilsyth, 166
Beaton, E.A., 183
Beaudry, M.C., 50–51, 57, 59, 62, 67
Bede, Cuthbert (Edward Bradley), 122,
 200, 202, 206–207
Beehive dwellings, 17, 18, 20–21
Ben Lawers Historic Landscape Project,
 30
Berry, C.J., 130, 131, 138, 140, 141
Bil, A., 34, 94, 124

Bishops' War of 1639, 166
Blackburn, R., 65
Blackhouses, 18, 20–21, 101–102
Bloch, Maurice, 68–69, 71
Boott Cotton Mill study, 50, 57, 59
Borgadale Glen (Kintyre), 91, 105
Borrafiach (Skye), 95, 97
Boswell, James, 15
Bounded communities, 51
Bourdieu, Pierre, 69–70
Bragar (Lewis), 88–89
Branigan, K., 28, 30, 101, 103
Broadie, A., 131, 132, 136, 139, 140
Bronze Age, 72
Building structures. *See* House
    architecture
Burial mounds, 73
Burke, B., 179
Burt, Captain, 15
Byres, 101, 102, 103, 107

Caird, J.B., 146
Cairns, G., 173
Caldwell, D.H., 28, 31, 87, 88, 99
Calves estate (Kilfinan), 178, 179, 180
Cameron, E.A., 205
Camic, Charles, 139, 140, 141
Campbell, G.D., 132
Campbell of Knockbuy, Archibald, 180
Campbell, Mungo Nutter, 177, 179, 188,
    189
Campbells, genealogy of, 162–163,
    169–170
Campbells of Argyll. *See* Argyll, House of
Campbells of Asknish, 178
Campbells of Ballimore, 179, 181, 189
Campbells of Loch Awe, 162, 163
Campbells of Otter, 174, 176–177, 178,
    181–182, 184, 188
Campbells of Stonefield, 94
Campbeltown (Kintyre), 113–114, 126,
    161, 165, 168, 208
Canopy clans, 155
Canuto, M.A., 51
Capitalism, social relations of, 1, 9–10,
    39–77
    cultural perspective and, 56–57, 58
    economic foundation for, 53–55
    Georgian Order and, 41–50, 55, 56, 60
    ideology and, 68–75

    individual and, 8, 55–56
    origins, 51–53, 60–61, 75
    social change and, 61–68
    social interaction and, 57–59
Cara House, 110
Carrithers, Michael, 58
Carter, I., 38, 195
Cattle droving trade, 183–184, 187
Ceramics
    Georgian Order, 43–44, 50
    shieling settlements, 95
Ching, B., 26
Chitnis, A., 138, 139
City countryside relationship, 64,
    65–66
Civil Wars, 92–93, 175, 177, 185–186
Civilizing of Kintyre, 167–170, 223
Clachan, 27, 82
Clan Campbell. *See* Argyll, House of
Clan Donald
    forfeiture and, 160–162
    Lords of the Isles, 158–160
    rebellion of, 165
Clan Dugall, 158, 159
Clan Ian Mor, 159, 160, 161, 166
Clan Ruari, 158, 159
Clan Somairle, 158–159
Clan system, 8, 26
    canopy clans, 155
    clan gentry, 8, 65, 157, 158, 185, 221
    community concept of, 157–158
    conflicts and disputes, 4, 153, 161, 162,
    165–167
    Crown and, 167–168
    hereditary occupancy and, 157
    kinship ties in, 155–156
    Lordship of the Isles, 158–162
    names, 157
    ritual practice in, 71
    territorial control by, 155–156, 166–167,
    168, 170–171
Class-consciousness, 56, 133
Class domination, 53–55
Clearances, 6–7, 33, 195–199
Closure, 52
Cognition
    ideological, 71–72
    nonideological (practical), 68–71
Cognitive landscape studies, 34–36, 40
Colquhoun, Dr., 178

Commercial Age, Enlightenment and, 11, 138–139
Commodification, 52–53, 148
Commodity production, 54
Communal practice, 124, 201–202, 220, 221
Community, and clan system, 157–158
Consumerism, 133
Conway, Henry Seymour, 131
Cook, L.J., 50–51, 57, 59
Cosh, M., 131
Cottage ranges, 107–109, 112, 121–122, 211, 218–219
Council of the Isles, 159
Courtyard farmsteads, 109–112, 113, 120–121, 125, 141, 142, 208, 211, 218, 219
Cowal estate (Inverchaolain), 92, 175
Cowan, I.B., 162
Craggans (pots), 22
Craignafeoch (Kilfinan), 87, 113, 211
Craigs (County Antrim), 87, 88, 95, 97
Creagan Fithich (Kintyre), 91
Creamware, 44
Creed, G.W., 26
Cregeen, E., 23, 85, 105, 150, 157, 164, 202, 206, 208, 209
Cressy, M., 95
Crofters' Act of 1886, 230
Crofting system, 198, 229–232
Cruck framing, 145
Cruden, S., 150
Crusies (lamps), 22
Cultural assimilation, Enlightenment and, 133, 145
Cultural hegemony concept, 50, 51
Currach Mor (Kintyre), 104–105
Curwen, E.C., 17

Dairying ceramics, 44
Dalglish, C., 173
Deetz, James, 40, 43–45, 46, 55, 56–57
Degenerationism, doctrine of, 19
Delft ceramics, 43
Description of the Western Islands of Scotland, A (Martin), 15
Devine, T.M., 38, 147, 148, 181, 183, 188, 189, 191, 197, 198–199
Dispersed settlement pattern, 89, 90, 103–104, 112, 142–143, 148, 201

Dixon, P., 28, 82, 91, 117, 118
Documentary-based research, 32–34
Dodgshon, R.A., 28, 31, 88–89, 90, 91–92, 95, 97, 98, 124, 155, 156, 157, 160, 168
Dominant ideology thesis, 67–68
Doorways, opposed, 103, 104, 218
Dower house, 110, 111, 121
Downes, J.M., 28, 29, 31
Driscoll, S.T., 36
Drumgarve (Kintyre), 107
Dunbar, J.G., 23, 27
Dunbeath project, 30
Duthchas, 153, 156, 158, 170, 171–172, 176, 198
Dwellings. *See* House architecture
Dykes
    curvilinear turf, 117
    head, 91–92, 97, 114, 117
    march, 92, 97
    stone, 97, 126, 218

Earthen boundaries. *See* Head dykes
Earthenware, 43
Easson, D.E., 162
Easter Raitts, 30, 85
Economic historians, 196–197
Emigration, 232
Enclosure
    cattle droving trade and, 184, 187
    changes in routine practice, 126, 148
    commodification and, 52
    in England, 144–145
    grid pattern, 115–116, 117–119, 144, 200
    irregular forms of, 116–117, 219
    in Lowland Scotland, 143–144
    pre-Improvement, 82, 83–85, 86, 90–91, 92–94, 95, 97, 218
    tree-lined, 93–94
England
    enclosure in, 144–145
    house architecture in, 147
    settlement pattern in, 142–143
Enlightenment. *See* Scottish Enlightenment
Entrances, opposed, 103, 104, 218
Ethnological studies, 13, 14, 15–22, 37
Evans, E.E., 26

Every-Day Life on an old Highland Farm
(Grant), 23
Evolutionary approach, 17
Ewart, G., 28, 87, 88, 99

Fairhurst, Horace, 27, 28, 30, 31, 33, 34,
82, 85, 101, 123, 124, 143, 208
Farm laborers, 5, 12
emigration of, 232
houses, 107–109, 209, 211, 218–219
tenure, 209
Farm machinery, 202
Farmers. *See* Tenant farmers
Fawcett, R., 150
Fences, wire, 115
Fenton, A., 23, 24, 25, 141, 146, 147, 148,
150, 231
Ferguson, Adam, 136, 139
Ferguson, J., 167
Fermtouns, 27, 141, 148
Field systems
Improvement, 114–120
pre-Improvement, 91–97
Fieldwork, on medieval settlements, 28,
29–31
Findlay, A.M., 80
Finlaggan (Islay), 87–88, 99, 103
Folk Housing in Middle Virginia
(Glassie), 40, 41–43
Folk Life, 23
Folk life studies, 13–14, 23–27, 31, 37
Foodways, ceramic forms and, 43–44
Forefeiture, 160–162
Fort Askamylnemoir, 166
Foster, P., 30
Foucault, Michel, 51
Fragments From Antiquity (Barrett),
72

Gailey, R.A., 29, 33, 34, 81–82, 83, 85, 91,
92, 93, 94, 95, 98, 100, 101, 102,
105, 120, 204
Gardens
formal, 143
Georgian Order, 47
kailyards, 82, 93–94
Gartavaich (Kintyre), 95
Gaskell, P., 181, 197, 201
Gatherer-hunters, 72
Gazin-Schwartz, A., 35

*General View of the Agriculture of the
County of Argyll* (Smith), 121
Gentry, clan gentry, 8, 65, 157, 158, 185,
221
Georgian Order, 40–51, 56, 60
ceramics, 43–44
garden design, 47, 48
gravestone design, 44–45
in historical context, 46–47
house architecture, 41–43, 55, 189
individualism and, 55
probate inventories, 49
resistance to, 50–51
social hierarchy and, 47–48
structuralist approach to, 45–46, 61
Giddens, Anthony, 53–55, 62, 64, 65
Gilbertson, D., 30
Gillies, W., 163
Glasgow University Archaeological
Research Division, 33
Glassie, Henry, 40, 41–43, 45, 46–47, 55,
56–57
Glen Breakerie (Kintyre), 116
Gomme, G.L., 22, 25
Graham, A., 95
Grant, I.F., 23, 24–25, 26, 124, 125
Gravestones, Georgian Order, 44–45
Gray, M., 197
Great Awakening, 44–45
Greig, J.Y.T., 131
Grid-pattern enclosure systems, 115–116,
117–119, 144
Grimble, I., 195
Gunna site, 87, 99

Habitus concept, 68–71
Haldane, A.R.B., 183
Harkness of Clachaig, Thomas, 177, 180
Harvey, K.J., 34
Head dykes, 91–92, 97, 114, 117
Hearth
central, 100, 101, 122, 123, 125, 127,
146, 147
relocation of, 25, 122, 147, 148, 219
Hebridean dwellings, 17–18
Hedge enclosures, 119
Herring trade, 183
Highland Clearances, The (Prebble), 196
Highland Folk Ways (Grant), 24, 26
Hingley, R., 27, 29, 32

Historical archaeology, v, 8
rural settlement studies as, 14, 27–32
Hodder, Ian, 8, 48, 61
Hood, F., 95
Hopkins, P., 164
House architecture
blackhouses, 18, 20–21, 101–102
cottage ranges, 107–109, 112, 121–122, 211, 218–219
courtyard farmsteads, 109–112, 113, 120–121, 125, 141, 142, 208, 211, 218, 219
dower house, 110, 111, 121
in England, 147
in folk life studies, 24, 25
Georgian Order, 41–43, 53, 189
in historical studies, 29
longhouses, 101, 102–103, 123, 208
in Lowland Scotland, 145–147
mansion house, 186, 189, 190
medieval, 43, 55, 98–100
patterns of change, 200–201
pre-Improvement, 97–103, 120, 125, 218, 220
range farmsteads, 105–107, 121, 125, 142, 207, 211, 218, 219
social structure and, 206–209, 226–227
subdivision of space, 121, 146, 209, 219, 220, 226
Hume, David, 129, 131–132, 136, 140
Hunter, J., 195, 196, 205, 229, 230, 232
Hutton, James, 140
Hypogea (souterrains), 18–19

Ideological cognition, 71–72
Ideology
discursive, 71
nonideological (practical) cognition, 68–71
resistance to dominant ideology, 67–68
ritual practice and, 71–74
Impostones (fishing weights), 22
Improvement
capitalism and. *See* Capitalism, social relations of
crofting system and, 229–232
defined, 1
English/Lowland Scottish exemplars for, 129–130, 141–149

Enlightenment linked to, 130–134, 150–151, 154, 224
farming population and. *See* Tenant farmers
historiography of, 195–199
ideological context for, 10–11
individual/group interaction in, 5–6, 39–40, 221–222, 227
landowner and. *See* Landowners
material environment of, 103–128
domestic space, 120–123, 200–201, 206–209, 218–219
landscape, 114–120
routine practice and, 10, 125–127, 201–202, 205, 220–221
settlement patterns, 103–114, 125, 211–214, 220
mercantile context for, 176, 184, 187–188
politics of, 6–7
See also Kilfinan parish, Improvement; Kintyre peninsula, Improvement
In Small Things Forgotten (Deetz), 43–45
Innean Coig Cailleiche (Kintyre), 91, 104
Innean settlements, 83, 85
Innens estate (Kilfinen), 180
Inveryne, Barony of, 175
"Invisible Centuries," 27
Irish Famine, 59
Irish landowners' landscapes, 57–59
Isaac, Rhys, 47

Jacobite rebellions, 80, 166, 167, 202
James, H.F., 28, 87, 99
James VI, 167–168
Johnson, Dr., 15, 122
Johnson, Matthew H., 39, 51–53, 55–56, 60–61, 62, 74, 142, 143, 144, 145, 147, 148, 149
Johnstone, A., 29, 33

Kailyards (garden plots), 82, 93–94
Kames, Lord (Henry Home), 130–131, 137
Kelly, D., 107, 110, 120, 200, 207, 208
Kerry estate (Kilfinan), 174, 175–176, 178
Kidd, C., 134
Kilchrist estate, 85, 86

Kilfinan parish, 11–12
  Campbell–Lamont relations, 92–93,
    175
  geography of, 4, 5
  Improvement
    enclosure, 116–118, 120, 184, 219
    house architecture, 121, 122, 123,
      194, 219
    Lowland exemplars for, 66, 150
    mercantile context for, 66, 176,
      182–185, 187–188
    middle class context for, 65, 189–190,
      224
    settlement pattern, 87, 107, 108, 109,
      110–113, 211–214
  landholding in, 154, 171–181
  location of, 2, 4
  pre-Improvement
    enclosure, 95
    house architecture, 99–101, 123
    settlement pattern, 86–87
  social change in, 65–66
  sporting estates in, 188–189
Kilfinan village, 113, 116–117
Kinship ties, clan, 155–156
Kintyre peninsula, 11
  under Campbells of Argyll. *See* Argyll,
    House of
  Crown annexation of, 161
  emigration to North Carolina from,
    232
  geography of, 2, 4
  Improvement
    as Civilizing project, 167–168, 223
    enclosure, 115, 119, 201, 219, 225
    house architecture, 121, 123, 194,
      201, 206–208, 219, 225
    landlord-tenant relationship in,
      153–154, 191, 222–223
    Lowland plantation, 168–169,
      170–171
    routine practice and, 201–202,
      225–226
    settlement pattern, 104–107, 109,
      110–113, 211, 225
    social divisions and, 206
  location of, 1–2, 3
  Lowland plantation in, 168–169
  under McDonald Lordship of the Isles,
    4, 158–162, 165

pre-Improvement
  enclosure, 91–92, 93, 94
  house architecture, 97–98, 100–101,
    102
  settlement pattern, 82–86, 87
  shieling, 94–95
  social change in, 65
  territorial conflicts in, 4, 153, 165–166,
    191
Kintyre school of sculptors, 160
Knocknahall (Kilchrist), 85, 86
Kus, S., 62

Laing, L.R., 27, 31
Lamont, N., 173
Lamont chiefs, 174–176, 178, 181–188,
  189, 224
Landowners
  Campbells (House of Argyll), 164–170,
    222–223
  changes in landholding, 174–181
  clearances and, 6–7, 33, 195–199
  crofting system and, 229–230, 231
  cultural landscape of, 58–59
  individual and hereditary claims, 11,
    153–154
  Jacobite rebellions and, 166, 167, 202
  McDonalds (Clan Donald), 4, 158–162,
    165
  mercantile role of, 176, 182–185,
    187–188
  middle class status of, 4, 11, 65, 154,
    172–174, 182, 185–190
  of sporting estates, 188–189
  relationship with tenants, 38, 65–66,
    74, 153–154, 167, 185, 191,
    202–203, 209, 222, 223, 226
Landscape studies in archaeology,
  29–30
Landscapes
  cognitive, 34–36, 40
  commodification process, 52–53, 148
  cultural, 57–59
  Georgian order, 42, 43, 58
  in Lowland Scotland and England,
    143–145
  open-field, 91–92, 114, 124, 143
  shieling, 17, 18, 91, 94–96, 120, 124,
    126, 144, 145, 147–148
  See also Enclosure

Langlands, Alex, 85, 117, 118
Langlands, George, 85
Largie estate, 85
Leases, written, 167, 193, 209, 223
Lebon, J.H.G., 144
Lelong, Olivia, 28, 30, 35–36, 85
Leone, Mark P., 39, 40, 45–49, 60
Levi, P., 15
Lime mortar, 145
Limecraigs House, 110, 111, 121, 122
Lindsay, I.G., 131
Livestock pens, 82
Lix (Perthshire), 123
Lloyd-Jones, J.S., 188
Loch Borralie (Sutherland), 30
Loch Tay, 30
Lochtayside, 95, 97
Lockhart, D., 113
Longhouse, 101, 102–103, 123
Lordship of the Isles
    Campbells and, 162, 163–164
    forfeiture of, 160–162
    rise of Clan Donald, 158–160
Lowland plantation, 168–169, 170–171, 186, 223
Lowland Scotland
    enclosure in, 143–144
    house architecture in, 145–147
    settlement pattern in, 141–142
    shieling in, 144

MacAlister of Loup and Torrisdale, Alexander, 180
McArthur, J., 113
McClement, J., 107, 229, 230, 232
McCullagh, R.P.J., 30
MacDonald, D., 102, 107, 206
MacDonald, J., 33
MacDonald, James, 165
MacDonald, M., 184
McDonald, R.A., 174
MacDonald, S., 26, 38, 195, 196, 197, 199
MacDonald, William, 117
MacDonald of Colonsay, Allaster (Alexander), 166
MacDonald of Dunnyveg, Angus, 165
McDonald of Dunnyveg, James, 161
MacDonalds of Dunnyveg, 159–160, 162, 163, 165, 222

MacDonnels of Antrim, 165–166
MacEwen's Castle (Kilfinan), 98, 99–100, 101, 103
McFarlane, A., 174, 183
MacFarlane, Andrew, 178
MacGregor, G., 30, 33
McGuire, Randall H., 62–64, 66, 67
Machribeg (Kintyre), 122
MacIlshenaich harpists, 160
Macinnes, A.I., 38, 65, 156, 179, 185, 186, 195
MacIntyre, S.W., 183
MacIvor, John, 177, 178
MacKay, D.A., 26, 29, 34–35
McKechnie, H., 93, 173, 182, 183, 184, 186, 187
MacKenzie, A., 195
McKenzie, W.M., 17
McKerral, A., 161, 163, 165, 166, 168, 169
MacLachlan, Colin, 178, 180
MacLachlans of MacLachlan, 180
McLeas of Lindsaig, 177
MacMhuirich poets, 160, 161
MacMillan, S., 180
MacNeilage, A., 107
McNeill, Charles, 85
MacVicar, A., 232
Magical charms, 22
Making of the Crofting Community, The (Hunter), 196
Malcolms of Poltalloch, 178, 179–180, 189
Mansion house, 186, 189, 190
March dykes, 92, 97
Markus, T.A., 52
Marshall, D.N., 98, 99, 100, 101, 103, 173
Martin, A., 113, 114, 120, 209
Martin, Martin, 15, 25
Master–slave relationship, 63, 64–65
Material culture
    capitalist social relations and, 52–53, 56–57, 70
    in empirical research, 34
    ethnological approach to, 16–22
    folk life approach to, 24–25
    pre-eighteenth century, 31
    See also Georgian Order

Meall Darroch (Kintyre), 122
Medieval house form, 43, 55, 98–100, 147, 148
Medieval settlements, 27–32, 87–89, 98, 142, 148
Medieval society, 54
Merrony, C., 101, 103
Middle class status, 4, 65, 132–133, 154, 171–174, 182, 185–190, 224
Military Survey of Scotland (Roy Map), 80–81, 90–91, 92, 93
Millar, John, 136, 138
Miller, D., 66
Mitchell, Arthur, 19–21, 22, 125, 183
Mitchison, R., 131
Moir, D.G., 80
MoLRS (Medieval or Later Rural Settlement), 27–28
Montrose, Marquis of, 166
Moodie, John, 178, 180
Morris, G.E., 80
Morrison, A., 13, 27, 30, 32
Mrozowski, S.A., 50–51, 57, 59
Muir, T.S., 17
Murrays of Blackbarony, 178, 179

Names
   clan, 157
   patronymic, 156–157
Nenadic, S., 132, 133
Neolithic, 30, 72
New Statistical Account for Southend, 207, 208
Newman, R., 142, 144, 148
Nicholson, R., 161
Nicols of Ardmarnock, 177, 178–179, 181, 189
North Carolina, tenant farmer migration to, 232
"Notes on Some Scottish Magical Charm-Stones or Curing-Stones" (Simpson), 22
Nucleated settlements, 113–114, 126, 141, 194, 214

Occupancy, tenant, 154, 193–194, 203, 205, 209–210, 215–16
O'Dell, A.C., 80
Oighreachd, 153, 156, 158, 170, 171–172, 176

Oldham, John, 178, 180
"On the Primitive Dwellings and Hypogea of the Outer Hebrides" (Thomas), 17–18
Open-field system, 91–92, 114, 124, 143
Orser, Charles E., 39, 50, 51, 56–59, 60, 74
Otter estate (Kilfinan), 174, 176–177, 178, 179, 181–182, 184, 188
Outline of a Theory (Bourdieu), 69–70

Paca (William) garden, 47, 48
Parker Pearson, M., 28, 30, 31
Past in the Present, The: What is Civilization? (Mitchell), 19, 22
Pastoralism, 72
Patronymics, 156–157
Paynter, R., 67
Pearlware, 44
Peate, Iorwerth, 23, 26
Pennant, Thomas, 15, 16
Pennyland estate (Kintyre), 117, 118
Pentland Rising of 1666, 166–167
People's historians, 195, 197
Petrie, G., 28, 30
Pict's houses, 18
Pitcarmick-type buildings, 29
Politics of Improvement, 6–7
Pont, Timothy, 80
Poor Law Act of 1834, 232
Potter, P.B., 39
Power
   economic, 53–55
   ideology and, 67–68
   in social relations, 66–67
Practice, archaeology of, 8
Praxis, 62
Pre-Improvement, 80–103
   domestic space, 97–103, 120, 125, 218, 220
   landscape, 90–97, 218
   in Lowland Scotland and England, 141–149
   routine practice and, 10, 11, 124–125, 220
   settlement patterns, 81–90, 112, 217–218, 220
Prebble, J., 195, 196, 197, 198
Pred, A., 8
Prehistoric archaeology, ethnography and, 16–19

Privacy, rise of, 41, 55
Probate inventories, 49
Proceedings of the Society of Antiquaries of Scotland, 21
Property rights, Adam Smith on, 137

Querns, 22

Ralston, S.M., 29
Range farmsteads, 105–107, 121, 125, 142, 207, 211, 218, 219
Rankine, Patrick, 177
Rankines of Otter, 179, 181, 189
Rannoch Archaeological Project, 30
Rectilinear fields, 117–119
Rennie, E.B., 100, 103, 179, 180, 188
Renwick, R., 173, 179
Rhenish stoneware, 43
Richards, E., 196, 197
Rig and furrow cultivation, 92, 114
Ritual practice, 71–74
Robert the Bruce, 159, 174
Robertson, William, 132
Roofs
  hip-ended, 100
  slate/pantiles, 146
  thatch, 100, 145
Rosal site, 33
Routine practice, 123–124
  Improvement, 10, 125–127, 201–202, 220–221, 225–226
  in Lowland Scotland and England, 147–149
  pre-Improvement, 10, 11, 124–125, 220
Roy Map (Military Survey of Scotland), 80–81, 90–91, 92, 93
Royal Commission on the Ancient and Historical Monuments of Scotland (RCAHMS), 1, 29, 31, 32–33
Rural settlement studies, *v*
  of cognitive landscapes, 34–36
  defined, 6
  empirical, 14, 32–34
  as ethnology, 13, 14, 15–22
  as folk life, 13–14, 23–27, 31
  as historical archaeology, 14, 27–32
  holistic/interdisciplinary approach, 6, 7
  new approaches to, 37–38
  rise of historicity, 9, 37

schools of, 13–32
  of social relations, 7

Saddell Castle, 111–112
St. Kilda, 17
Scott Wood, J., 29, 33
Scottish Country Life (Fenton), 24
Scottish Enlightenment, 10–11, 129–130
  Commercial Age and, 129, 138–139, 223
  on human independence, 139–141
  on human nature, 138
  link to Improvement, 130–134, 150–151, 154, 224
  Lowland and English model in, 129, 133, 224
  stadial view of society, 129, 135–137, 223
  Whig-Jacobite debates, 134–135
Scoular of Innins, Arthur, 180, 189
Sculptural tradition, Lordship of the Isles, 160, 162
SEARCH (Sheffield Environmental and Archaeological Research Campaign in the Hebrides), 30
Sellar, Patrick, 33
Sellar, W.D.H., 163, 169
Settlement patterns
  in England, 142–143
  Improvement, 103–114, 125, 211–214, 220, 225
  in Lowland Scotland, 141–142
  pre-Improvement, 81–90, 112, 217–218, 220
Sharples, N., 28, 30, 31
Sheep grazing, 120, 126
Sheepfolds, 105
Shepherd, I.A.G., 29
Shieling, 17, 18, 91, 94–96, 120, 124, 126, 144, 145, 147–148, 219
Simmons, A., 15
Simpson, J.Y., 16–17, 18, 22
Skelton, R.A., 80–81
Skene, W.F., 21
Slate roofing, 146
Slater, T.R., 143
Slipware, 43
Smallholders, 5
Smith, Adam, 131–132, 135–137, 140
Smith, J., 121, 126, 200, 207

Smout, T.C., 28, 97, 113, 126
Social archaeology, v–vi
Social change, 61–68
Social contradiction, 63–66
Social genealogies, 51–52
Society of Antiquaries of Scotland, 16
Society for Folk Life Studies, 23
Souterrains, 18–19
Southend (Kintyre), 113
Sporting estates, 188–189
Stackyards, 82
Stark, J., 107, 120
Statistical Account, 131
Statutes of Iona, 168
Steer, K.A., 158, 160, 161, 162, 163
Stephenson, George Robert, 178, 180
Stevenson, D., 161
Stewart, A., 22
Stewart, A.I.B., 91, 92, 124
Stewart, Arthur MacArthur, 179
Stewart, Dugald, 132
Stewart, J.H., 30, 34, 158, 181
Stewart, MacArthur, 180
Stewart, M.B., 30, 158
Stillaig (Kilfinan), 107, 108, 109, 122, 211
Stone, J.C., 80
Stoneware, 43
Storrie, M.C., 23
Strone Point (Kilfinan), 87
Structuralist archaeology, 45–46
Superstitions, 22
Sutherland Clearances, 196
Sutherland estate, 33
Sutherland, S.R., 197
Swanson, C., 29
Symonds, J., 30

Tacksmen, 110, 158, 169
Talatoll (Kintyre), 95, 96
Tarbert Castle, 161
Teignmouth, Lord, 15, 122–123, 201, 206
Tenant farmers, 5, 12
  acceptance of Improvement, 200–205
  comparison of Kilfinan and Kintyre, 194–195, 214–215
  emigration to North Carolina, 232
  houses, 109–112, 146, 200–201, 206–208
  leases, 167, 193, 209, 223

Lowland plantation, 168–169, 170–171, 186, 223
  occupancy concerns of, 154, 193–194, 203, 205, 209–210, 215–216, 222–223, 225
  political loyalty of, 166–167, 202–203, 226
  regional variation in Improvement, 210–216
  resistance to Improvement, 195–199, 214, 228–229, 231–232
  social structure of Improvement, 205–210, 208–214, 226, 227–228
Territorial control, by clan, 155–156, 166–167, 168, 170–171
Thatch roof, 100, 145
Third, R.M.W., 143, 144
Thomas, F.W.L., 17–19
Tigh Vectican, 33
Tilley, C., 66
Timperley, L.R., 85, 93, 94, 173, 179, 180
Tipping, R., 30
Tourism, 188
Towns and villages
  consumerism in, 133
  in England, 142
  growth of, 113–114, 126
  middle class in, 132–133
Traditional ways of life, folk life studies of, 23, 26
Transformation of Virginia 1740–1790, The (Isaac), 47
Travel journals, 15
Tree-lined enclosures, 93–94
Trigger, B.G., 17, 19
Turf walls, 100
Turner, R., 29

Walker, B., 141, 146, 147
Walls
  cruck framing, 145
  lime mortar, 145, 146
  slate, 146
  stone, 100, 117, 146
  turf, 100, 145
Waternish (Skye), 90
West of Scotland Archaeology Service, 33
Wheelhouse, 18, 21
Whig–Jacobite debates, 134–135

Whittington, G., 80
Whyte, I., 141, 142, 143, 144, 145, 146,
    147, 148
Whyte, I.D., 145, 146, 147
Whyte, K., 141, 142, 143, 144, 145, 146,
    147, 148
Williams, B.B., 87, 88, 95, 97

Withers, C., 230
Wolf, Eric, 198
Wood, J., 85
Wordsworth, Dorothy, 15, 125

Yaeger, J., 51
Yeoman, P., 27